The Incredible Light Beings of the Cosmos

ANTONIA SCOTT - CLARK

A Dedication

This book is dedicated to my son John who accompanied me for better, for worse every step of the way, not only through the highs and the lows of life itself, but also on our common journey as photographers of the 'Light Beings'. We may not have found all the answers John but we have walked some of the path and more will be revealed one day.

And of course it would be a very serious oversight on my part not to include here in this dedication, all those thousands upon thousands of nameless 'friends' who suddenly manifested in my life and who I call the 'Incredible Light Beings of the Cosmos'. This book is for you and it is about you.

The
Incredible
Light Beings
of the
Cosmos

Antonia Scott-Clark

Adventures Unlimited Press

The Incredible Light Beings of the Cosmos

ISBN 13: 978-1-931882-90-3

Published by:
Adventures Unlimited Press
One Adventure Place
Kempton, Illinois 60946 USA
auphq@frontiernet.net

www.adventuresunlimitedpress.com

Acknowledgements

My very grateful thanks are due to Belinda Carlisle for motivating me to write this book in the first place and for writing the foreword to it; to Anne (Cloudy) McGregor for never losing faith in me; to Mike Cook for being my friend and to his daughter Heidi Cook for her love and trust; to Adam Clayton for his friendship and for keeping an open mind about the 'Light Beings' and not laughing at them; to Pat Swain from New York for taking it all so seriously; to Tim Wallace-Murphy for being a skeptic (got to have at least one and you're it Tim); to Laurent Mathieu from G.E.E.S.A. for teaching me to recognise fake photos; to Christopher Needler for all the great times out on the boat and to Delphine Coquatrix for all the Christmases; to James (Dukey) Mason for reading the original draft of this book and giving it the 'thumbs up'; and to all those many, many friends from all over the world who are too numerous to name (you know who you are) who have given their love, encouragement and support through all the good times and the bad.

I am sure that first time authors are very often a headache for publishers – and speaking strictly for *this* first time author who didn't have a clue what she was doing, it was at times quite frustrating to get the format of the transcript right! So here is a big vote of thanks and gratitude to my editor David Hatcher-Childress for guiding me through the editing process with real kindness, patience and encouragement!

Contents

A Foreword

I remember meeting Antonia, in early April 2005. I walked into her sumptuous apartment on the Croisette in Cannes, sat down and was immediately drawn to the bookshelves (a habit that I have, as it reveals so much about a person). I could not believe it! Her shelves were filled with books on Rennes le Château, Mary Magdalene, the Cathars, the Templars and many other subjects that I have been passionate about for years. I thought "Oh, a kindred spirit!"

As we have gotten to know each other since that particular afternoon, we found that we both have so much in common on the more esoteric subjects.

I don't know why she never mentioned to me then the fact that she was able to photograph orbs, but when over a dinner party with mutual friends I was asked if I had seen "Antonia's balls", I of course did not understand what was meant by that rather strange question and was stunned to learn that she had this ability to photograph orbs and was equally shocked that she was so nonchalant about it.

The Incredible Light Beings of the Cosmos

She never told me of this extraordinary gift of being able to pick up these light beings on film, even in daylight and even before the digital camera had been invented. I guess it was such a 'normal' occurrence for her that it slipped her mind to mention anything about it.

She showed me several pictures of the orbs she had taken at a U2 concert and then proceeded to show me many photographs of orbs she had been capturing for years. They were gorgeous, unmistakably 3D in quality and with these intricate patterns. There was no question that they seemed to be attracted to her and had in fact been following her for years.

I was envious and wanted to photograph them for myself. I bought myself a digital camera, put out the 'Orb Vibe', but nothing ever showed up for me -- that is until one night in September 2007, when Antonia, myself and a couple of friends took a trip up to the mysterious Col de Vence, a reputed place of many mysteries, including being able to pick up strange things on film that were invisible to the naked eye. I was hoping to finally get lucky and I did.

I was snapping away into the black void, hoping for the best, frustrated that she was picking them up easily on her camera (I wasn't), when finally I captured my first little orb that was very dense in quality, had the pattern of an eye ball with a ring of blue around the outside.

That evening I took about 10 photos where these beautiful spheres showed up. Since that evening only rarely have I been able to photograph orbs, and only in India in very holy places. In fact recently in Varanasi I did get some tiny, very sparkly ones.

I have no idea what orbs are. I do know that they are real -- and I do have my own theories about what they could be. I think we are entering into a new phase of Universal Consciousness which is gaining quick momentum with the dawning of the Age of Aquarius. This is perhaps one of the reasons why more and more they are being captured on film by people -- to open our minds to a new way of thinking, and that can only be a good thing considering where we are at as a civilization.

I feel that Antonia has been chosen by 'The Light Beings' to introduce them to the world in a gentle but instructive way that removes fear from the populace in general and it is for this reason that I suggested that she put down in writing all her experiences and actively encouraged her to write this book.

I hope that you will find this book as eye opening as I did and that it will inspire you change your thinking and discover that there is much more to our everyday life than meets the eye.

Magic does happen all around us, even if we can't see it.

Belinda Carlisle

June 2008

The Incredible Light Beings of the Cosmos

Introduction

There is a principle which is a bar against all information, which is proof against all arguments, and which cannot fail to keep a man in everlasting ignorance. That principle is condemnation before investigation.

Quote attributed to: Herbert Spencer

If this book had started and ended its life with the publisher's dreaded phrase "Thanks but no thanks", and had never seen the light of day, it really wouldn't have mattered. I would have nonetheless gained huge satisfaction out of getting my amazing adventure with the 'Light Beings' down on paper, even if it had only been for myself. I would have considered that not the least of my achievements while writing it, would have been that I learned to spell the word 'phenomenon' and that the plural of phenomenon is 'phenomena' and believe me that was no mean feat in itself! But amazingly the book didn't get red-pencilled and here you are reading it, so let's, you and I together, explore the Cosmos and those mysterious and strange creatures that I call 'Light Beings' and between us let's try to come up with a few answers to the infinite number of questions about the orb phenomenon that still remain unanswered.

When I first started photographing them and it looked as though they were here to stay, my very first question was "Why me? Why, of all the billions of people in the world am I one of those relatively rare few who have the ability to consistently photograph those mysterious spheres of light which have come to be commonly known as 'orbs' or 'spirit orbs'?" This question is just one, of so many about the orbs, that to this day remains unanswered -- and as baffling as it was to me, especially at the beginning, it was even more baffling to my friends.

By and large, my friends were intrigued and they found the orbs quite fascinating, good for a laugh even, and there were plenty of ribald jokes about 'Antonia's balls'! "There she goes photographing her balls again!" They were prepared only to give credence to any logical, natural explication for the mysterious phenomenon, as long as it was rational and they weren't being challenged to believe any mumbo-jumbo about ghosts or spirits or that it just might be something else really weird that was coming from realms beyond our own. Most of my friends seeking the logical explanation, were convinced that I had the ongoing bad luck to buy a string of faulty cameras. Then, when that first 'faulty' camera turned into a second faulty camera and then the third, one or two of them began to sit up, take notice and say "Hey maybe there's something odd going on here! You should write to 'Canon' or 'Olympus', or whoever else the current camera happened to be made by, and ask them what they make of all this." *Not*, please note, "Hey maybe there's something going on here! These things are a bit weird! You should try to find out what they are. Maybe they're coming from another world!" Naturally there had to be a rational explanation like a faulty camera or memory card which the camera companies would know about.

To their constant suggestions to write to the camera companies which at times bordered on nagging, I'd sweetly say "Yes, p'raps I'll do that one of these days," but I never did write those letters because deep down I knew that I was the recipient of something very special, possibly bordering on the sacred and that by writing to the camera manufacturers I was only going to get some adroitly formulated, non-committal reply about dust motes, dirty lenses, moisture in the air, lens flare, refraction etcetera -- all the arguments already trotted out by the orb debunkers.

It Predates Digital Photography

There is another even more valid reason why I never wrote those letters to the digital camera manufacturers and that is because I had in fact taken several photos of orbs well before I owned a digital camera and I already knew that the phenomenon was much older than digital photography. My last 'normal' camera had been an ordinary 35mm Nikon which used ordinary film and the film I usually bought was probably ASA200 if I remember rightly. I took several photos of orbs on this old Nikon camera -- not many admittedly, maybe five or six in total, but of course certainly nothing like the number taken since I converted over to digital cameras. Those few photos taken on the Nikon however, were enough for me to be aware of the phenomenon already and that was well before I started getting them in great numbers on the digital.

I had some years previously, as a consequence of those early photos, already been on the internet and found a few websites with information on the subject of orbs and I had even sent in one or two of my photos for publishing on the 'net' by those websites; but in those days no one had any real idea of what they were -- except that they were possibly 'Spirits of the Dead'.

Having Faith – Is It So Naïve?

I am one of those people who has a tendency, when confronted with something new and exciting, to put doubt, misgiving, logic and all that, temporarily on the back-burner and allow my imagination and the romance of the new idea to prevail. I allow myself to 'believe until proven otherwise', in something new and mysterious even if I don't understand it in the least little bit. To systematically rule something out, just because it's strange, not understood and is at present unexplained is most certainly to deny oneself the joys of discovery through delving deeper into a subject and through so doing, opening up new vistas and experiences. After all, America didn't exist did it and didn't appear on any known world map, until it was discovered.

Thus it was with 'The 'Light Beings'. They challenged me to accept the existence of something which, I could see only through the eye of the camera but not with my own eyes. Neither could I touch, taste nor smell them and I could not even begin to formulate any sort of explanation as to what they might possibly be. It was very much a question of taking them on-board as something weird and wonderful but totally mystifying and until more was revealed, putting all prejudice aside and 'believing' in them through a simple 'Act of Faith'. Is it so naïve of us to take on something as an act of faith? Actually, I think not. Aren't we all at practically all times in our growing-up expected to take on-board just about everything that we are ever taught without question -- as an act of faith?

"Why is the sky blue Mummy?"

"Because it's blue"

"Yes but *why* is the sky blue?"

"Because I say it is."

"Oh."

From that point on ever after and for the rest of his life, Junior is going to believe without ever stopping to rethink or to question it again, that the sky really and truly is blue. And he in turn, will teach his own offspring the same.

Isn't blind unquestioning faith exactly what 'Religion' in its many and various guises has demanded of all of mankind throughout all its history? Even in this day and age, not only in Third World countries, but in more of the so-called 'civilized' countries than I would care to name, people are still denied the freedom to choose their religious denomination. For millennia man has been bludgeoned over the head with the big religious stick to forcibly make him accept without question or protest, or as much as a 'how-do-you-do', according to where he happened to have been born, the prevailing church dogma as an act of faith. There will be no arguments thank you very much. It was 'sinful' not to believe exactly what you were told, so you wouldn't dare argue would you?

When we were children, they made us learn and recite by heart 'creeds' and a 'declaration of faith' which deep down some of us may have secretly thought was a whole load of bollocks, but did any of us dare to stick our tiny hands up in Sunday School and say "Er, s'cuse me Miss! Umm -- what would have happened if Mary had had a girl?"

Actually I *did* dare once and *only* once (it had something to do with virgins having babies) and I got myself into a whole load of trouble for my pains. After a humiliating punishment in front of my peers, I settled down into a state of outward compliance with the-rules-according-to-those-in-authority, but with a fierce resentment at the unfairness of it raging in my rebellious little thirteen year-old heart and that fierce resentment has never really gone away. Someone should have warned me to think twice, before daring to ask *'them'* any searching questions about anything so serious as My Personal Religious Instruction – especially when they're telling me by force-feeding what I'm to believe for the rest of my life and what I'm to pass on to my own children.

Wow! Do you realize that I was actually being indoctrinated and *'they'* expected me to live my whole religious and spiritual life believing in random, totally unconnected Biblical freak-show oddities that happened thousands of years ago, like raining frogs, babies floating in baskets, animals two-by-two in boats, chaps who could walk on water, pretty ladies turning to pillars of salt, or whales swallowing a man who lived to tell the tale (now you know where the expression 'whale of a tale' comes from!) Well I've got news for you. They *did* expect it! This was *religion* and I had better swallow *all* of it hook, line and sinker and if I didn't, then I'd better watch out because something really, really scary would happen to my eternal soul after I died.

Religion. Figure this -- it's weird! Countless millions have gained their immortal souls by killing in the name of it -- and willingly continue to do so. Countless millions have gained their immortal souls by dying for it -- and willingly continue to do so. So what's the big deal? It's a win/win situation. Hey! Let's all go out and start a good old religious war. It seems like you're just can't lose! Or have I missed the point? Oh dear! I vowed before starting this book not to bring religion into it because religion is not what any of this is about!

However before we get back to the real subject of the book there's just one more thing I want to mention that illustrates with frightening clarity the degree of control that is wielded over the 'ignorant masses' who can't or won't think for themselves any more. It should send out loud warning bells about the sick state of humanity today. It is this. According to a recent survey, the terrible truth is that statistically sixty-two percent (that's way over half!) of the population would be prepared to go out and kill, torture or maim in the name of religion or any other praiseworthy principle if someone they *perceived* to be a Figure of Authority told them to do so. Moral is: Be careful who is placed by us in a position of power. Learn to think for ourselves, trust our own personal judgement and always be ready to follow our own personal Truth without fear.

A Gift From Beyond?

Among the various ideas on my list of who or what the 'Light Beings' could be (Chapter 4), is that they could be the perfected souls of those who have undergone successive reincarnations and who, having completed their incarnate earth journeys, are now spiritually evolved beyond the restrictive bonds of the physical plane of paltry physical needs, and now dwell in the realm of light, as pure and perfect consciousness. True 'Children of the Light'. Did not Jesus himself, who came to teach and to reveal, declare himself to be the 'Light of the World' by saying . . . . .

"He that walketh in darkness knoweth not whither he goeth. While ye who
have light, believe in The Light, that ye may be the Children of Light."

Belief in The Light . . . . . It's that simple really. But it does require an act of absolute Faith.

Once the 'Light Beings' showed up in my photographs, it occurred to me quite early in the piece, that as I seemed to be able to capture them with such constancy and in such quantities, it might in truth be a 'gift' from '*Them*' whoever '*They*' might be. It occurred to me that they might be using me for some specific purpose which would be revealed to me at some time in the future. Right from the outset I really held onto those ideas and kept on believing in them because the 'Light Beings' have something going for them that shifts this particular ballgame into a whole new category of believability, and puts it way ahead in the blind faith stakes. It is this: We may not be able to see the orbs with our own physical eyes, but we can see them in photographs so we *do* actually know what they look like and therefore we positively *know* they exist. The debunkers can argue the point here until they're blue in the face but the proof of that particular pudding is in the photograph. The camera never lies!

In The Spirit of Love Not War

This needs to be said right at the very beginning to reassure those who are afraid of seeing orbs in their photos. Fear of the unknown is a most normal human reaction. I have already met several people who are spooked by the appearance of orbs, especially when the photos are taken in the home environment. Folks fear that they are ghosts or spirits of the dead or something. Maybe they *are* ghosts -- or maybe they're something else that we haven't thought of as yet -- but whatever or whoever the 'Light Beings' are, and whatever it is that they are here to achieve or do (if anything), the one thing that I can positively say about them is that they are very, very 'people friendly' and their purpose is certainly not to harm us human beings. I am positive that if they are on a mission, it is a peaceful one and should it be that they are indeed intelligent beings from another realm, then I believe that they are here to 'reveal' not to cause us harm.

Let me state unequivocally that I have never had a frightening experience of any description with the 'Light Beings', neither before, during nor after a photographic session. No scary poltergeist activity; no negativity or bad vibes in my environment; no strange things that go bump in the night. Over many years, there has been nothing whatsoever to scare me or to make me think or feel that I was dabbling in something in any way dark and dangerous. It has been quite the opposite in fact. I believe that my life has vastly improved in every area since the 'Light Beings' have been in it. And it just keeps on getting better! Long may they stay.

The orbs need to be investigated and that has to be done with an open mind so that we do not remain in 'everlasting ignorance'. We need to take off the blinkers of prejudgment and to be courageous enough to open up the human spirit and not shut that self-limiting door of contempt and condemnation. We need to allow ourselves to grow by welcoming new possibilities with an open mind -- at least for as long as it takes to make that journey of thorough investigation.

Which of your inner voices will you listen to? Will it be the quietly whispering, intuitive voice your psychic being? Or will you squash all that silly 'flight of fancy' stuff and not listen to any of it for fear of having people think you might be a bit of an odd-ball? With all the evidence that I will be presenting to you in this book, I am convinced that even the most skeptical amongst you will have to admit (even if it's reluctantly), that there *is* something happening out there that is definitely real – no question about it.

To anyone who is still teetering on the brink between belief and disbelief and not quite sure which way to jump, I am sure that after reading this you will be convinced of the existence of the 'Light Beings'. You are already half-way there – after all you bought this book didn't you!

And for those of you who are already believers, well you are going to love the book because there are so many stunning photos and some great stories of my experiences with the 'Light Beings' which will confirm what you already know -- and build on it.

So read on, tuck your feet up, buckle-up your seat belt and welcome aboard this flight of fancy towards new horizons and into the real world of the strange!

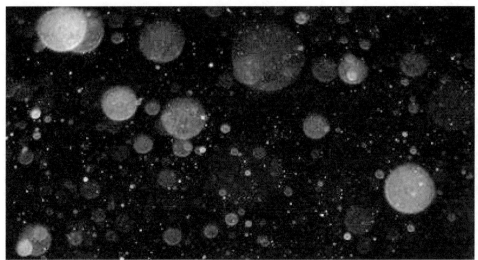

Welcome aboard this flight of fancy into the real world of the strange!

PART ONE

Introducing the 'Light Beings'

CHAPTER ONE

Something About Me

Let's start by getting introductions out of the way before we get to the real subject of this book -- those fascinating spheres of celestial light which I call 'Light Beings', aka 'orbs' or 'spirit orbs' to the populace in general.

As it happens, I have quite a considerable relevance in the story, so it's fitting and only polite that I begin by telling you something about myself.

I was born way down there at the bottom of the world in a great little country once romantically known as 'Aotearoa', or the 'Land of the Long White Cloud' but which these days, goes by the more prosaic name of New Zealand, presumably named after the 'old' Zealand wherever that might be. In terms of chronological age, I am strictly speaking no longer in the prime of youth, having been born a few days before World War II officially broke out -- but in terms of mental age I think that I've discovered how to reverse the process and I'm getting younger day by day. I have this permanent feeling that I'm a relative newcomer on a planet where each and every day holds a fresh adventure to be lived and enjoyed to the fullest.

Today the world is indeed my proverbial oyster and I consider myself to be a fully paid up member of the human race and too, a creature of the Universe.

It used to amuse me when I was a girl to write my own name and address over and over wherever and whenever I could find a place or an excuse to do so. It went into the fly leaves of books, school text books, school exercise books and on the backs of envelopes of letters when I wrote to people. It went like this:

Antonia Patricia Scott-Clark,

'Chimneys',

Ilam Road,

Fendalton,

Christchurch,

New Zealand,

The Southern Hemisphere,

The World,

The Galaxy,

The Universe,

The Cosmos.

So you can see can't you, that even as a youngster, I had a predisposition to think rather large and not limit myself to a simple home-town postal address like most 'normal' folk. Even then I was thinking in terms of the Cosmos! No way was I ever normal! In those days I saw myself very much as a princess-like ethereal creature, a denizen of the vast Universe and maybe it was for that reason that I first got myself noticed by the 'Light Beings'. Maybe they spotted me way back then and earmarked me as a likely candidate who, at sometime at a much later date, would be in the right frame of mind and in the right time and place to spread 'The Word'.

Meanwhile though, even for ethereal princesses and messengers-in-waiting, life had to go on. There was growing up to be done, an education to be got, exams to pass, careers to be followed, and girlhood dreams to be pursued. The life of an ethereal princess preparing for a golden future was an extremely busy one.

Then one day, at the age of twelve-going-on-thirteen, when I was happily settling into the exciting new adventure of boarding school, I received a letter containing the shattering news that was to change my life forever, and bring my childhood, and indeed my very life it seemed, to an abrupt and cruel end. The letter was from my father to tell me that my beautiful mother, that Goddess who I had placed upon the highest of high pedestals, had left home. She had committed the worst crime and had run off with another man. She never came back.

With that letter all my childhood castles and girlish dreams collapsed in a crashing and thunderous heap of wreckage to be replaced by a darkness that never completely lifted until I was finally released from her by her death just a few weeks before I began writing this book. It seems that this planet is too small for an abandoned child who could not forget and an unloving mother who refused to remember.

I was pole-axed by her death and for the first four or five days after I received the news I was all but bed-ridden by a massive attack of what seemed to be a type of acute Rheumatoid Arthritis. I think that it was the release of a lifetime of stored pain finding a way to leave my body. When the cloud lifted, and the joint pains went away, it slowly dawned on me that it was all over and I felt as though some Karmic score had been settled. A debt from some long-ago lifetime had been paid. I had lived through the pain and I had suffered the consequences. I had not failed I believe, to learn the lessons which needed to be learned and I somehow know that I will have the power to make the choice as to whether or not she is in my life the next time around.

Where Darkness Dwelt

Those days after the defection of my mother, were dark days indeed. I survived and I somehow grew up without a mother's presence. I somehow survived my father's rapid descent into alcoholism and his subsequent remarriage to a local beauty queen who, being just five years older than I, was not much more than a girl herself. I somehow survived incredible mental cruelty and a certain incident of unpardonable physical maltreatment which imposed serious psychological scars which have I lived with all my life until relatively recently, when with help I was finally able to let it go. I somehow survived a sick see-saw of raw insanity and emotional torment in that horrid house that had nothing to do with the principles of family 'love'. And I could never tell anyone what was going on. No one would have believed me. "What those ever so 'nice' people? Never! The girl must be unbalanced!"

All considered I somehow got through school with surprisingly good grades and even topped my class in certain subjects. Then out of the blue one day, for no apparently justifiable reason nor for anything that I had done, other than to 'exist' in that accursed household, which held no semblance of a 'home', the beauty queen made a bonfire in the back yard and just about everything I possessed which made up my life to that point, including my 'Cubby' the threadbare bear cub, that I'd had since I was a baby, were all consigned to the flames. I can still get tears in my eyes when I think of Cubby. My 'Inner Child' would like him to be with me still.

My books from each stage of my childhood went; so too did my school reports, my photographs, my schoolbooks and projects that I had worked so hard at and had been so proud of. My drawings, the poetry I had written, my personal 'Dear Diaries' (not before they had been thoroughly read), my little white calf-skin prayer-book which my Godmother gave me for my First Communion, clothes and makeup -- all went onto that bonfire.

I Was Erased From My Own World

The only token of remembrance that I had of my grandmother which was her long amber necklace, my mother's diamond engagement ring from Dad which she left behind on a shelf in my bedroom when she left, plus my 'precious' (precious to my mind anyway) Woolworths pearls which I had saved to buy out of my small allowance, I never saw again. My beautiful doll Emily-Leigh, given to me when I was six by an aunt of the same name, the beauty queen told me that she had given away to someone else. I never had either the heart or the courage to ask who.

Everything that was 'Me' or mine was obliterated that terrible day. I had been erased. With that inferno I suddenly had no past. I felt as though I was standing bare, ship-wrecked on a desert island. My bedroom was sanitized of all trace of me and very shortly after, based on some 'trumped up charge' which had no basis in any truth that I was aware of of, I was tossed out of my father's house, where full-blown, certifiable insanity, alcoholic paranoia, perverted thinking, jealousy and hate and the beauty queen now ruled. Besides, she was expecting a baby and the unborn infant would need the room which had been mine. I was not yet eighteen and suddenly I found myself homeless.

What happened immediately after that is not for this book, but it was an ongoing nightmare. Somehow I got through it. Somehow I completed my training and passed my exams with good grades and graduated in conservative dentistry.

Deep wounds such as those, can remain engraved forever upon the human soul but with the passage of time an uneasy state of 'truce' and semi-forgiveness may be achieved. Such was the case here -- but that came only after many years and the truce was not lasting. You see, memory is long and the trust was gone.

Yes, time passes and even though the broken pieces of the past may have been painstakingly glued together as one might mend a broken vase, the fractures, although not always visible, remain just beneath the surface -- forever.

Marriage Motherhood & Divorce In Quick Succession

Life at the dawn of the early sixties was a very exciting epoch for those who lived through it. It was an iconic age which was happening to others all around me but not to me. I went through each day with a heart which felt as though it was made of lead. I was a tragic shadow of the girl I was born to be. Gone was the natural gaiety. Gone was the ethereal princess with shining brown eyes and dark bouncing curls, who once danced and cart-wheeled everywhere she went, and who galloped her pony across the carefree, sunlit plains of happy childhood. In her place was a sad teenage girl on the brink of womanhood, with a wistful smile, a broken family and a dazed sense that nothing that she had been born to believe in was real anymore. She had already made a half-hearted attempt at suicide. She no longer dwelt in her father's house and she had nowhere in the world to go that she could call home. That sad girl carried in her heart an all-invasive aching yearning for her parents as she remembered them once being. She yearned too for the lovely, rambling old family home of her childhood which had been sold and downgraded to the small, ugly modern bungalow with not enough bedrooms for baby and her.

She had a desperate need to be approved of and loved by someone -- anyone -- so maybe it was not altogether surprising that at the age of twenty, came an ill-advised marriage to a twenty-two year-old jazz pianist who smoked opium and marijuana. The marriage was closely followed by motherhood and then just as closely followed by abandonment and divorce. It was no one's fault. We were both too young. We were two mal-functioning children playing at house. He got away, but all of a sudden there I was coping alone as a solo parent with a six month-old baby. It seemed like a life sentence. My youth never happened.

By the age of twenty-one, I had already been married, become a mother and had a divorce underway. I was the one-and-only wage earner, chief cook and bottle-washer, laundress, gardener, chauffeur, baby-sitter, homework supervisor and so on and on, while desperately trying all the time to stay beautiful on the outside in order to snare the new husband who was going to sweep into my life on a galloping white charger to rescue me and erase the pain of the past. This man was going to unburden me of all my troubles and I'd live happily ever after. Like in the fairy stories.

That I needed rescuing, no-one looking on could have been in any doubt. I was very young and had no one to turn to. Some kind people tried to help but I didn't want *them*, I only wanted my own mother and my father. Any love, kindness and guidance that I was getting was coming from the wrong people.

Nothing that was happening to me then was going according to the plan that had been originally mapped out for me by sending me to a good private school where I was being taught how to grow up to be a 'Lady'! Suddenly, all the scandal and shoddiness that was happening at home was in direct conflict with the principles I was being educated to value. My parameters were fudged and I was living in a constant state of confusion and fear. I no longer had the ingrained sense of identity of who I was. I was totally ill-equipped to cope out in the big world fending for myself. I was nowhere near tough enough. I was not street-wise and the street was virtually where I found myself.

It is only now with the clarity of vision that I enjoy today, that I can look back on all this and other 'stuff' that life dished up, and understand with compassion for that poor lost girl, that even ethereal princesses are not super-human and are liable to fall down under the 'load of life' itself when things go so terribly wrong. I was no exception. I have had to learn not to blame myself.

Mother's Little Helper

The 'load of life' was not an excuse for what happened, but was perhaps part of the reason why it was that I fell into the habit of partaking of a small glass of 'Mother's Little Helper' to relax me from the stresses of the day during those incalculable days and nights while I was waiting for my very small son to grow up. The years stretched ahead like an interminable road with no destination -- there was no ending in sight. I was only twenty-one; I was a pretty young woman in the full bloom of youth with plenty of young energy, but I felt tarnished both inside and out and the future looked just about as bleak as the past.

I discovered very early on that that a 'little something' in the glass not only relaxed me, but it also eased the gnawing pain of grief which constantly gripped me somewhere in the region of my solar plexus and so began the gradual journey down the slippery slope which gathered momentum and eventually took me right to the bottom. My increasing alcohol consumption no longer had anything to do with relaxing at the end of a stressful day. It became a physical and mental need and after years and years of nightly tippling, it finally spiralled way out of control. The 'Mother's Little Helper' became 'Mother's Ruin', while the nightly drink became the nightmare drink with me quite often waking up wherever I happened to have passed out the night before. I was in deep trouble and I knew it.

To Be Or Not To Be

Any lingering traces, even in my heart, of the ethereal princess had definitively vanished. The new husband who was supposed gallop up on his white horse, never looked like showing up, and the former grandiose address which had once declared me a citizen of the Universe became whittled down to read something like: Antonia Patricia Scott-Clark, The Bedroom.

Then one day in July 2000, which started out like every other – that is too say badly – I knew that I couldn't go on. The day of reckoning had finally arrived. It was decision time. Either I pulled myself together and shaped up or I shipped out altogether. It was going to have to be either "Hello life or bye-bye cruel world". I took the first option and I chose to live. I thank the Universe to this day that I had just enough survival instinct in me to want to tidy up my act and reach out for the pinpoint of light that I glimpsed at the end of the tunnel. I promptly got myself qualified help for my drinking and sobered up. There was a glimmer of hope on the horizon. The long and wearying battle was at last over. I was re-born.

Walking In The Light Once More

With hindsight, I understand now that the drinking was a desperate attempt at applying bandages to my bruised soul. It was the palliative and anaesthetic for the intense pain that I had suffered over my mother's defection from the family after which my father piled more pain upon existing pain. His alcoholism, his mental cruelty and his absolute rejection of me from that time when he tossed me out of home, kept the original wounds inflicted by my mother, open and bleeding.

My father became entrenched in his own alcohol-sodden world. He was unreachable and he stayed that way for the rest of his life. Not even the birth of his first grandchild, my son, ever opened that door to him again. He became a pathetic parody of his former debonair self, and was no longer capable of managing his own life. He took the line of least resistance and handed over his personal power and his responsibility as a parent into hands which were unqualified to navigate the domestic ship through those stormy seas. That the ship foundered on the rocks and sank should not have been a surprise to anyone. People had to go down with the ship and they did -- I was one of them. I could not possibly have understood this then. Today I do.

You might wonder why I have told you these extremely personal details of my life which most people would very much prefer to leave unmentioned. There are two reasons why I have deliberately chosen to tell this part of my story. One is because it might help someone else still trapped in the terrible prison and the private hell of The Bottle to know that there always is a way out. If by chance someone in pain is reading this, my message is this: Get help. There is a life after the bottle richer than it is possible to imagine. Believe me, if I could do it anyone can.

Enter The 'Light Beings'

The other reason why I tell this part of my story is because I now know without a shadow of a doubt that all the years of drinking, all the horrible addiction and the numbing oblivion produced by a dangerous daily cocktail of alcohol, tranquillizers and sleeping pills, plus very heavy smoking were a terrible and effective block not only to the physical world and those who inhabit it, but also to the world of the spiritual. It was like living permanently on the dark side of the moon unseeing and unseen. I was cut off from my fellow human beings and from any contact with the Universal Spirit, and cut off too from my personal God and the realm of angels.

I do not in any way consider it to be mere coincidence that very shortly after I knocked all my addictions on the head and made my re-entry into the land of the living, it was then that the 'Light Beings' showed up in my life and allowed me to photograph them. Not just the occasional photo like I had taken in the past, but in such profusion that it was awesome -- even a little frightening.

I believe it was a message from the Universe. Now that I was living a live clean and sober and was free of all forms of addiction, it was as though I had emerged from behind an impenetrable screen of total radar block and the Universe was once again able to receive the faint blip of my signal and was now beaming in on me. I was humbled and awed by what seemed to be a sign from 'Them up There' simply saying "Good girl, stick with it!"

Ever since that night when the 'Light Beings' came onto my life for real, I have never felt alone. And it seems that 'They' have never left me.

I have never felt the urge to drink or to take tranquillizers and/or sleeping pills again; and I smoke no more. What came to pass was a truly mysterious miracle of physical, mental and spiritual healing from the blackest hell-hole of multiple addictions which I have since come to understand was beyond my or any human power to break free of. I now believe that for this miracle of physical, mental and spiritual healing to have taken place, that I somehow tapped into a source of spiritual power which was a thousand times more powerful than any of the addictive substances that had held me a prisoner for so long.

I am free at last and I am walking in the light once more -- in the dazzling sunlight of the spirit. It's the sunny side of the street.

Free at last and walking in the dazzling sunlight of the spirit!

CHAPTER TWO

How It All Began

I now live in Cannes on the French Riviera. Cannes is mostly inhabited by the retired, the rich and the famous and is best-known for the glitz of its famous Film Festival. It is a town where ugliness of any description has no part -- at least not visibly on the main drag La Croisette and the famous Rue d'Antibes where all is brand-image, designer clothes, diamonds as big as pigeons' eggs, grand hotels like royal palaces and convertible Rolls Royces, Bentleys, Mercedes, Aston Martins and so on.

La Croisette is a glamorous palm-tree lined boulevard which runs alongside the white sandy beaches of the sparkling Mediterranean where stars of all descriptions are still able to stroll, shop and dine while remaining relatively unmolested by the population in general. Cannes people are used to stars and their presence is an almost daily occurrence which arouses not much more than a pleasurable passing curiosity. The locals are very protective of 'their' stars and that very urbane attitude allows celebrities to go about their day in Cannes in relative peace -- just as long as the tourists don't bother them.

La Croisette is a four kilometre stretch of over-the-top elegance where the apartments are some of the most expensive in the world and where the loudest and most annoying noise to be heard is the vroom-vroom of sleek and shiny Ferraris. Either you hate it or you love it. I happen to love it. Probably it's that teensy, lingering wisp of the old ethereal princess which still pops up in me from time to time. But what the hell It's all a lot of fun as long as you don't take any of it too seriously!

Film Stars Ferraris Fireworks & Orbs

Apart from international film and rock stars, Ferraris, Film Festivals, and a sparkling azure bay where the world's mega-yachts gather to doze in the Mediterranean sun like great basking whales, Cannes also has a very big reputation on the world stage of International Fireworks Competitions. (Yes, yes more inconsequential frivolity I know!) But that's Cannes for you, and I guess that someone, and I hope that it's Cannes itself, gets a big spin-off from the eternal fireworks displays we locals have to 'suffer' on an almost twice-weekly basis throughout the months of summer.

Anyway one night I was at home quietly cruising around the Internet when I heard the familiar whistling and bang-banging of yet another of the famous Cannes fireworks displays getting underway. Reaching for the new digital camera which I had recently bought in Hong Kong Duty Free, I quickly ran out into the garden wanting to find out how it would handle fireworks. Holding the camera high above my head in order to clear the garden hedge, I aimed it in the general direction of the fireworks and clicked and clicked and clicked.

When the show was over, I went back inside and downloaded the photos onto my computer. Looking through them to see how they had come out, I suddenly stopped dead in my tracks. There were huge balls of white light in two of the photos which as far as I could make out, had absolutely nothing to do with the fireworks! What were they? Could they possibly be orbs? I suddenly remembered that some time before I had taken several orb photos on my old 35mm camera but nothing since. Those orbs back then had been quite small. Did they

There were huge white balls of light in two of the photos which as far as I could tell, had absolutely nothing to do with the fireworks! What were they? Could they possibly be orbs? I had read about them on the internet .

come as big as this? Little did I know it then that a whole new world had opened up for me that night. From that moment on taking photographs of anything at anytime was never to be the same again. The 'Light Beings' had entered my life and were to accompany everywhere I went and they would lead me into an ongoing journey so exciting that I could never have dreamed up such an adventure. Neither could I have asked for anything more wonderful to happen.

What happened after that, is the story which I will be telling you in the pages that follow.

A Shower Of Orbs That Night

I studied those photos on my computer with great excitement. Would the orbs still be there? Could I do it again? I went outside into the garden to see if I could get any more shots of these mysterious giant white balls. I pointed my camera aimlessly at nothing in particular in the dark, but more or less concentrated on a Magnolia tree and the Cyprus hedge in the bottom corner of the garden which was where I had been standing when I took the photos of the fireworks. At first there seemed to be nothing and then suddenly there it was! An orb – not a big one, but an orb all the same -- floating in the vicinity of the Magnolia. And then there was another, and another, and lo and behold suddenly it was like a shower of orbs snowing down from the heavens. There were dozens of them in one spectacular photo after the other. All night it continued like that. It was amazing!

My excitement at the phenomena was tinged with mixed feelings of real fear, awe and reverence, because I knew without a shadow of doubt that I had tapped into a paranormal field of something that night, which I did not understand but which was surely coming from beyond the realms of our perceivable dimension. I had absolutely no idea what that something could possible be. Were they spirits of the dead? This is what it was largely claimed on the internet. I must admit that this needed to be given serious consideration because, believe it or not, that very night was Halloween or All Saints: 'Toussaint' as it is called in France.

The next morning I was up with the larks and with my camera. Were they still going to be there? I didn't have to wait for long. They were still out there in the garden; not in the great numbers of the night before but there they were, most particularly around the fountain like the last guests at a party who are reluctant to

The above picture was taken out by the fountain in my garden early in the morning after the 'fireworks' night . It is one of my very first batch of orb photos taken on my old 2.5 mega-pixel camera. The orb here is one of the lingering 'Light Beings' from the night before -- rather like the all-night party reveller who is going home the next morning. Knowing what I know now about orbs today, this one because it is slightly elongated is an orb in motion. It also has a lovely electric blue aura. The fact that it is hanging out by fountain and is very opaque, shows me that it perhaps came to the fountain to drink – or to re-hydrate. Orbs need to do this in order to remain in optimal good health. They will always search for a source of water.

go home. This was the start of my long career as a photographer of the 'Light Beings' and despite an initial tinge of fear because I was not at all sure what I was meddling with or which doors to what unknown realm I was opening, I was instantly and irretrievably hooked! I became obsessive about photographing them both day and night and it paid off. The more I photographed the more orbs I got. I had the impression that they were enjoying it just as much as I was. That night, as it turned out was just the beginning of the adventure.

Suddenly it was like a shower of orbs snowing down from the heavens. There were dozens of them in one spectacular photo after the other. All night it continued like that. It looked like they had turned a Cosmic ballet for me. This was my first experience of orb photography. No wonder I was 'hooked' from the outset! The orange light behind the Magnolia tree is a street lamp shining through the leaves.

CHAPTER THREE

The Paranormal Butterfly

Since as far back as I can remember I have been a enthusiast of the paranormal, and although I had read many books on various aspects of the paranormal world and had even dabbled in one or two areas over the years, I had never gotten myself too deeply into any one aspect of it. I have always been a great fan and follower of Uri Geller, and had done my fair share of ghost hunting and séances with the ouija board -- all with mixed results. I also made brief forays at various times into disciplines such as astrology, the Tarot and reading palms, becoming an overnight expert for a few months and then letting it drop. I had also been through several sessions of 'past life regression' with an old school friend who is seriously into this for the purposes of healing. This, I have to say, produced some spectacular results for me personally and convinced me that there is definitely something in all that which I would like one day to investigate further.

A Run-Away Boy & A Lost Dog

As far back as I remember from the very first time that I tried, I seemed to have a natural ability to 'divine' with rods and also to use a pendulum which come to think of it, I took pretty much for granted, like it was really no big deal. I once found someone's lost Poodle dog, which being stone-deaf, couldn't hear its owner's frantic calling. I did this by dowsing with a pendulum over a map of my city. The dog had wandered for miles and was in a field on the outskirts of town, not far from the airport and having a grand old time romping with the cows when we found it thanks to the pendulum.

I also once found a run-away adolescent by working a pendulum and the rods over a map of the South of France. He was mentally challenged and had slipped his mother's vigilance in Nice. I 'located' the boy out of Toulon which is a port town in the south of France nearly 200 kilometres from Nice. It seemed a real long-shot and extremely far-fetched, but with the aid of the pendulum and a psychically inspired guess, I told his near-hysterical mother that I thought that he might be on a train heading for Paris. I must have sounded a lot more confident than I felt, for on giving her this rather extraordinary piece of information, she immediately acted on it by telling the police, and much to my surprise, that was in fact, exactly where he was -- on the night train bound for Paris! Fortunately, there was plenty of time to organize a 'reception committee' for the boy at the Paris train station, where he arrived safe and sound the next morning. Unharmed and suffering no ill effects after his big adventure, he was returned to his mother under escort on the next train bound for Nice!

That incident and finding Lucy the Poodle, I have to say were perhaps my only two great moments in the world of the paranormal. The rest of it was decidedly more in my imagination than in reality. But I often wonder if I would have been any good if I had concentrated on the pendulum and the divining rods. I might have made a fortune as a water-diviner somewhere in the desert in the Middle East!

My Collection Of Uri Gellar Spoons

My friend Belinda knows Uri Gellar personally and she is a total believer in his mind powers: She's had them demonstrated for her and her family on a private basis at home. As Belinda always says: "He's amazing – the real thing!"

One day we were discussing Uri in a general sort of way and Belinda says "Hey! This is making me feel really uncomfortable! We shouldn't be talking about him because each time I do that, something weird happens."

"No way!" says I – not really believing that it could be all that bad. So imagine my astonishment and utter disbelief when I got home a couple of hours later to find that there's a teaspoon on the bench in my kitchen – and it's bent!

A few months later the subject of Uri Gellar comes up again with Belinda: Same scenario: "We'd better stop talking about him," says she, "Remember what happened last time!" This time I'm not quite so skeptical and agree – so we stop the conversation! Too late. The next day I notice a golden spoon on the dresser in my dining room – yep it's all bent and twisted! Three times this happens and I am sure that Uri would be the first to understand -- we discuss him no more!

The Honey Pot Remained Empty

Hands-on healing and healing with quartz crystals and gem-stones has always fascinated me as well and I have had more than just a passing interest in this field but never really got into it seriously. Crystals still do fascinate me and I use them all the time on myself for various aches and pains and have done so for a number of years. I have had some very positive results with this, even for certain quite serious disorders and I'd be amazed if crystal healing had not been one of the principal medical skills of the ancients. I seriously believe that medical researchers need to do some urgent research into the non-invasive healing powers of quartz crystals on the human body. On second thoughts, I suppose that this kind of research will not be in the interests of the drug companies -- so of course it is highly likely that it won't happen.

I believe though that it is probable that the immense power of quartz crystal is still relatively untapped by us today. If miniscule quartz crystals chips can drive the timepieces of the world and run the world's computers what else are they capable of? Easing my chronic rheumatisms that's what! Instead of reaching for the pain-killers and anti-inflammatory drugs, I sleep with a clear quartz crystal in my bed and as long as I've remembered it, I wake up feeling supple and pain free. When I've forgotten it, I really know it! Try it sometime. Can't possibly hurt.

One of my regular 'party tricks' which was a guaranteed crowd gatherer was when, as the night wore on and after 'a few', I would start reading palms. Incredibly, I was often right on the nail but how much of that was actual psychic ability or educated guesswork combined with a bit of lucky fluke I'm not sure. (Or could it give new meaning to the old Latin phrase 'In vino veritas' ?)

So that's about it for me and my paranormal background – I had always had this tendency to dip into the paranormal honey pot without ever developing any particular skills in any particular field. A bit of this here and a bit of that there of anything and everything that caught my imagination. Truth is that I was always way too lazy to commit myself to any one thing or to study anything in any depth. It all seemed like too much hard work and my 'mother's ruin' days got seriously in the way because the heavy drinking interfered with my powers of concentration, so I never developed any real skills in any particular area.

Over the years, I managed to collect a vast library on every imaginable mysterious subject, much of which I hardly read or at best only skimmed through. I was a sort of paranormal butterfly going from mystical flower to mystical flower -- a roving 'Jill of all trades' and of course, I ended up being the proverbial mistress of none. Until that is, the orbs floated into my life!

Internet & Inter-lect

Long before the night of the fireworks, I had been surfing the web and found a website with pictures of orbs – it seemed that at the time the general belief was that they were the spirits of the dead and they called them 'Spirit Orbs' in those days. Me being Moi, I was immediately riveted by the subject. People were finding that they had these white spheres of light turning up in their photos and they were associating them with the spirits of the dead. I was utterly fascinated because I when I saw them, I remembered that they had shown up in several photos I had taken in the past on my old Nikon 35mm camera. Those orbs had been fairly small hovering around people lurking high up in the corners of a room by the ceiling or in trees! The orbs of the night of the fireworks were similar but much bigger.

There is now a lot of material on the subject of orbs posted on the internet. Some of it spooky; some of it very intellectual and scientific-sounding, yet difficult to understand because it doesn't seem to make a lot of sense. Some of it is spiritual and some of it downright wacky. Very recently I have found several books which have been written on the subject. I have read them and enjoyed them to varying degrees but with all due respect to my co-photographers and fellow seekers, I have to say that having read their books with great interest, I am still absolutely none the wiser as to what these orbs actually are.

I truly believe that it is infinitely better to say "I honestly don't know", than to make up a theory and try to pass it off as fact, or to give the orbs names or an identity which is going to lead the whole gullible world up the proverbial garden path. To my mind, that is a form of commercial dishonesty. It's called riding the band-wagon of sensation -- all the way to the bank!

Orbs are truly a complete puzzle to me and even though I think that I probably know as much as anybody else about them, and possibly quite a lot more than some, I am as yet totally incapable of telling you exactly what thy are. From that time in 2000 when I photographed those first orbs during that fireworks display, until today, nearly eight years, hundreds of photos and many thousands of orbs later, I can say that I still know practically sweet nothing about them and in spite of what they might try to tell you, nobody else does either. Not yet. But before you put this book down without reading any further, let me tell you that this does not mean that I don't have plenty to say about them. I have several theories as to what they *might* be and I am sure that by the time you get to the end of this book we will all be much more enlightened and hopefully you too will have formed your own ideas on the subject.

CHAPTER FOUR

First Define Your Orb

The definition of an orb in my 'American Heritage' dictionary is given as "A *sphere-especially a celestial sphere. A heavenly body. One of a series of concentric, transparent spheres thought by ancient and medieval astronomers to revolve around the earth and to support the celestial bodies"*.

Let's check this out! How closely does this description fit 'our' orbs? That is to say the orbs that you and I have been photographing lately -- and if you haven't started as yet, then the ones that you soon will be!

✓ They are spheres.

✓ They are 'celestial spheres' in that they float on air or in the sky.

✓ Photos clearly show that they appear to be composed of concentric circles.

✓ They are transparent because (with certain exceptions) you can see right through them.

✓ They *do* revolve around the earth in a manner of speaking – appearing as they do everywhere in the world from Australia to Arabia to Europe.

That's five points out of six that check out affirmative. Not too bad. But are they the 'concentric transparent spheres' that the ancient and medieval astronomers believed supported the celestial bodies? (Presumably by that they meant the stars) Er, well quite frankly, they appear to be a bit too flimsy to perform that weighty task. But who knows what they are capable of? As I said earlier, who could ever have imagined not so very long ago that a miniscule chip of quartz crystal could drive the world's timepieces and computers? Or who would have been able to foretell that a few invisible neutrons and atoms arranged according to a certain formula, could lay waste vast areas and flatten whole cities such as happened in Japan in World War II? So can we really know what invisible force would be able to 'support the celestial bodies'? For me the above description begs a million-dollar question: What exactly were those concentric, transparent spheres that the ancient and medieval astronomers obviously believed existed and described in such detail? And if they believed they existed, doesn't it mean that someone at sometime, somehow actually had the physical ability to see them either with the naked eye or through some sort of optical instrument, and was therefore able to give that precise description of them? You can't after all, describe something in detail that you have never seen, can you. So what were they describing? Can you think of anything else that these 'celestial spheres' of the ancients might have been?

Sometimes you really have to wonder about those 'ancients'. They seem to have had the ability to experience, see and describe all sorts of weird and wonderful things that are totally unknown to us mere 'moderns'. A quick flick through The Bible, especially the Old Testament, speaks of all sorts of phenomena from fiery chariots to pillars of salt, that the ancients claim to have seen which are totally baffling to us in this day and age. Where did all that stuff - all those weird miracles go to? Why aren't they happening to us today?

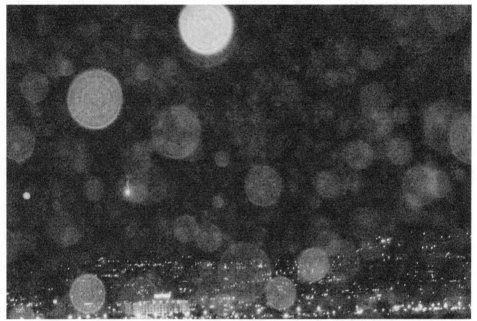

Trying to get a glimpse of the lights of Cannes through a dense curtain of orbs!

Seems that the ancients either had some sort of extra-sensory powers which we have somehow lost through the millennia, or they had huge imaginations, or they were into using hell-fire tactics big-time to terrify the living daylights out of the ignorant and through fear, gain control over the minds of the masses. Sounds rather familiar doesn't it. It's a tried and true technique that the modern politician is in fact highly skilled at -- and which is extensively used in this our own day and age. We need to learn to recognize the methods. They can be pretty subtle: Like for example: 'Homeland Security Colour-coded Terrorist Threat Levels!' It's a *daily* subconscious reminder to us to stay locked into 9/11 and stay scared. But we need to know that to be scared is not to be free. A scared person is a person who is locked in the firm grip of someone else's control. A scared nation is a nation of people who, sheep-like, are not thinking for themselves -- it is a nation which is looking to the Big Master to tell them what to do, rather than seeking good, moral government through inspired leadership.

I Think Therefore I Am

The orb phenomenon is not entirely new. In the past orbs were frequently captured on traditional cameras using film (I myself took several) but the incontrovertible fact is that with increasing frequency within the last decade, these mysterious balls of light have been suddenly showing up all over the world in everyone's digital photos in such numbers, that they will be labelled a phenomenon belonging specifically to the 21st century -- beginning with the last decade of the last millennium.

These mysterious balls of light are starting to demand our attention whether we like it or not. It's got to the stage where we can't ignore them and can no longer write them off as 'nothing'. Make no mistake about it, these orbs are definitely *something*. We can actually see them in our photos and presumably *something* that is visible to the camera's eye actually does exist even though we may not be able to see it with our own human eyes.

To quote René Descartes with a slight variation on his famous theme "I think therefore I am", it can be also said of the orbs or 'Light Beings', "*They* exist therefore they *are!*" They're physically *there* so they're not *nothing* and because they appear *everywhere*, it categorically means that they *are* everywhere.

Furthermore they appear with such consistency of shape and structure, that they can no longer be dismissed as being caused by faulty cameras or memory-sticks.

Not even the most skeptical debunker with a pair of eyes that function at least moderately well, can deny their presence, once he removes his blinkers and accepts (and I am afraid that he's going to have to), that there is no global photographic conspiracy afoot out to 'get' him by playing some massive but pointless hoax on him personally, or for that matter on the world at large.

Descartes him-very-self would have agreed that these light manifestations *are something* because they are there and we too, through the sheer weight of visual evidence stacked up in front of us, have to admit despite our 'Doubting Thomas' selves, that they exist whatever or whoever *'They'* might be. So with no place else to hide, we now need to start asking ourselves what the phenomenon could possibly be.

It's Not Our DNA They're After

It's extremely important that we keep strictly to those possibilities that are relatively believable and I am therefore going to try to avoid any thing that borders on the too insanely crackpot, so as not to totally discredit the whole phenomenon as nothing more than something weird and wonderful picked up on by a band of New-Agers during meditation or channelling from another galaxy.

There have indeed been some pretty crazy New-Age ideas about orbs bandied about which are very easy to dismiss because they are perhaps a mite too fanciful. Not that I've got anything against New Agers, I'm bordering on being one myself, but sometimes -- well, let's just say shall we, that we should leave the more extreme amongst them spinning out there lost in their galactic channellings.

There's a New-Age theory that the orbs ('Light Beings') are here to warn us Earthlings to look after our environment or we'll end up like Atlanteans at the bottom of the sea. I don't think so. There's another that says that they come from the 'Pleiades', and that they wrecked their own environment by some cataclysmic event and that they are seeking another life-supporting environment in which to live. I don't think so. Yet another says that they are here to steal our DNA and to create a super-race of mutants from human beings. I don't think so.

All that hocus-pocus is supposition, sensational is fear-based and provokes fear and has no place in this book. First we need to try to identify for ourselves what or who they are and then, and *only* then, can we begin to ask ourselves the actual whys and wherefores of it.

Let me state unequivocally that neither I nor anyone else truly knows what or who they are, what they are made of or what they are here for, if anything; and what I don't know I am not about to make up in order to make a sensation of this book or to frighten the gullible. But I will be making suggestions throughout the book, some of which may seem extreme, and it's going to be up to you whether or not you pick up the ball and run with it.

I have composed a list of several possibilities which need to be given fair consideration in order to be able to begin to penetrate the truth. These are listed very roughly in my own personal order of preference and while you are reading the list, please keep in mind the very high possibility that at least *one* of the suggestions put forward here could just possibly be the right one. But which one? "Aye, as Hamlet said, there's the rub!"

- Intelligent, non-physical 'Beings of Light'. That is to say, a perfected form of pure 'being' which needs no exterior material life-support such as food, shelter, clothing etc.
- A hitherto undiscovered and as yet undefined category of intelligent animal life-form like insects, birds or jellyfish, which has always existed but until the arrival of digital photography has been rarely captured on film and therefore has remained unknown.
- Blobs of intelligent or semi-intelligent plasma.
- Balls of pure, concentrated energy.
- Elemental organisms of hydro-charged gaseous concentration.
- Cosmic 'fallout' of some description

- The perfected souls of those who have undergone successive reincarnations and who have completed their requisite earth journeys and the lessons involved and who now dwell as 'The Light'. (Jesus claimed "I am The Light", What actually did he mean by this?).

- Personal 'attachments' like 'spirit guides' who accompany each individual throughout his or her lifetime.

- Disembodied souls of family and loved ones who have passed on.

- Ghosts or earthbound spirits.

- The physical manifestation of pure thought or consciousness.

- A micro universe in its own right.

- Part of an individual's 'soul-pool'.

- Angels or Heavenly messengers.

- Sprites, Fairies or Faeries.

- Aliens from another planet.

- UFO probes from a mother-ship.

- Portals or doorways to another world in another dimension

And who knows? Perhaps they are even Cosmic Torch Bearers sent to light the way for us into this new 'Age of Aquarius', the promise for which is that all which has hitherto been covered-up, secret and hidden will come to the surface and will be revealed. The 'Age of Aquarius' is the age of Truth with a capital 'T'.

You too are sure to have your own pet ideas as to what you think that the 'Light Beings' could be and also your own order of preference of the ideas presented here on the list. I would be very interested to hear them.

CHAPTER FIVE

An Orb Is An Orb Is An Orb

How do you describe an orb? I've given you the 'American Heritage' dictionary's definition in the first chapter, however despite my favourite dictionary's worn, tattered and coverless condition, my trusty old friend ('old ' being the operative word -- it was written about thirty years ago), the definition given is almost as good a description of 'our' modern day orbs as could be found anywhere today. But isn't *this* strange ... 'our' kind of orbs hadn't technically speaking, been discovered thirty years ago when my version of the American Heritage was written, so how do you describe something that hasn't yet been discovered? Someone must have known something back then too.

I then got to thinking about how, if the folk at 'American Heritage' were to ask me to write a modern definition for them of orbs today as we understand them, how would I describe them? This is what I came up with: *"An orb is a sphere of light which has neither the appearance of nor the substance of a physical body and which manifests in a wide variety of colours, sizes and opacity, from opaque white to completely translucent."*

Further definition of an orb could go something like this: *"The orb's environmental element is primarily in the air although marine divers are now producing photographs showing that they are also present in water. Rarely reliably reported to have been seen by the human eye, orbs appear recurrently and with increasing frequency in photography, especially digital photography, which makes them primarily a phenomenon dating from the middle of the last decade of the 20th century."*

Hmm so far so good. What else can we find to say about them? How about: *"Their sudden appearance on the paranormal stage has resulted in a surge of speculation as to what exactly, these mysterious bodies of light might be. Everything from ghosts to alien probes and a whole range of other possibilities in between, has been proposed but until some verifiable results of a legitimate investigation into the phenomenon are produced, we must meanwhile remain in the realm of ignorance and conjecture."*

Hey I'm warming to this, maybe I missed my vocation as a dictionary writer! *"Mediums, ghost hunters, and UFO spotters have respectively populated various locations from haunted houses, graveyards and mountain tops in the quest of these elusive denizens from, it is generally widely believed, the 'spirit world'. A growing deluge of reports of hauntings and other supernatural occurrences, is being submitted to the increasing number of Internet websites dedicated to the subject of orbs, along with accompanying photographs of genuine orb manifestations 'proving' the veracity of these 'hauntings' which are wholly presumed: a) to account for the presence of the orbs and: b) thus provide further 'proof' of the existence of ghosts or spirits of the dead."*

Not too bad huh? I like that word *'denizen'* -- nice touch. Now, in order not to appear biased and much as I hate to, I think we had probably better mention the debunkers and what they have to say about it otherwise they'll only have a go at me later: *"The orbs do not come without their detractors however, who claim that the spheres of light are frequently caused by the presence of various debris in the environment such as water droplets, high humidity, dust or pollen, which accumulates either on the camera lens or in close proximity to it and which reflects the camera flash in a bounce-back effect and produces the materialization of anomalous globules which have come to be known as orbs."*

There you are all you debunkers, you can thank me for that -- I think that it was a fair and impartial reporting of your soap-box for you wasn't it.

The Camera Company Disclaimer

I had got about this far with my book and the telephone rang one bright and sunny morning. It was my friend Richard who lives in nearby Valbonne which is a very picturesque medieval village nestled up in the hills behind Cannes.

"Is that you Antonia? It's Richard here. You can stop writing your book!"

"What d'ya mean I can stop writing my book Richard?"

"I've discovered what your orbs are!"

This bald statement was followed by a long drawn-out "Okaaaaay" from me: "I see -- What are they then?"

"Listen to this -- I just bought myself a new digital camera and in the trouble-shooting part of the user's manual there's a whole section on them!"

Richard then proceeded to read out the section in the manual which dealt with 'orbs' and which went roughly like this:

"You may occasionally detect the appearance of round white spots in your photographs: This is no cause for concern, neither does it imply that either your camera or the memory card are faulty. These white spots are caused by dust particles or moisture droplets in the environment which, when the flash is used, bounces back reflected light and results in the appearance of 'orb-like' objects in your photographs."

"You see!" Richard ended triumphantly, "They even call them orbs! So you can stop writing your book! The camera people know what they are!"

"The camera people are more likely covering their proverbial backsides" said I. "That dear Richard is what is known as a 'disclaimer' and it's put there because they are getting flooded with calls from people who, finding that they are photographing genuine orbs and not knowing what they are, are bombarding them with complaints about faulty cameras!"

"Oh!" said Richard sounding just a mite deflated, "I hadn't though of that."

"Darling Richard" I cooed with my most honeyed voice which is when, in fact, I am at my most dangerous. "Trust me! If I thought I was writing a book about dust motes, or rain-drops or insects on the wing, I would give you full permission to come and lock me up in one of your 'special' wards. (Richard happens to be a doctor.)

In fact, I was/am particularly grateful to Richard for phoning me that day, because I was more than interested to know that the camera companies had addressed the subject in that way. I need to pass it on to you because then you won't be tempted to fill my mailbox with letters telling me that your camera manufacturer knows what orbs are because they have written about them in the

'Trouble Shooting' section of the user's manual.

It is perfectly understandable that you (or anybody for that matter), would believe that the camera company 'knows best' – after all it's their business -- and that of course is your choice, but why not put all prejudice aside for the moment and let's see what you believe by the time you have read right to the end of this book. I have studied the subject in depth and take it from me -- no matter what the camera companies say in their disclaimers, just know that capturing dust particles in the flash, even by making a deliberate effort do so, is extremely difficult to achieve. So difficult in fact, that the chances of doing so are remote. I've tried!

There is a vast range of types and colours of orbs and so many different photographic conditions that are not covered in those brief statements put out by the camera companies. Believe me those statements are simply an attempt by the camera companies to stem the constant flow of enquiries which they probably receive in their hundreds on a daily basis. However when confronted by genuine orb activity the camera companies will be just as baffled by it as you and I because it is inexplicable and the more you get to know about it, the less you realize that you do know!

Debunking The Debunkers

Before I go any further, let me get something off my chest right here and now! I've got a thing about debunkers! Debunkers of *anything* – not just of orbs or Crop circles or UFOs. The very word 'debunker' makes me feel like I'm about to break out in a rash.

There is a whole category of people in this world who are simply in no way prepared to understand *anything at all* if it's outside the norm. It's way, way too scary for them. To ask them to come down off their soap-box just for a moment and to accept for a micro-second that there might be something out there that they don't comprehend -- something that's bigger than them, bigger than any of us -- would be asking far too much of these types. Instead of saying "Yes how fascinating! Maybe there's something in that", they slam the door of their brains tight shut and promptly launch a debunking campaign intended to deride the whole phenomenon and to show how smart they are. "There you go; doesn't exist. Sorted!" Well I've got news for you! So listen very carefully for I shall say this only once.

A *genuine* orb (i.e. the orb which appears as a phenomenon as opposed to an anomaly) is *not* repeat *not* a grain of pollen. It is *not* repeat *not* a mote of dust.

I have studied the effect of grains of pollen as shown on the internet and it is true that they can produce globule-like spheres which to the untrained eye could be seen to resemble orbs and which to the green horn could even be taken for genuine orbs. But they are *not* orbs. To someone with my long experience studying orbs in all their states and forms, grains of pollen don't even remotely resemble an orb, neither by 'look' nor by structure. Anyone with any reasonably long experience looking at genuine orbs is not likely to mistake a bit of pollen or a seed for the genuine article.

The same goes for dust. In fact dust like rain, is extremely hard to photograph even using the flash. But being by nature an extremely fair woman, I have tried very hard to prove the debunkers right, and on a dusty road in the middle of nowhere I have been known to screech to a halt, descend from my car, jump up and down and scuff the ground for all I'm worth with my new Gucci loafers, stir up as much dust as possible into the air and then before it has had a chance to settle, run off a few rapid shots of the resulting dust cloud and got some magnificent photos of err, a dust cloud, sadly with not an orb in sight and alas not even a teensy mote of dust posing as one! Clearly this line of research needs to be worked upon and obviously it needs to be not just any old dust, it needs to be the *right* sort of dust. I promise I will not give up! Err-pass me the Kleenex someone: I've got me-self a nasty attack of sneezes from all that dust and pollen I've been stirring up in the interests of scientific research!

All joking aside, while still on the subject of dust, I have this really strong mental image of a good Robert De Niro action movie where he's being chased by the baddies. It takes place in an old disused factory with rays of light beaming in through broken windows -- with dust motes stirring lazily in the air, lit by slanting shafts of sun (looking like orbs of course). Robert takes cover behind concrete pillar, takes pot-shot at villains who fire back. Our Hero hastily runs to cover of next pillar amidst a spray of bullets. Bullets miraculously miss him and ricochet off pillar. More dust stirs in air – more sunlit particles – more orbs – more action. But that is a movie scenario and it takes place in a disused factory under the harsh glare of studio lights! Never mind -- next time you are out walking and find a disused factory with sun streaming through broken window pains, lighting up the dust motes, promise me you'll get your cameras out and send me the results! Can't wait! In truth, real orbs are already difficult enough to photograph but false orbs in my experience, are extremely difficult to get. I should say that with one or two exceptions which you will find pictured towards the end of this book, I personally have never had any great success in turning a dust particle into an orb look-alike but I'll keep on trying.

Nevertheless much as I dislike debunkers, they do have their place in that they oblige us to be as discerning and as honest as we can be -- so as not to confuse the issue. Someone did point out to me that whether we are dealing with 'true' orbs or with 'false' or 'simulated' orbs, the fact remains that they are *all* photographic anomalies. An excellent point. But are they all phenomena? There-in lies the burning question.

Water, Water Everywhere & Not A Drop ..... Is Round!

Another hobby-horse that the debunkers ride for all its worth, is that when it's raining, orbs are caused by the flash reflecting off the raindrops! Really? Did

you ever hear anything so silly! What shape is a raindrop? What shape is an orb? I guess if you were to ask one hundred people the question what shape is a raindrop?", ninety-nine point nine percent of them without even stopping to think, would most probably say round or

This is a portion of a photo reproduced elsewhere in the book and it shows Belinda Carlisle out at the crop circles in Wiltshire England. No photo could more eloquently illustrate the point I am making about the impossibility confusing a rain drop and an orb. The rain is pelting down here and Heidi's fast, ten mega-pixel camera has caught both the raindrops *and* an orb. Note that the rain is stretched into ribbon-like lengths after its long and stressful fall from a great height -- its shape is determined by the pull of gravity. (Photo by Heidi Cook) pear-shaped. A *round* rain drop? No way! Think, think and think again! Rain drops aren't ever round -- they're like streamers. Long and thin. Think about it. Rain comes hurtling earthwards at practically super-sonic speeds from a great height of a couple of thousand meters or more, and into the bargain, it is very often driven by gale-force winds. Anybody out there still going to think that it arrives on the ground in the form of perfectly pristine *round* drops? Sorry!

Quite apart from all of the above, old Grandma Gravity has most assuredly got quite a lot to say in the matter and she definitely has her part to play in it.

Photograph of a fountain playing in a Cannes property. I have studied this photo minutely in its highest definition and nowhere to be found is there a drop of water which is round! This doesn't occur because the water is tossed into the air by the fountain and is then pulled down to earth again by – old Grandma Gravity. Debunkers of the phenomenon of orb photography base some of their argument on water droplets reflecting the camera flash and producing orb-like anomalies. I think that we can prove otherwise.

Every time it rains, Grandma Gravity pulls all that water which constitutes rain down to earth in the cruellest and most unkind fashion -- and the higher it comes from the harder and faster it falls – just like some people. By the time rain has arrived here on earth, it has been through enormously stressful forces and has suffered all sorts of terrible tortures -- it arrives positively deformed!

The fundamental nature of water is that it goes everywhere. It flows, it seeps, it drips, it drops as rain, it oozes and finds its way into the tiniest nooks and crannies because whatever it does and wherever it goes, it adapts its form to suit whatever shape is required of it -- but it is *never* round. Not even the most perfect raindrop sitting on a rose petal is round -- because the side which is in contact with the rose petal is flat! It follows therefore, that a photo taken during a rain shower of an orb which is round in shape, is not and cannot be mistaken for a raindrop – because quite simply, raindrops are not round. Elementary dear Watson!

Simulated Orbs

Recently I found something on the internet which I viewed with a slight sense of disquiet as I am very keen that the honesty and integrity of the 'art' of orb photography remains intact and therefore beyond reproach. There is a man who has spent a lot of time and effort simulating orbs, both in still photographs and in videos. This man is not a debunker of the phenomenon per-se, neither does he seem to have issue with anyone who photographs genuine orbs so I am not entirely certain exactly what it is that he is actually setting out to prove, but what he has proved to me is that with the help of a few stage props, orbs are in fact quite easy to simulate and therefore the veracity of the genuine orb phenomenon could become fuzzy around the edges and hamper a serious study of them. However this man's work as long as it is kept in its own category and is distinct from the real thing, could have a definite place in a serious study of orbs by providing a us with a definitive work of reference on fakes.

He demonstrates that many orb photos and other phenomena published on the internet, could be unintentional fakes not necessarily put out there with any dishonest intent to deceive. He shows how various materials such as house dust, dust from a blanket which has just been shaken, a stray hair, water droplets, reflections from glass and so on, can produce effects which closely resemble a genuine orb or orbs in motion etcetera.

Although the uninitiated eye would perhaps have difficulty in distinguishing between these simulated orbs and the genuine article I myself was able to detect that the orbs he produced were simulated as there was a 'look' about them that I have never seen in any of my orb photos and I have taken hundreds of them remember. However what did amuse me greatly about his photographs was that here and there I noticed that he had a genuine orb or two mixed in amongst the fakes. I wrote to him about it but 'Monsieur' who took his 'false orbs' very seriously indeed, was not amused by my revelations and didn't want to know about the presence of the genuine article in his photos -- or so it seemed. It was probably our friends having their little joke with him. That would be typical of their zany sense of humour! They always get the last laugh you know -- especially if you are trying to disprove their existence.

I've done quite a lot of photographic research of my own on water and how it behaves expressly for the purposes of this book and the photographs on the previous pages should prove the point that water is never round and should calm down any of those lingering debunkers who keep on insisting that it is.

In the closing chapters of the book, I have included an entire chapter on fake orbs, ectoplasm and other anomalies which are what I call 'False Friends' or 'Posers' but in the next chapter I shall be describing the structure of genuine orbs.

Went for a wander after a curry dinner with friends in Nice one night in May 2008 to admire the refurbished Place Massena and the new 'Tramway'. Sensing the presence of the 'Light Beings', I took several photos of the fountain, all with orbs. The orbs, cannot possibly be mistaken for water. This really lovely photo shows that orbs often gather around sources of water. They need to re-hydrate in order to stay healthy.

CHAPTER SIX

What Are They Made Of & How Are They Built?

Of all the living creatures in our three-dimensional environment, I think that the orb most resembles one of those little flat, coin-like jellyfish that float around in the sea, but until someone actually manages to catch one (an orb I mean, not a jellyfish) and lie the poor thing out on a laboratory table for dissection and proper analysis, no one can say for sure what they are made of. Meanwhile, until that happens, lots of theories have already have been proposed about their structure. I believe however that perhaps a study of jellyfish could help us to understand their internal structure and why it is that no matter from which angle we photograph them, they always seem to be presenting the same 'face' and the internal design always looks the same.

I have almost never taken or seen a photo of an orb in any shape other than near-perfectly or perfectly round. Occasionally I have taken a shot of one or two which seem to be slightly flattened on one side, like the one shown here – but while not entirely uncommon, it is relatively rare.

Although orbs look as though they are flat, disc-shaped objects, I have never yet managed to take one in profile, three-quarter face, or lying flat like a saucer. This proves that they are spherical and three dimensional like balloons or soccer balls. They cannot possibly be otherwise, because if they were discus-shaped objects, then they would appear like plates or saucers when caught from any angle other than face on. They therefore must be spherical. But what about that flattened side in this orb here? Must have bumped into something.

The Eight Basic Types

According to my observations to date, there are eight basic types of orbs. I have described those orbs and their structures in the list which follows. Other authors have come up with other types and shapes not familiar to me with interior markings which I have not seen in any of 'my' orbs so I will stay only with those orbs as it has been my personal experience to observe, in order to maintain my own integrity and to leave other peoples' classifications out of this book. Any mistakes therefore shall be my own and not those of others! So here we go. Here are the eight types of orbs that I have catalogued:

Type 1.   Semi opaque with a clearly defined internal structure which usually shows approximately seven concentric circles like age rings in a tree, bisected by a wheel-spoke formation radiating from the centre out towards the perimeter making countless clearly marked segments within the orb. There is a definite nucleus in the absolute centre of these orbs. These can range in size from the size of a tennis ball to huge -- up to ten or more metres in diameter. They usually show a slightly phosphorescent aureole or aura around the perimeter. Objects such as leaves and other orbs can clearly be seen through them.

Type 2.   A very recent type of orb new to me, which I encountered as recently as November 2007, closely resembles a pot-lid or a gladiator's shield. It has a dish-like formation and the outer edge casts a clear shadow itself in relief. There is a convex area with no apparent markings which culminates in a slightly protruding and very clearly defined nucleus. I know people who have photographed this type of orb who compare it to an eyeball. This type of orb usually shows a slightly phosphorescent aureole or aura around the perimeter.

Type 3.   Opaque and white resembling a ball of cotton-wool and with a slight fuzziness around the edges but having no aureole or aura. Nothing can be seen through them. There is no apparent nucleus.

These can vary in size from very small like snow-flakes to quite large e.g. the size of a bread plate. This type will be covered more fully when discussing photographing orbs in the rain.

Type 4.   Opaque and white almost resembling cotton-wool with a very strong electric blue coloured phosphorescent aureole or aura around the perimeter. Nothing can be seen through them. There is no

apparent nucleus. These can vary in size from quite small like a ping-pong ball to quite large e.g. the size of a bread plate. The specimen shown in the picture here is a classic example of a Type 4 orb.

Type 5.   Milky white and slightly translucent with a hint of poorly defined internal structure discernable. It is seldom seen with a nucleus but usually with a slightly phosphorescent aureole or aura around the perimeter. Objects such as leaves, other orbs etcetera can faintly be seen through them. These can range in size from the size of a tennis ball to measuring up to and in excess of 1-1½ meters.

Type 6.   Completely translucent and see-through. Objects such as leaves, other orbs etcetera can clearly be seen through them. A nucleus which is quite often off-centre can frequently be seen in this type of orb.

Type 7.   Very faint with no internal structure visible, no discernable aureole and no discernable nucleus.

Type 8.   All coloured orbs which are not white. These colours include gold, pink, blue, green, various shades of violet and very rarely red.

This is a perfect example of a 'Type 1' orb. It was taken without flash in my garden in full daylight. There is a clear blue/gold aura around its entire perimeter. The orb excellent health; it is neither too opaque nor is it too transparent. It is actually behind the Magnolia leaf which is important to our research.

The two beautiful orbs shown on this and on the previous page, both have something very important in common. They are both *behind* objects. The one on page 65 is behind a leaf on a Magnolia tree in my garden while the orb below is behind an ornamental post in an abandoned garden in Cannes. Of these two orbs the one in the abandoned garden is by far the larger as the ornamental post would be approximately 1m20cms high thus giving the orb a diameter of approximately one meter. The orb behind the Magnolia leaf, when I measured it against one of the actual leaves on the tree, I estimated to be between twenty-three and twenty-five centimetres – about the size of a big dinner plate which makes it a very respectable size all the same!

An orb in an abandoned garden. The post beside it is at least one meter twenty centimetres high so this is a large orb with a circumference of approximately one meter. Note that it seems to be hugging the post very closely and is slightly behind it which gives us a good spatial reference and allows us to measure its size with a reasonable degree of accuracy. This also proves that the orb is not floating in front of the camera lens and therefore cannot be a speck of dust or dirt on the lens causing the orb.

The significance of orbs being *behind* other objects is of enormous value to us in the serious study of the orb phenomenon. There are at least four good reasons why this is so.

1) It gives a point of reference to the size of the orb because it can be compared with the object it is behind and measured accordingly.

2) It gives a spatial reference of the distance from the camera which can be measured to an extremely accurate degree.

3) It proves that it is not a dust mote a rain drop or any other foreign matter which could be clinging to the camera lens and therefore . . . .

4) . . . . . increases its veracity as a material object in is own right which has body and substance.

Further observations of orbs reveal that they have...

- A high water content which they need to replenish from time to time.

- A source of energy which allows them their tremendous mobility This 'fuel' could well be electricity which accounts for the fact that they are often seen in greater numbers before and after electrical storms and also around high-tension wires. Therefore they possibly have electrons circulating at high speed in their bodies.

- They have a very high luminosity and leave a trail behind them when in motion. This internal light source is possibly phosphorus which could also be one of the elements in the physical make-up of orbs and which could account for the highly luminous electric blue aureole or aura which they often display.

A distinctive feature of most genuine orb types which distinguishes them from fakes, simulated orbs, seeds or pollen is that they very often have an aureole of bright phosphorescent light. This aureole or 'aura' borders the orb in varying widths from narrow to very wide and can come in a range of colours from blue to green to pink to silver and gold.

The interior design of the orbs can very often look like a maze with a nucleus or they can appear to be constructed of concentric circles, usually seven in number, with a bicycle wheel spoke-like structure radiating out to the circumference looking very like a cross-section of a tree trunk showing the annual age circles, with the 'bark' being the aura of the orb. The maze-like design gives them the appearance of flattish discus shapes which in fact they are not. They are spherical. Somehow their design must be consistent right through the body of the orb, so that no matter from which angle you are viewing it, the pattern always shows the same. Intriguing!

How Big Are They?

Orbs can come in any size through from tiny pin-points to the size of a marble, to a ping-pong ball, to a tennis ball, to a football and so on right up to such an enormous size that it can be counted in several meters in diameter. I suspect that they come even larger than we have measurable comparisons for. At a certain point, they could be so massive in size that we no longer realize that we are in fact taking a photograph of an orb. We maybe looking into it not *at* it. We might even be *inside* it!

The picture on the facing page provides an excellent example of the great diversity of size between one orb and another which can be from quite small to really huge. This photograph also gives us some depth perspective. The larger orb is very much further away and although it has very nice markings they are a little fuzzy and out of focus because of the great distance. The small orb in front of it is much closer to the camera and is therefore much better defined.

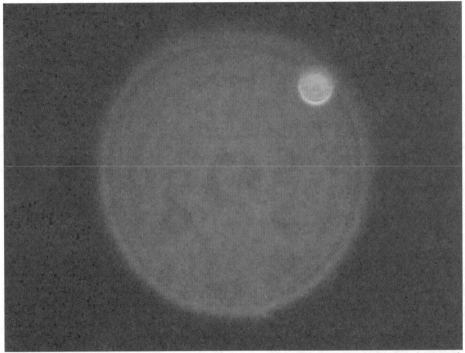

A small orb in front of another orb. The perspective here is important. The larger of the two orbs is much further away than the small orb. The size difference here could be like comparing the moon to planet Earth. Or planet Earth to the Sun -- or some other Galactic goliath! As above – so below!

Making Funny Faces

Some people claim that they can see faces in orbs. I can't -- or is it that I just haven't looked hard enough or maybe I don't have a big enough imagination!

Recently someone sent me a beautiful orb photo which she had taken and included a note saying that she could see a small child's head in it, and she gave me instructions as to how to look for it. I have to admit that after a long moment of studying the orb, all of a sudden by squinting my eyes, I could see the head quite clearly. I don't think though that physical representations or portraits of loved ones who have passed over are what orbs are 'about'.

Someone else sent me a picture of her favourite orb stating that it was a 'Smiley'! Sure, I could see that quite well too, but to actually claim that there was a clear message to us Earthlings from another planet, contained in the image of a 'Smiley' face in this particular orb, I felt was stretching things a bit! But hey! Perhaps it *was* intended as a message and the 'Light Beings' were just showing us

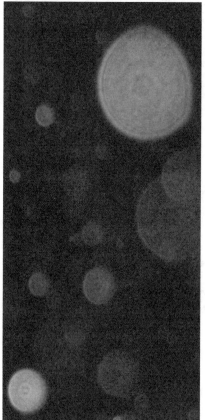

that they have a good sense of humor. That would be entirely characteristic of their loony behavior. At the end of the day it's up to you to make of this anything that you want to – if you find that your Aunt Gertrude's face turns up in one of your orbs – well then say a big hello to Aunt Gertrude from me and send me the photo pronto!

Baby Are You Mine Tonight?

Having made that flippant remark about Aunt Gertrude's face, it is actually not as silly as it sounds and I have included this orb photo here because I am intrigued by it and I want you to see it too. It is a big orb with the flattened side. Does this give you a sense of déja-vu? That's right! We have seen it earlier, at the beginning of this chapter and we will be seeing it again many times as we make this journey together -- so let's give him a name shall we? How about we call him Old Flatface!

Because one orb looks very much like another, I once asked the 'Light Beings' to send me a clearly recognizable orb to 'prove' to me that they have different identities. Old Flatface here is so distinctive with his flattened side that I think that this is the answer to my request and is my 'identifiable' orb. A lop-sided orb is so rare that I seriously believe that it has to be the one and the same orb. Should this be so, then the implications are staggering because the two photos were taken at a geographical distance of at least forty miles and at a lapse in time of six or seven months.

If Old Flatface *is* one and the same orb, it would mean that he travels with me and so belongs to me and not to the area where it was photographed. It could therefore be one of my personal orbs and would support at least three of my theories of what orbs could possibly be.

Vis:

- 'Personal Attachments' like 'spirit guides' who accompany us throughout our lifetimes --
- or the souls of family and loved ones who have passed on –
- or part of an individual's 'soul-pool'!

CHAPTER SEVEN

Who Knows Where Or When?

The most frequently asked question about orbs by those who have never photographed one is, "Where do these Orbs hang out?" The answer to that is simple; everywhere and anywhere. Least of all where you expect them to be, and most of all where you least expect them to be. They're kind of a law unto themselves. They can pop in uninvited when one is trying to do a spot of serious photography and on the other hand they can and do, remain maddeningly absent when one is trying for all one's worth to capture them!

Graveyards And Lost Souls

When I first started reading about Spirit Orbs on the internet, back in 2000, the general consensus seemed to be that they were the souls of the departed, lost spirits trapped in our dimension and unable to pass through 'the curtain' onto the other side'. Consequently orb hunters were bravely venturing out at night photographing in and around graveyards and they seem to have had some degree of success judging by the number of graveyard photos with orbs to be found on the web.

I have a flip-side to that cemetery coin. As it happened at about the time when I was first aware of the existence of orbs, I was doing a lot of family research in the north of Scotland. My work of tracing ancestors took me into just about every graveyard all over Caithness, Orkney and the Shetland Isles, where all the auld kin were buried. Some of these graveyards were very often in the middle of nowhere and were downright spooky having been long since abandoned, with the graves almost obliterated by turf or overgrown with stinging nettle and brambles, while others were significantly more civilised, weed-free with mown grass, the dead often being kept company by the local rabbit population out foraging for the free lunches provided by the flowers left on the graves.

During those numerous cemetery sorties, I photographed an awful lot of graves, tombs, headstones etcetera – and I mean a lot! Yet never once was there even the slightest suspicion of an orb and believe me I was trying! Nevertheless on any same day that I'd been out in the graveyards, an evening family get-together with the living relatives (as opposed to the departed ones), would produce an unexpected orb or two, much to my excitement.

I should perhaps mention here that my days of hunting down relatives in cemeteries were actually well before I had a digital camera and yet I was taking orbs even back then. Not often admittedly but often enough to be highly significant as far as proving that they are not necessarily uniquely a product of digital cameras.

So it was/is therefore not my experience that graveyards were or are a place of especial preference for orbs and I thank the saints for that because if they are indeed the spirits of the dead, then I find it very disturbing to think that some poor disembodied, disoriented spirit might be wandering aimlessly, lonely and confused in a graveyard trying to connect with its earthly remains which have been long since laid to rest six feet under. Brrr! Horrible thought.

Churches & Fervent Prayer

Now we're talking! I live in continental Europe where churches are nearly all very ancient and I travel extensively by car, especially around the South of France where I seldom miss an opportunity to investigate an old Church and I think I can pretty safely say that I have very rarely visited an old church, chapel, cathedral or sanctuary without capturing an orb lurking in there somewhere. Why should this be? Is it perhaps that many of these places are associated with certain cataclysmic events in history, and were silent witness to intense human emotions from great joy to great personal suffering, together with fervent prayer? It's an interesting thought, and it could be a partial explanation of their presence in churches. It could be that great joy or great pain builds up in the micro-environment within one of these religious buildings and leaves behind it a physical but invisible form of spiritual energy. Or could it possibly be that our orbs are the souls of departed Christians with a deep-rooted attachment to their church which they are unable to relinquish even after death?

Somehow I don't think that anything that went on in or around churches in the way of humans in prayerful worship and the residual energies of intense emotion or prayer is the full answer, because I have captured much bigger and

I took this photo of three orbs in Toulouse Cathedral in 2002. The graininess is because lighting conditions in religious buildings are very seldom adequate for photography. As is often the case in churches and as was the case here, we were not allowed to use the flash. This provides us with yet further proof that orbs do not need flash to be visible to the camera's eye. (I used some light enhancement here for improved reproduction for the book.

more dramatic, better defined orbs and manifold manifestations in places which have nothing to do with religious buildings. Or do they – could there be a connection?

Could it be that it's not actually the churches or cathedrals per-se that bring into being the orb phenomenon, but is it in fact, the actual *physical places* where those churches or cathedral were built? Now I think that perhaps we are getting closer to a possible truth.

It's a well-known fact that throughout early Christian history countless places of so-called Pagan Worship were hijacked, and by using the old temples shrines and sanctuaries as foundations for the new Christian structures, anything from a small church to a great cathedral, was built on top. This is why so many church crypts are of a much earlier date than the main churches above them. It's quite fascinating: It's actually all about 'layers'. Seek beneath the top layer and you'll find something else lying beneath it. Very often what is found beneath the surface layer speaks more eloquently of what went on in the past than any history book can.

What invariably happened after consecration of the new buildings in the name of Jesus and the newly created Christian Saints, was that those old religions were declared to be heresies and their places of worship were eventually swallowed up so entirely and forcibly, that within a generation or two they fell into oblivion. It might be worth mentioning here as a sort of 'by the way', that this seldom happened without an additional bit of unfriendly persuasion with the stick and the sword, or a quick roasting at the stakes and pyres of the mass burnings. (Exceptionally nice people those early Christians – just as long as you agreed with them that is!)

Underground Streams & Ley Lines

We know that the ancients, the Celts and the Druids, had an uncanny ability to tune into earth energies and built their temples and other places of worship above underground streams and along the magnetic 'power-points' of electrical forces in the earth's surface 'grid'. In other words, they found and built along those veins in the earth which we know today as 'Ley Lines'; those invisible 'train-tracks' which resonate with a mystical source of energy. 'A mystical source of energy'. Let's keep that phrase very much in mind. I'll be trotting it out again very, very soon, meanwhile we should bear in mind that these energy spots on the earth's surface could very well be the places where orbs and other phenomena congregate and manifest most easily.

In The Wide Open Spaces

Oddly enough it is in some incredibly wild places like for example, high in the mountains where there is not a vestige of human habitation that I have takes some of my most beautiful orb photos. The Col de Vence is just such a place. It is an extremely weird and wonderful area in the pre-alps of the Alpes Maritimes in the South of France with a supercharged atmosphere, where 'things' happen. There have been many reports of UFO activity up there over the years and in late summer 2007 a mystifying 'crop circle' with a huge diameter measuring thirty two meters appeared overnight in an uncultivated field of wild grasses. This was by no means the first and only circle to be found traced in the land up there. Could there be a possible link between this slightly hostile, wild and desolate environment high in the mountains and the cathedrals and churches in more 'civilised' surroundings? The answer to this is a resounding "Yes, yes and yes again!" And the reason for this is that the Col de Vence is one of those spots on our planet, where abides a 'mystical source of energy' in heaps. You see! I told you I'd be trotting out that phrase again very soon!

In Human Company

Yes without doubt, orbs seem to adore human company and can invariably be found around people whenever and wherever they are gathered together for family occasions such as weddings, baptisms, dances, discos, parties, rock concerts and so on. Especially rock concerts. We'll be taking a closer look at this in upcoming chapters. I also have an idea that the orbs could be your 'personal attachments'. By that, I am saying that you have your own 'Light Beings' from your personal collective 'soul pool' which actually 'belong' to you and which watch over you and accompany you wherever you go, rather like Spirit Guides which of course until proven otherwise, it is perfectly possible that they could indeed be.

By their behaviour patterns, my observation of orbs is that they actively and intelligently seek out human company quite deliberately and that they seem to know where and when their presence would not be required and certainly not appreciated -- as for example where they sense fear or in the case of professional photographers -- then they make themselves scarce and stay away.

Protective Role

I once heard someone say that orbs flew with aircraft and protected them in flight. To be perfectly honest with you, I'd much rather put my trust in the pilot and his experience, the reputation of the airline, it's safety record and its maintenance staff on the ground. However, always curious, I couldn't help wondering if there were any orbs around my aircraft when it landed in Dubai on a recent trip there. As we were disembarking, I took a quick photo to find out which showed me that there were indeed several orbs around the plane.

Nice to know all the same!

Various Other Places Where Orbs Are Frequently Photographed

- Restaurants and night clubs
- Old theatres and music halls
- Psychic Church meetings
- Pubs, especially old ones, where people hang out in an atmosphere of conviviality
- Near any source of water
- Anywhere and everywhere
- Where you least expect them!

Those are not orbs neatly lined up at the bottom of this picture but the stage lights at the U2 concert in Nice. Bono and Adam are the two scintillating stars lighting up the Big Screen! Orbs love to go to rock concerts and we will be looking at the attendance of the 'Light Beings' at the U2 concert and rock concerts in general in another chapter.

CHAPTER EIGHT

Are They Intelligent?

This is the chapter where I am going to be putting the status of my mental wellbeing on the line and you will either judge me as fully certifiable or give me the benefit of the doubt and take me for what I am trying very hard to be, which is an objective observer of orbs and their behavioural characteristics, reporting her findings and who first and foremost trusts that she will remain entirely open-minded, while attempting make some small pioneering break-through in understanding this new paranormal phenomenon.

As it happens, I have not been able to avoid noticing that the orbs positively demonstrate a very real level of intelligence and according to my interpretation of their behaviour, they most frequently show a discernable ability to think and act. Therefore as from here onwards I am going to be obliged to attribute certain personality traits to the entities I call 'Light Beings', I hope that you too will keep an open mind, stay with me and realise that I am merely passing on to you the result of many years of close scrutiny of their manner of behaving and nothing that I have to say from this point on is to be taken as evidence (conclusive or not), that I have either totally lost it, or whether or not I personally believe that the 'Light Beings' are --

i.   living, intelligent creatures capable of thought process or --

ii.   merely random blobs of accumulated plasma making a very good job of passing for intelligent creatures capable of thought process!

Here are just a few of the characteristics and behaviour patterns which I have observed in them over the years.

- They seem to be playful and show a marked sense of fun.
- They can be either absolutely adorable or downright maddening depending on their mood.
- They can get up to all sorts of silly antics.
- They seem to adore babies, small children and animals and seem to want to play with them.
- They definitely appear to love human company and have a strong tendency to show up at family get-togethers especially those where there are children involved.
- They seem to respond to telepathy.
- They seem to like being photographed and will show up for a session often placing themselves right in front of the camera.
- They don't show up in photographs of professionals. They definitely seem to know that they would not be welcome.

- They seem to understand fear as a human emotion and do not reveal themselves in photos of people who are afraid, or make their presence known anywhere where they sense fear.

- While vast numbers of orbs have been photographed inside homes especially at parties -- by and large I believe that they prefer to be out of doors rather that 'trapped' inside.

- They gather in vast numbers for musical events and often seem to have travelled great distances to get there.

- They appear to be capable of assembling in pattern formations and adapting their colour to suit certain occasions or to demonstrate a point.

Telepathic Capacities

I know that this is going to sound a little crazy, but I have found, that the 'Light Beings' seem to have the ability communicate in a two-way exchange of mental telepathy and although I can't physically see them, I am beginning to believe that after all these years of working with them that I have 'learned' to tune-in to them psychically. I have found that I can more or less summon them up at will just by concentrating and thinking about them. More often than not if I mentally ask them to show up for a photographic session, after just a few clicks of the camera or (if it's at night), after a few explosions of the camera flash they invariably come flying in for the rendez-vous. I rarely have to wait more than a minute or two before they appear. They in turn, seem to know how to get their message across to us humans if we learn to 'listen' closely. When they are present, I definitely seem to have an ability to sense them by some sort of telepathic message which is almost audible and seems to filter through from somewhere out there in the ether. At those moments I get an overwhelming feeling; in fact it's more than a feeling, it's a positive knowledge that they are there, so I drop whatever it is that I am doing, grab my camera and start clicking. I am invariably spot-on and that with such a high percentage of accuracy that it has to be more than a mere coincidence.

This proves to me almost conclusively that they have an ability to make their presence felt to those who have a certain level of sensitivity and can pick up on their vibes. It's all about radio waves and being tuned in on the right band.

Yes, I know it sounds slightly loopy but I am just reporting what has been my experience with them. Can't be more objective than that can I?

They Know How To Get The Message Across

In one of the books I read recently on the subject of orb photography, the author got this great photo of a group of orbs looking as though they made up a formation of some kind. His wife said "Looks like we should join up the dots!" No sooner had she said that, then this guy got this rather off-the-wall idea of making a tracing of the orbs onto paper and checking it against a star map of the heavens. He didn't have to look for very long before he found surprise, surprise that the configuration of the group of orbs corresponded exactly, down to the very last star, to the constellation where the Dog Star is -- Canis Major. Now I must admit that I found that pretty amazing but what I found absolutely incredible about this story was the fact that the idea to check the orbs against a star chart came to him *out of the blue*. Why did he get that slightly way-out idea? Where on earth did it come from? It would seem clear that The 'Light Beings' deliberately formed the configuration of Canis Major so that they could prove a point about something which he and his wife had been discussing earlier and then to further 'prove' themselves, they *told* him what to do and where to look. This demonstrates to me is that the 'Light Beings' are highly intelligent and that they

have the ability to get their message across telepathically which is exactly what they did here. He was tuned in and he picked up on it. Even his wife's idea that they should be joining up the dots looks like a really significant part of the telepathic experience that was going on there, because that's exactly what happens with charts of star constellations. The 'dots' are joined up!

So to ask the question again. Are the orbs intelligent and can they impose themselves on us telepathically? To that I have to tell you that I think that there is a very high probability that they are extremely intelligent; that they can think and act and that they can impose simple ideas on us telepathically. However for us to be able to communicate with them, we need to find their broadcasting frequency and learn to tune into it.

Are Orbs Vain?

Mirror, mirror on the wall – who is fairest of them all?

The orb here is a perfect specimen of a Type 1 orb and could well be looking at its own reflection by using the window as a mirror! It is a valuable photo in the study of orbs as it shows that they can cast a reflection and what's more, its own reflection is visible through its own body. This photo was taken on my terrace early evening on 2nd July 2004. This orb is very conveniently placed so that I was able to get a precise measurement of its diameter. The door is exactly one metre wide and the amount the orb overlaps the door frame is by about ten centimetres, so it measures around 1m.10cms in diameter. This was getting very big and slightly scary! But I was still a beginner when I took this photo. I had no idea then that in the fairly near future I would be photographing orbs ten times this size!

They Have A Zany Sense Of Fun

They also seem to love to play hide-and-seek which appears to be fairly consistent with their silly sort of sense of humour. It's a kind of peek-a-boo game they have which goes like 'now you see me – now you don't'! They can be out in force and then suddenly turn all camera shy and go into hiding so that you can be clicking away out there in the freezing night air and not get a single shot. Then just as you've had enough and have decided to go inside out of the cold, bingo they show up again!

Another extremely annoying trick of theirs is that the best and brightest of them with the clearest markings, the very one which would make the best candidate for enlarging and studying, has this infuriating tendency to just peek around the edge of the frame so that all you get is no more than a tantalizing portion of it. I have noticed too that they're probably quite vain because they seem to love being photographed and will more often than not put themselves right in the camera's line of vision which is very convenient and makes them easy to photograph; and yes, as the photo on the facing page shows, I've even caught them admiring themselves in mirrors and windows. Truly, I think they're vain!

A-List Party Goers

The 'Light Beings' adore parties and are first class gate-crashers. Birthdays, weddings, christenings or parties of any description where friends and families are gathered together, seem to give them a really good excuse to show up, so of course there's a very high chance of capturing them at a social event, especially if

you happen to have your digital camera with you. Point it up to the ceiling in the corners of the room – they very often skulk about up there until they get over their initial shyness, feel more confident and come on down to join the party. Of course people will ask you why you're photographing the ceiling. Just smile mysteriously and tell them "No particular reason -- just fooling around with the digital!

CHAPTER NINE

Are Orbs Visible To The Naked Eye?

Are orbs visible to the naked eye? No. Not that has been reliably reported to date. Some folk, particularly people who have psychic abilities, claim that they can see orbs. I can't, and the best that I can say is that from time to time I think that I have caught a glimpse of something in my peripheral vision; either a fleeting movement or a small flash of light which when I turn to look is not there. And then if I'm photographing at night, there is a moment, a split second when I see a confetti-like tinsel sparkle just as the flash goes off. They're always there when I see that.

The very best answer I have yet found to this question is provided in the quote below by David Icke from his book 'The Biggest Secret'. (I hope you don't mind me quoting you David! I'm sure you won't -- it proves that I buy your books!)

"Creation consists of an infinite number of frequencies or dimensions of life sharing the same space in the way that radio and television frequencies do." This compares with our ability to see or hear a fourth dimension by tuning a T.V or a radio in and out of a station. Turn the tuning knob on the radio and you no longer receive the station even though the station is still out there broadcasting. I can grasp that simple fact! (David Icke "The Biggest Secret page 26.)

I can grasp that simple fact too. When I read this passage in David's book, it leapt off the page at me and hit me like the proverbial ton of bricks. That's it! I said to myself. That's exactly what orbs must do. They are there all the time sharing the same space, the very air we breathe, but they dwell in another dimension of that space. A fourth or fifth or sixth dimension and, like an out-of-tune radio we can't pick up on anything coherent because it's operating on a different frequency. The radio is still merrily broadcasting along its invisible wavelengths but we can't receive it because we're not tuned into the station.

Spiritual ambassador and healer of the planet, Drunvalo Melchizedek has this to say in his book 'Serpent of Light': *". . . . . . . the Universe is seen as purely sound or vibration. The relationship between the dimensions is also purely vibrational and corresponds perfectly to the laws of music and harmonics. The dimensions are separated from each other in exactly the same proportions that notes on the chromatic scale of music are separated from each other. Instead of cycles per second as in music -- for dimensions they are separated by wavelength, but the proportions are the same." (Drunvalo Melchizedek 'Serpent of Light' Page 133.)*

Just because we can't see something, doesn't mean it isn't there. Imagine electricity. It's totally invisible but it lights up the entire world. I guess that the bottom line here with the 'Light Beings' is that we humans don't see them because we can only look with our physical human eyes which aren't built for the job, and if they are trying to communicate with us by using sound, we can't hear them because we can only listen with our human ears -- but despite these handicaps, we can try to open up our psychic eyes and ears and learn to see and listen with our hearts.

It seems to me that at times, we humans are a pretty arrogant bunch of know-it-alls and tend to pooh-pooh anything that we can't see, smell, touch or taste. We've still got a lot to learn and I suspect that Mother Nature has plenty of surprises in reserve for us yet. Surprises that will replace atomic and hydro-power and render them so totally obsolete, that we will laugh at them one day. Don't forget it's only in very recent years that we've used solar energy and wind power.

There is surely much, much more out there to discover and uncover. Crystal power for example. There I go beating that old drum again! And who knows, we might yet discover that orbs are a rich source of energy too waiting in the wings to be discovered and harnessed.

What About Babies & Small Children – Can They See Them?

Yes, I believe that it is extremely likely that infants can see the 'Light Beings'. I've no doubt that with their ability to float and to move extremely swiftly, they can dance and play and are probably able to make themselves highly entertaining to babies and animals alike. Orbs also come in a variety of beautiful colours and although I have only for the most part photographed white or translucent orbs, I have also had the occasional golden one, one possible beautiful pale green one (picture on next page) and of course, pink as we will soon see.

The Incredible 'Light Beings' of the Cosmos

These colours would add enormously to their appeal to young children so that tells me that maybe the 'Light Beings' have the ability not only to change size which they can do with amazing rapidity, but to change their colour as well.

I'm sure we have all been intrigued and amused at some time or another to see a baby in its cradle waving its arms and kicking its little legs while smiling, gurgling and focusing unwaveringly on something in close proximity as though there was an invisible presence there. What could it be that babies are seeing

My friend 'Cloudy' from New Zealand took this charming photo of her grandson Corun. Behind him is a beautiful pale apple-green orb. This is the first and only orb I have seen of that colour. Could it be that these pastel-coloured orbs come in to play with children? If you look closely there is also a very faint lolly-pink orb to the left of and slightly higher than the green one. I actually had some reservations about including this orb photo because Cloudy's son Sam, who is an airline pilot believes that the green and pink is light refraction and I figure that an airline pilot should know light refraction when he sees it! On the other hand, it is my understanding that light refraction produces hexagonal and octagonal shapes so I decided to run the photo anyway and Sam and I can argue it out later. The orbs do however lack definition which is unusual and causes me some doubt as to whether or not this is a genuine orb manifestation. Doubt is normal and not a bad thing. It makes us ask more questions which is another good reason for running this photo. (Photo courtesy of Annie McGregor).

when they do this? Fairies? Is it the spirit of an ancestor leaning over the crib, playing with baby? Or could the infant perhaps be seeing orbs? I think that it is quite possible that this is a physical and psychic ability which like animals, infants possess, until it is crowded out as the stimulus of the material world gradually intrudes upon and deadens the child's other levels of consciousness.

My son John, who like me is an orb 'initiate' and regularly takes photographs of the 'Light Beings' has taken many photos of his last-born infant at just a few months, smiling at something and sure enough there is invariably an orb in close proximity floating somewhere above the baby's crib. Makes you wonder

So Why Not Us Poor Old Grown-Ups?

So what about us poor grown-ups -- why can't we see them? Much as it would be fun and fascinating to be able to see these marvellous heavenly creatures, we simply don't seem to have the right sort of eyes for the job, and our inability to see them will almost certainly have something to do with our eyesight's operating range in the electromagnetic spectrum in relation to the 'Light Beings'' millisecond vibrational frequencies. In all honesty this is getting into territory that's rather technical so I'm therefore going to hand over explanations of this sort of thing to the scientists who know what they're talking about -- and who can write their own books on the subject. I'm happy to stick to David Icke's explanation about radio stations and their broadcasting frequencies. As I said, it is easy to grasp and as an explanation it resonates well with me.

Fascinating though it would be for us to be able to see the 'Light Beings', perhaps we really shouldn't have too many regrets about it. Maybe the Creator of all things Bright and Beautiful in His or Her or Its wisdom has deliberately seen to it that orbs are invisible to the adult human eye. Try to imagine a life where everyone is constantly distracted by the marvellous light-show displays of these beautiful multi-coloured orbs and their ability to turn on a celestial ballet. We'd never get used to it any more than we never get used to a beautiful sunset, and we'd be forever side-tracked watching them. We'd be constantly bumping into people, running into lamp-posts, and having terrible accidents -- so we will have to accept that it's for our own safety that we can't see them with the naked eye -- and we'll just have to depend on our cameras!

With their ability to turn on a spectacular celestial ballet, it's probably just as well that we can't see them!

What About The Vision Of The Future?

It's not too much of a distortion of the truth to say that we *can* in fact already 'see' them -- with the aid of our digital cameras -- and we can get quite detailed information about them which I will be teaching you how to read in later chapters. I predict that it is only a matter of time before (and here mark my words of prophecy), someone, somewhere invents specially tinted glasses which, like digital cameras will have the ability to tune into and pick up on their wavelength.

My Photographer Friend Pat & The 'Light Beings'

Now -- by an amazing synchronicity (and the world of the paranormal is all about strange co-incidence and synchronicity), no *sooner* had I written the above

sentence about 'specially tinted glasses', than I received the e-mail on the following page from my American friend Pat who talks about the soldiers in Iraq being able to see orbs through their night goggles. Pat Swain is a career photographer and a university lecturer in the

subject, who until she first met me in September of 2007, had never heard of orbs. During a conversation over coffee, I told her about the Col de Vence where so many strange 'happenings' had of late been taking place including the appearance of a 'crop circle' in a field up there. Being an 'instant' sort of person and also because she was travelling and on a tight schedule, Pat wanted to go up to the Col de Vence there and then – no two ways about it! Would I take her? I told her that it was a pretty spooky up there after dark, but she was still game to go even though it was nearing the end of the day! I agreed but said that I was not at all keen to stay up there once it got dark; especially as we didn't have the right clothes. So we leapt into my car and broke all speed limits to get there before nightfall! We arrived just in time to see a magnificent sunset and the very first photo I took when we got out of the car was of Pat while she was checking her camera settings -- and sitting right behind her shoulder was a big, bright orb! She was dumbfounded when she saw it for herself on the LED screen of my camera and was immediately fascinated. She needed no extra convincing and was instantly 'hooked'. She couldn't get over how 'solid' the orb was and vowed to look into the subject when she got back to New York.

Almost immediately after her return to New York, Pat found that she was taking photos of orbs in her apartment. She was slightly spooked by this but it made her decide to follow up on the 'orb phenomenon' and this led her to attend a lecture by someone who had recently written a book on the subject. Here is Pat's letter written from New York a couple of weeks after she left France.

New York-October 2007

Hi Antonia,

I went to a lecture on orbs last night. It was quite astounding. They said a number of things; one is that the orbs are celestial, or that they are spirits: they are human spirits but without bodies, some say they are truly celestial beings. They showed pictures of funnels of orbs and compared them to religious paintings from different centuries and it looks the same or very, very similar. Also some pictures of angels also look like orbs in these paintings. They talked about photography and orbs. They do show up only on flash digital cameras though some people see them without cameras. It is the frequency of the digital and flash. Also they come with music because of the frequency of music. I asked if they are in the battle zones in Iraq. They are. The soldiers with their night goggles see them constantly all over and with the dead.

Many people have started to see them within the last five years. Some believe they are here because the earth is in deep trouble. Perhaps they have always been here and digital frequency can pick them up.

At the end of the program. one of people who made the documentary played music and in the flyers it said to bring your digital camera so I did. And I got orbs! I wanted to share this with you. I plan to go to be in Nice on Dec. 23ʳᵈ to Jan 1ˢᵗ . If you are there, I would love to go back to that place on the Col de Vence.

Love Pat.

Interesting letter huh? There's just one thing though that I wish people would 'get over' and forget all about – and that is the hypothesis that orbs can *only* be seen at night with the flash. This is simply not true. Orbs have a light source all of their own and are perfectly visible to the camera without depending on the flash to jog them into life by illuminating them.

Further proof of this is in the orb photo on the next page. It was a bright day and not only is the orb clearly visible against the backdrop of garden greenery, but in the original size of the photo, all its markings are clearly defined too. An enlargement of this particular orb is the example of a 'Type 1' orb shown in chapter six on the subject of how orbs are constructed. It is a perfect orb. I took very accurate measurements of the orb by measuring it against the actual Magnolia leaf closest to it and I came up with an estimate of 23-25 centimeters which makes it about the size of a dinner plate. This particular orb is in perfect health. It is neither too opaque nor is it too transparent. This is an important photo because it gives a 'spatial' perspective for the orb. It is three to four meters away from me, between the Magnolia tree and the Olive tree behind it. It is therefore not up against the camera lens so it cannot dismissed as something like pollen or dust clinging to the camera lens itself. Distance from the camera is one of the most difficult aspects to guage in orb photography and to assess this, we always need to be on the lookout for clues such as this.

This magnificent orb was taken without a flash in my garden in full daylight.

Call me a nagging female if you will, but before I close this chapter let me repeat once more, orbs do not need to depend on the photon explosion from the flash to illuminate them as it is currently believed and is being promoted by other authors. I can only imagine that they persist with this idea that orbs can only be captured at night, because they have never actually gone out and tried to get them in the daylight. It is a great pity and this totally false notion needs to be nipped in the bud. The beautiful photograph on the following page is yet another example of a daylight shot high I the mountains on a plateau on the Col de Vence.

Following Page: I really love this picture because of the breath-taking bleakness of the vista and I was going to find a place for it in the book no matter what and this seems as good a place as any for it. The orb was lurking all by itself on a very high plateau at an altitude of 1000 meters on the Col de Vence in the South of France. There is no doubt that the Col de Vence is a highly charged crossroads in the earth's grid and because it is extremely important in this story, I shall be dedicating several chapters to it later.

CHAPTER TEN

Dyed-In-The-Wool Rock Fans

In my friend Pat's letter she says *"Also they come with*(or to) *music because of the frequency of music"*. I have absolutely found this to be my experience with them. It seems they positively adore rock concerts and they show up at these in their hundreds (or is it in their thousands?) They'll be right in there amongst it, there if there's anything happening in the way of entertainment especially if it's rock music, and it seems that the louder it is, the better it is with them! But before we go any further, let me first assure you that before anyone questions these amazing photos on the next few pages, those are *not* dust motes. Neither did I have a dirty camera lens as some debunking smart-aleck-know-all once accused me of. While I'm not one of those obsessive before and after 'wipe-click-wipe-click-wipe' people, like some orb photographers claim to be (do you really believe them?) I absolutely *do* make regular routine checks making sure that the camera lens is clean especially before I go out for a session; just as I routinely make sure that the battery is fully charged. I've been photographing orbs for long enough to consider myself pretty clued up in this rather 'specialized field', therefore by now,

'Buena Vista Social Club' concert in Vence in the South of France. This photo shows how translucent the orbs can be. A second orb is plainly visible through the body of the orb in front of it. The large orb which annoyingly is half hidden shows the seven concentric circles which are typical of the orbicular structure.

I think know the difference between a dust mote and an orb. Sheer size might actually have something to do with it – unless of course anyone has ever seen a dust mote with a ten-meter diameter! If you have let me know and I'll get out of its way – it'd be terrible wouldn't it to get a dust mote that big in your eye! Ooh those debunkers, I'll get 'em one of these days!

I took some amazing photos at an open air concert given by the 'Buena Vista Social Club' in the town square in Vence in the South of France' on 17th July 2004 which surprised even Moi. I'd love to show you all of them but this book only allows space for two as we have lots of other goodies to see as well and we

Buena Vista Social Club concert – Vence. The people watching the concert have no idea that they're standing in the middle of an extraordinary phenomenon -- a cloud of orbs so dense that it all but blocked the camera's ability to photograph the scene. In fact I took one particular photo that night in which that was the precise effect. You could virtually not see the stage at all as it was almost completely blotted out by the mass of orbs and so too were the people. I took photo after photo like this that night – so many in fact that it was very difficult to choose which one to put in this book.

need to leave room for them all!

The town of Vence is on the lower slopes of the hills which give rise to the famous Col de Vence which is an extremely active area for orbs and it is also an area where UFO activity is very often detected. I will be talking a lot more about the fascinating Col de Vence in much more detail in later chapters.

I have found that orbs always congregate in their hundreds; read that as in their thousands at concerts. I think that 'word gets out' in the orb community and I believe that the orbs travel towards concerts perhaps drawn by the huge crowd of humans gathered together. Either word gets out that there's a concert on and the orbs go for the music, or the orbs travel to the concerts with everyone who goes to concerts because the orbs actually belong' those people. So -- big crowd of people gathered together equals lots of orbs.

I have another theory which is that a large group of humans congregated together is a source of 'nutritional' energy for the orbs. But more about that later.

RU4 U2? Yeah!

I have a very special and valued friend who apart from being my friend and confidant, also happens to have a most unusual and much coveted job. He is the bass guitarist for one of the world's greatest rock groups U2. Adam has always been fascinated by my orb photographs and while not quite going so far as to actually admitting to being fully fledged believer, right from the start I could see that he was highly intrigued by them, especially when he saw the ones I took at the Buena Vista Social Club concert. "Hmm, I wonder if you could get them for us," he mused (*us* being U2), "That'd be interesting!" He didn't have to wait too long to find out, for on Friday 5th August 2005, U2 gave a mega-concert in the big stadium in Nice as a leg of their 'Vertigo' Tour, and of course Adam gave me 'Friends and Family' VIP tickets for the concert. Here too the 'Light Beings' did not fail us, they turned out in full force as you can see in these pictures.

Facing Page: I took this photo and many others like it, at the mega-concert given by U2 in Nice while the group was on a leg of its 'Vertigo' tour. Here too the orbs turned out in full force. This photo was taken just before U2 came onstage and I am sure that the 'Light Beings' were attracted by such a huge crowd. There was an estimated 56,000 at the show. Are orbs attracted by huge crowds and is this how they refuel their energies?

The big orb at the U2 concert in the picture on the previous page, probably rates as one of the biggest orbs that I have photographed to date but to even begin to appreciate its size, you have to have some idea of the immense size of the stage which was a really colossal structure. At a very rough guesstimate, this big orb had to measure at least ten meters across. One or two of your average suburban bungalows would probably fit quite snugly inside it.

This is just another of all the amazing photographs taken at the U2 concert. Here the show is really rocking and everybody is jumping and waving their arms about but the stage is almost obliterated by the orbs. Is anyone out there still going to try to tell me that the "Light Beings" don't enjoy a good rock concert when one is on offer? Dust motes kicked up by the crowds? I don't think so – as you can see I was seated well away from and high above the crowds in the big grandstand at the rear of the stadium.

Needless to say Adam was really surprised by all the photographs that I took at the concert and I have no doubt the boys in the band were all very pleased too that they drew such a huge crowd of 56,000 jumping and screaming fans, who paid for their tickets that night. But I have a funny feeling that Adam might have secretly been even more pleased and intrigued by those numerous extra spectators who got in for free!

Adam is a very spiritual person and I believe that he has his own personal orbs in attendance wherever he goes, as on most occasions when I've been with him, sure enough there are usually orbs somewhere in his environment. And he can now photograph orbs for himself!

More Fireworks & Orbs For Adam

One night in the summer of 2007, we were out on a private yacht belonging to our good friend Christopher to watch yet another of the fabulous Cannes fireworks displays from the sea. On a scale of one to ten in terms of 'big boat' sizes our boat was absolutely not small, and there we were parked in the bay facing Cannes, (Okay you seadogs we were 'anchored'!) cheek-by-jowl with some of the world's biggest super-yachts (or are they now called 'mega-yachts'?) As usual I began taking photographs left and right to see what was doing that night, wondering of course if the 'Light Beings' would turn up for the fireworks display and as usual I didn't have to wait long before they made their presence known.

Of course by now, everybody in my entourage is getting a bit 'ho-hum' about my orbs. They are starting to treat them as a perfectly normal state of affairs whenever Antonia is around. My friend Tim Wallace-Murphy who (by the way), is a widely published author on spiritual and esoteric matters was also on the boat that night. Strangely enough for someone so deeply into the mystical as is Tim, when it comes to my orbs, he is my greatest skeptic and debunker. But this particular night once my orbs started to show up, even Tim just grunted into his goatee beard and said laconically "You know Antonia you really *should* get your camera checked!" -- but with none of his usual verve. I think he too is starting not to be surprised by my 'Light Beings' and I have a sneaky suspicion that he might even be beginning to half believe in them but doesn't want to show it!

"Yeah Tim, I'll do that -- one of these days!"

Suddenly, an awed little voice piped up from Adam's quarter on the boat: "Hey, Antonia! I think I just photographed an orb!" He passed his camera over to me and sure enough there was a beautiful orb in the picture he had just taken. Another convert joins the ranks! Awesome!

If Music Be The Food Of Love Play On!

Those huge orbs taken at the U2 concert were probably amongst the most beautiful, best marked, well-defined and healthiest-looking orbs that I had taken at that stage. There must have been something about the overall conditions that night that suited them particularly well. What can explain this? I'd love to be able to tell you unequivocally that it's because they love and adore rock music and perhaps they do. There's a part of me that definitely believes it, but maybe it is something else as well.

Could it be that a manifestation such as a mega rock concert provides yet another supply of that 'mystical source of energy' we were talking about earlier? It is entirely possible that, as Pat said in her letter, orbs come with (or to) music and are attracted to it.

I believe that music sets up a harmonic resonance that the orbs respond to in some way and which, because it suits their vibrational wavelength allows them to recharge their batteries. Whatever it is, something definitely attracts them to rock concerts because they *do* show up at those in their thousands and the result seems to be that they grow bigger on the spot and their markings become clearer.

Until I received Pat's letter, it had not occurred to me that it would be intriguing to experiment with this possibility and the moment that spring comes, and the roads are clear of snow and ice, I plan to go up to the Col de Vence taking a variety of CDs with me of a wide range of music from Mozart to U2 and play them loudly through the car's speaker system and see what gives. We'll soon find out what their musical preferences are!

The Sharks Of The Skies!

Perhaps their need to recharge their batteries can be achieved through the tremendous force of energy given off when a crowd of many thousands is gathered together especially at an event like a football match or a rock concert where the crowd is very often in a state of mass excitement which can border on hysteria. Maybe the orbs can revitalize their energies by feeding off mass human energy and, rather like sharks who can smell blood in the ocean miles away the orbs can 'sniff out' a massive concentration of energy somewhere, and travel great distances and in great numbers to gorge themselves in a kind of feeding frenzy on this 'foodstuff' and so recharge themselves. Yikes!

Should this be so, then it gives rise to the rather amazing thought that if they can 'sniff out' vital energy at a distance and travel to it, *or* if they come to rock concerts because they love the music and the party atmosphere, either way it really doesn't matter because either way it shows a fundamental and primal intelligence plus the use of reason. The orbs clearly demonstrate the ability make a 'decision' and to travel towards something they want, be it a primary necessity like 'food', an energy source or a situation which is appealing, simply because it is entertaining and they can be in human company.

Maybe it's a little bit of both! It's up to you to decide what you think but I would like to add here that some of the biggest orbs by far that I have ever photographed have been of those taken at rock concerts and most particularly at the U2 concert. Could it be that they have just had a big feed of nutritional human energy from the crowds and got fat and bloated on the spot? Eek!

Bella, Bella Belinda

Another person who I am convinced has a personal retinue of orbs in permanent attendance is my soul-sister, iconic super-star Belinda Carlisle. Lead singer of the GoGo's and one of the world's most beautiful women in every sense that that word implies, Belinda is also a very well-informed and spiritual person. She takes her Yoga very seriously, is a constant seeker, a very deep thinker and she is an avid reader on anything that touches the paranormal and the higher realms of existence. Belinda is also a firm believer in the 'Light Beings', so much so that she is the one who positively nagged at me to get this book written and wouldn't let up until I had made a start.

In June of 2007, Belinda gave a concert in London to launch her new French album *'Voila'*. A whole crowd of her friends, myself included, travelled over from

Belinda in concert in London June 2007: This spectacular orb which appeared right over her head, floated around during most of the concert. After the show, I showed the photos to Belinda who is a very psychically 'tuned-in' lady, and she said that she rather hoped that they were there and she kind of knew they were there and she thought she knew who they were.

France to London for the show to give Belinda a good turn out and lots of moral backing from her biggest fans -- her closest friends! Not that she needed it, there was standing room only and we could hardly get near the place!

Before the concert started, she asked me to take plenty of photos to see if there were any 'Light Beings' around her when she performed. She said that she suspected that they were always there with her but she wanted to know for sure. Maybe with my gift for photographing them, I could provide proof for her. She told me that of late she had been feeling the 'spiritual presence' of her husband's Godmother Lesley Blanch, a renowned beauty of her day and a famous explorer and writer, who had at the time, recently died at the grand old age of 104. She and Lesley had been very close and Belinda sensing that she was around her a lot at that particular time, wondered if I could 'pick up' on her. Sure enough there were several orbs around her all through the performance and one in particular which was very large and bright seemed to hover over her head all night. Perhaps Lesley came to the concert and brought some of her celestial friends with her! Whoever they were, they stayed all night.

Speaking of friends, Adam was among Belinda's 'earthling' friends who came along to the gig that night, so on the assumption that orbs are personal attachments that accompany us wherever we go, between Belinda, Adam and myself acting as magnets, for the 'Light Beings', can anyone imagine that there would be a shortage of orbs in the club that night?

Since that concert Belinda had discovered that whenever she sings, anywhere in the world, there are orbs around her.

The Kevin Spacey Fan Club

Not only do the 'Light Beings' love a good concert, but it would seem that they like to take a really close up look at celebrities too! I took a whole series of photos during the 2008 Cannes Film Festival and there were some spectacular orbs in many of them. I particularly liked the one shown on the facing page. A huge banner of Kevin Spacey the American actor and film director now-turned artistic director of the Old Vic theatre in London, was strung across the main street in Cannes for the duration of the Film Festival and lo and behold there was strong orb activity in every one of the photos I took of Kevin. The 'Light Beings' it seemed, had floated right on down to take a really close look at him (who would blame them -- certainly not Moi). To give you some perspective on the size of these orbs; this banner was huge -- the width of the street probably -- at least 15 metres and so I estimated the orb covering Kevin's face to be just about the size of a large dinner plate.

Kevin Spacey and the curious 'Light Beings'. This photo taken during the Cannes Film Festival in May 2008 shows that the 'Light Beings' are like all of us; they love to get a good close look at a celebrity!

CHAPTER ELEVEN

All About Interaction With Animals

If (psychics apart), your run-of-the-mill, average, grown-up human being like you and me can't see the 'Light Beings', I am firmly convinced that animals can.

Many years before I started photographing orbs and long before I even knew of their existence, my dog Tinkerbell, a scatty Cocker Spaniel that lived to the grand old age of seventeen, would have us in hysterics with her mad antics. She would chase an imaginary something around and around on the lawn, leaping in the air as though to catch a ball, trying to scramble up the wall of the house, dashing like a quarter-horse, turning and spinning on a sixpence until she'd drop with exhaustion. We'd all roar with laughter and say, "There's Tinkerbell going mad again!" In hindsight perhaps she wasn't in 'mad mode' after all. Perhaps she was chasing something we couldn't see, but which was very real to her. Perhaps she was chasing orbs.

Milou the Pekinese surrounded by orbs: I took this photo because of the dog's unusual behaviour. He seemed to be watching something intently in the garden, which he appeared to find rather amusing because he was wagging his tail. I can count at least twelve orbs in this picture and they are floating at a much lower altitude than usual as though they have come down to play with, or investigate the dog. If this should be the case, then it shows that they have a large measure of curiosity in their character..

I am convinced that the 'Light Beings' love animals most animals -- especially dogs, although I suspect that they might show a bit more caginess around cats because cats have nasty scratchy claws and as proof of this I've seen photos in which the orbs seem to be smart enough to hover just high enough to stay out of batting range of those naughty feline paws!

I have taken many photos which definitely seem to show that to play with animals (especially dogs) they appear to purposely come right on down to the animal's level, that is to say near ground level, instead of floating up in the air at their normal cruising altitude. Could this be so that they can better interact with the animal? And could it also indicate a real curiosity about an animal and so they come right on down to get a better, closer look at it? And couldn't this indicate a real intelligence too?

After scatty Tinkerbell the Cocker Spaniel passed over to Doggy Paradise, came sensible Milou the Pekinese; a venerable Chinese gentleman imbued with all the infinite wisdom and beautiful manners of thousands of years of selective breeding in the Imperial Palaces of his ancestors.

Milou would very often sit meditating and contemplating the world in general, and then suddenly he would seem to be giving a very real demonstration of watching an invisible something which appeared to be in his immediate vicinity. With head moving from side to side and up and down, he would follow it/them gazing intently, and occasionally give a languid wag of his plume-like tail as though he found their antics amusing. He could obviously see something that we couldn't.

I took many, many photos of orbs in the vicinity of the dog. It was easy. The dog's comportment was invariably a dead giveaway. So watch your animals very carefully. Anything unusual in their behaviour, could well indicate the presence of orbs. Don't delay, get the camera out and start clicking.

Was It Pete Or The 'Spirit Of The Bees'?

The beautiful white orb in the picture coming up on the next page, is also associated with animals. Has it come out of curiosity to find out what the swarm of wild bees is all about? Or is it the spirit of the bees? Or could it be Pete's spirit?

Peter Mulgrew was a very close friend who was killed in the disastrous Air

New Zealand crash on Mt Erebus in Antarctica on 28th November 1979, in which 237 passengers and all 20 crew lost their lives.

In 1958 Pete crossed Antarctica and reached the South Pole as part of Sir Edmond Hillary's team during the highly publicized New Zealand South Pole Expedition, therefore being very familiar with the territory he was the commentator- guide on the fatal Champagne flight to Antarctica that day.

Pete's many brilliant achievements as an explorer, yachtsman and mount-

'The Spirit of the Bees': This beautiful orb photo was taken in my garden in March 2002 when a swarm of bees landed there. The area in the photo which looks like a tree trunk was a in fact the slender cane of a climbing Peace Rose and was no larger than my index finger. Under the weight of tens of thousands of bees it is bent double and would be the size of an average man's thigh. The bees are 'protecting' the poor Queen Bee who was probably suffocating half to death somewhere in the middle of all those bodies.

aineer were legend in his day, and he still had a great deal to give, both as an explorer and also as an inspiration in the field of adventure to a whole generation of young New Zealanders. The 'other' Pete was a bee-keeping hobbyist in his spare time, an interest he picked up from Ed Hillary who was a born and bred professional bee-keeper. I think that Pete would have loved to have been there if a swarm of bees had landed in my garden and I feel without any doubt that if he had been able, he would have come right on down to direct operations when the local beekeeper came to take them away! This orb turning up on an occasion like this is just the sort of photo which almost convinces me that orbs could very well be the spirits of loved ones who see what is happening in our lives and pop in to take part.

When I saw this photo the 'psychic' in me instantly felt a strong conviction that it was Pete. And I really don't know why I should have thought that: after all Pete had been gone for something like twenty-three years, so why think of him all of a sudden and right out of the blue like that? Was it just a simple association of ideas? Or is it further evidence that orbs can impose themselves psychically and give us the information that we need to know?

There's No such Thing as 'Mere Co-incidence'

I believe that we need to learn to trust these sixth-sense intuitions. This is what the developed psychic medium is trained to do and without a shadow of a doubt if and when we learn to do this too, our thoughts and ideas can be trusted as being more than mere hunches but concrete information which is being fed to us from a place in the 'Beyond'. And why not from the 'Light Beings' themselves? Who amongst us has never had the experience of thinking about someone just as the telephone rings and sure enough . . . . . ! Or having a tune on the brain all day and turning on the radio just as that very tune is playing?

Just co-incidences you say? Maybe -- but there is a saying which goes "There is no such thing under the sun as a co-incidence!" I believe that the phenomenon of co-incidence is the way the Universe gets to sit up and take closer notice of what is really going on around us. It's about reading the signs. I believe that *They* whoever they are, are reaching out to us and sending us a multitude of signs in an attempt to bridge the communication barriers between our two worlds. It is possible that they have come to instruct -- and if we ignore them, it could be at our peril for in times of conflict, unawareness and ignorance are the bluntest arms to carry onto the field of battle. We need to begin to trust our intuition, fine-tune our sixth-sense and listen and learn.

Pink For Love

Here we have another spectacular photo this which was taken by my son John. The orb seems to be showing an inordinate interest in an unusual animal. It seems to have floated right in for an eyeball to eyeball introduction to the baby Wombat being held by Michiyuki-san, my son's Japanese father-in-law at the Sydney Zoo. The wombat looks extremely docile and appears to only have eyes for the orb! I'd be interested if anyone can come up with other examples of pink orbs around any babies or animals. Could it be that this is because the colour pink is usually associated with love -- or with toys and play-time which simply goes best with small children and babies including baby animals?

While we are looking at this extraordinary pink orb, I would like once again to stress that it absolutely disproves that orbs depend on the photo flash to

Photo of Michiyuki-san and the wombat in the Sydney zoo. (Photo by Courtesy of John Goodland)

be visible. As you can see not only is the photo taken in full daylight, but it is a bright sunny day too and what's more, it is under the Australian sun which is probably amongst the harshest and brightest sunlight in the world. However a point very much worth mentioning here, is that the orb, which would most likely have been invisible to the camera's eye if it had been floating high up in the sky with no colour contrast is in this case clearly seen set against the dark colour of Michiyuki-san's jacket. Have I convinced you yet?

CHAPTER TWELVE

The Fragility Of Those Gossamer Substances

I've always had dogs, and in my long chain of various canine companions, were variously scatty Tinkerbell the 'mad mode' Cocker Spaniel and Zen, Meditating Milou, followed by the 'Terrible Two'; Adam and Ava the Pekinese pups (no prizes for guessing Adam's namesake).

One night when Adam and Ava were still very much babies, I took them out into the garden for late night 'walkies'. Once outside and the sniffing around for the 'right spot' was underway, all of a sudden Adam started making this weird nibbling action in the air as though he was biting at something. At about the same time he began chasing an invisible (to me) something; at first it looked as though it was along the ground as though he was playing with a ball and then he started making little jumping movements as though the 'thing' was slightly up in the air. He then stopped abruptly, sat down and seemed to be chewing on something unpleasant and trying to spit it out in the way dogs do when they have tasted something they don't like and want to get rid of it. It was almost as though he had chewing gum in his mouth.

Celestial Food For Thought

From long experience of observing animals in action when the 'Light Beings' are around, I recognised the signs and thought "O-ho there's something going on here! I sense an orb!" I dashed inside, grabbed the camera which was usually on hand near the door and started shooting. When I downloaded the photo onto the computer I was stupefied to see that I had captured a bright lolly-pink orb; exactly the colour you would give to a baby to play with. But much, much more than just that! When I looked closely at the right hand edge of the orb, I saw that it was all tattered and torn as though it had been nibbled at . . . . . by a puppy! The pup had actually damaged it.

If you look at the photo closely, you can see that on the right hand side of the orb there is a definite break in its border aureole or aura which glows an electric blue. The conclusion here is unavoidably staggeringly obvious. Orbs are not just insubstantial balls of pure light but they actually have a physical substance which can be damaged. You can't tear something that has no material stuff or body to it, can you? And furthermore, judging from the way Adam was trying to spit out whatever it was he had bitten, some of it had actually gone into his mouth and had an unpleasant taste to it into the bargain.

Now take another look at that orb: you will see that it is clearly sitting half *inside* the garden pot and is probably partially sitting on the soil in the pot. It is as though it is resting in pain in there after its traumatic experience with the pup. But even more importantly for our purpose of research and study into orbs, is that it yet once again proves that orbs are not some sort of free-radical floating in front of the camera lens to be picked up by the camera flash. The spatial reference is very clear and the also the size of the orb can be measured against the pot. By later taking a measurement against the flower pot itself, I guesstimated this orb to have had a diameter of seventeen centimetres which is exactly the size of your standard saucer. This makes it quite a big orb in fact.

Adam and his pink orb: The photo was taken quite late at night and very possibly without flash because it is so grainy. Therefore I have lightened two areas of the photo which are of chief concern – one to show up the pup who was practically indistinguishable on the stony ground and the other to highlight the orb. On the upper left hand side you can just make out the Pekinese ball of fluff, Adam who looks a bit like a grey orb himself and on the right, the bright lolly-pink orb. It is damaged and is tattered and torn along the right-hand side after the puppy had chased and chewed it. This tells me that orbs have a physical substance and if they are foolish enough to be caught by an animal, they can get hurt.

It's really, really strange -- celestial food for thought? One last suggestion Had this orb started life as a pink orb? Or had the puppy injured it to such an extent that it went pink? Like it was bleeding to death, orb fashion -- poor thing. This was one orb that wasn't smart enough to keep out of the way. Oh dear! Accidents *do* happen!

I really can't bear the thought that these beautiful creatures can suffer injury or be hurt in any way.

Rain Hail Or Shine

Before we move onto our next chapter which will be an exciting one, because it deals with some 'Close Encounters of real people with the 'Light Beings', I would like to take a moment here to speak a bit more about the question of the fragility of orbs as was demonstrated in the previous section with Adam the Pekinese pup's injured pink orb.

I now believe without a shadow of a doubt that orbs, although they seem to be insubstantial and see-through gossamer fine, they actually do consist of a real substance which is easily damaged.

In April 2008, a heavy hail storm cut a path across certain districts of Cannes and as I am a great believer in photographing for orbs in all weather conditions, I went out onto my terrace after the storm with my camera just to see what (if anything) was doing out there. I immediately got orb photos which was not surprising because I now know that they come out to drink in the rain. But what about hail? How do orbs get on when something as potentially devastatingly and as damaging as hail comes hurtling down through the skies like bullets set to tear into anything in its path, often leaving havoc and devastation in

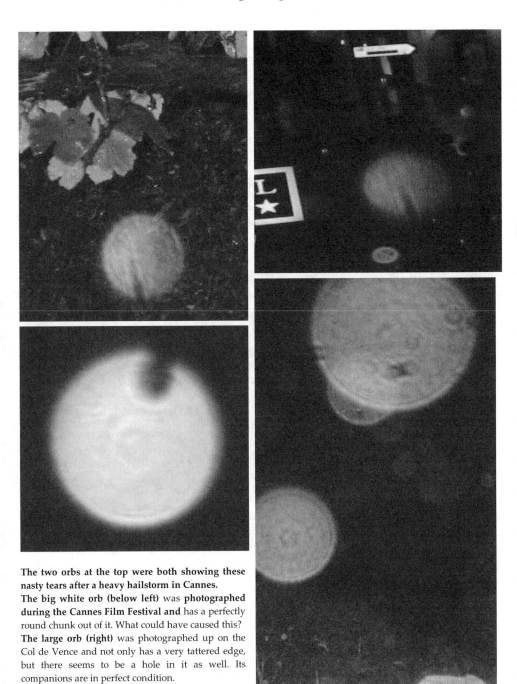

The two orbs at the top were both showing these nasty tears after a heavy hailstorm in Cannes.

The big white orb (below left) was **photographed during the Cannes Film Festival and** has a perfectly round chunk out of it. What could have caused this?

The large orb (right) was photographed up on the Col de Vence and not only has a very tattered edge, but there seems to be a hole in it as well. Its companions are in perfect condition.

in its wake? I was soon to find out.

Definitely Damaged!

That night I took several photos of orbs which appeared to have been shredded or torn. I had not seen this in an orb before. If you take a close look at these two orbs you will see that they each have a definite nasty gash cut right through them. Furthermore, a closer look at the orb on the left, shows that there is a clearly visible luminous electric blue aura on the lower left hand side of its body which is totally absent on the right hand side where the orb has a much darker appearance as though its luminosity is fading and it is dying. This was a revelation to me and gives us yet another good reason to go out and photograph them in all conditions. We are on a constant learning curve and little by little the veils will be lifted as we learn more and more about our mysterious friends the 'Light Beings'. The spectacular pink orb shown here was photographed in my garden on the morning of 3rd November 2000. At first sight it looks as though this is only half an orb. The orb *is* in fact intact but because the light is shining through it on the top half, it has caused a 'white-out' in the part above the hedge. The lower edge of the orb shows a scalloped effect which is most unusual. Has this orb been damaged by something? Also note the strong electric blue aura to its right. There is a second small pink orb on the ground by the bird bath.

The two brown orbs pictured below were both photographed on the same night up on the Col de Vence. They appear to be badly damaged too. There is a clean-cut rectangular chunk missing out of the perimeter of the orb on the left. It is almost as though it has been cut with a knife. What could cause such an injury? The orb in the photo beside it also shows an oblong scar. I believe that there is a very strong possibility that both these photos are of the same orb but taken at different angles – one in profile and the other face on.

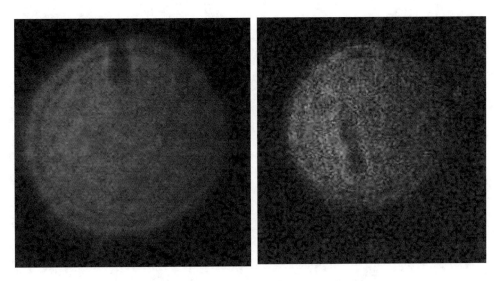

The deeper that I delve into the world of the 'Light Beings', the more I find that my mind is being challenged to reach out and grasp new possibilities and ideas which were hitherto unthinkable such as the very real likelihood that what appears to be non-matter is not insubstantial after all. If matter has the possibility to sustain tearing and injury and suffer death just as we ourselves do, it is therefore a material substance -- as real as you and I.

I firmly believe that we are living in parallel worlds with the 'Light Beings' and by beginning to understand this we are truly poised on the brink of pushing through to new frontiers with the prospect of going beyond our own limitations and finding out what exists on the other side of the curtain. This my friends, is just the beginning. Do not laugh at these strange ideas for the loudest laugh might well be the laugh which is the first to be stifled!

CHAPTER THIRTEEN

Close Encounters

In this chapter you will see some even more stunning photographs than we have seen so far which lend support to one of my theories that the 'Light Beings' accompany us wherever we go rather like 'Spirit Guides' who, it is believed, remain close to each and every one of us throughout our lifetimes.

We have already seen that the 'Light Beings' love family occasions and will show up for parties and play around children and animals and the following photos underpin this premise. We will now see some 'Close Encounters' of the very friendly kind!

The Ghost Of Muness Castle

Our first 'Close Encounter' is not an orb but it definitely merits a place in this book as it is a rare and most extraordinary thing. It is a photo of a real ghost!

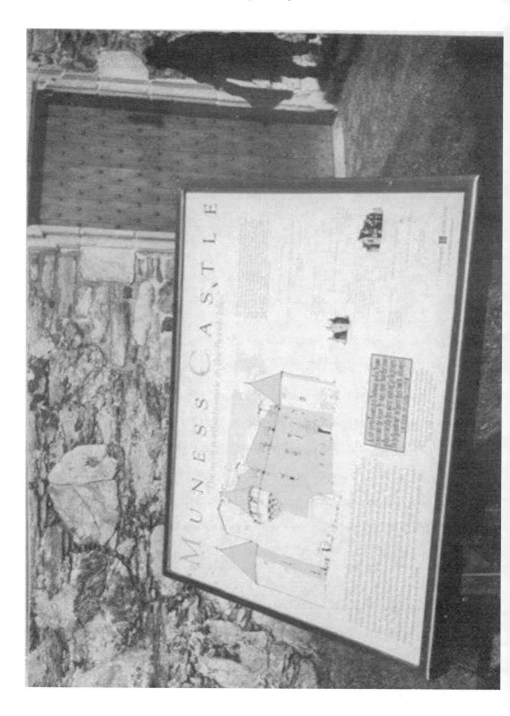

This incredible photo was taken by my cousin Margaret Clark in about 1996. It was during one of my Find-the-Old-Scottish-Ancestors forays to the North of Scotland and Margaret came with me this time.

Our travels took us up to the remote Shetland Islands -- a widely scattered archipelago of more than a hundred wind-swept islands way up in the North Sea, far off the Scottish coast and lying much closer to the coast of Norway than to Scotland. We found a wonderful hotel in the township of Lerwick, the 'capital' of Shetland, right on the water with great views of the islands and the shipping port and declared it our base-camp. Each morning we ate a huge, typically Scottish cooked breakfast of bacon and eggs, with mushrooms, tomatoes, sausages and hash-brown potatoes that would really set us up for the day but just in case, we also organized a picnic to take with us on our day-long sorties out into the wilds of Shetland -- to see what we could find. Our great-grandmother Mary Scott-Russell came from Shetland and it is through her that I get my name Scott. She married the 'Clark' – Peter Clark from Caithness Scotland when they both immigrated to New Zealand back in the 1850s. But that's all another long story and would be a book in itself.

One of these day excursions to discover our Great-grandmother Mary's old life in her native Shetland nearly 150 years earlier, took us, by catching a series of small inter-island ferry boats, to Unst, Shetland's most northerly inhabited island. Our destination was 16th century Muness castle – Europe's most northerly castle -- built in 1596. It was a glorious day and quite hot for those northern climes, considering it was the last week of September and technically the Shetland islanders had already had more than their six weeks of summer. When we arrived at Muness Castle, we ate our picnic huddled in the recess of the big oaken front door which, although it wasn't cold, gave us some shelter from the North Sea wind which, even though it was a warm, sunny day still had a slight bite to it. When the time came to be moving on to catch the last ferry back to the relative civilization of the 'main island', Margaret decided to take one final photo of the castle – or should I say of the Historic Places Trust's information panel so

that she would be able to remember the castle's name later. The photo on page 134 was the photo she took! But who is the 16th century gentleman who seems to be about to enter the castle door? He is dressed in the style of his day and he is clearly carrying a bundle of something in his hand which is casting a well defined pointed shadow which spills over the doorframe and onto the door itself. Are we seeing the man himself or are we only seeing his shadow? I have puzzled over this photo all these years and can't come up with an explication for it.

Needless to say, we were totally alone up there that day and the strange personage is *not* my shadow. I was standing right beside Margaret when she took the photo and even if you argue that it could only have been me, let me assure you that there is no way that I would have cast a shadow like that. I'm just not built that way! I was wearing jeans and a t-shirt that day and my hair was tied back in a ponytail. It's a strange one. Is it a ghost? Or is it a goblin, a hob-goblin a troll or is it one of the 'wee folk' that so many stories of local legend are written about?

Of all the aspects of this very strange photo the most mystifying thing for me is that little point of shadow cast by the hat or whatever it is carrying in his hand which spills over the doorframe and onto the door itself. It implies a solidity of substance which I would not have hitherto associated with a ghost.

Orbs can cast reflections and sustain physical injury – ghosts can cast shadows! Clearly we are beginning to see that the world of the immaterial is not so insubstantial after all!

By the way Margaret's photo of the Ghost of Muness Castle was taken on an old Kodak 'Instamatic' using traditional film. It just goes to show that '*They*' turn up if they feel like it, when we least expect it and that it is usually without any conscious effort of trying on the photographer's part!

The American Grandmothers

Kevin and Charlie are old friends from New York, who were visiting Cannes in April 2008 for the annual International market of television products which is much like the famous Cannes Film Festival only for television. They both work in the 'animations' industry ('cartoons' to old-timers like myself). Kevin is a very talented artist while Charlie is more in the executive side of things.

While they were here, they kindly took me out to a dinner one night and left the choice of restaurant up to me. I opted to introduce them to a very special restaurant 'Le Jardin de Madeleine', which I wanted them to get to know which is owned by friends of mine of many years standing, Madeleine and Didier. It is a restaurant I always choose for overseas visitors because it is unadulterated French home-cooking and the food is amazing! During the course of the dinner I told Kevin and Charlie about my 'Light Beings' and this book in progress. They were highly intrigued and I was somewhat amazed that neither one of them had ever encountered an orb and neither had they ever heard spoken of them. This seemed especially odd to me, as their industry involves a tremendous lot of photography: But then why should I be surprised? I had long ago learnt that the 'Light Beings' give professionals a wide berth out of politeness and respect for their trade! They simply know that they would not be welcome showing up in professional photographs, movies and TV documentaries etcetera; so it really was not at all surprising that neither Kevin nor Charlie had ever seen one. "We shall soon rectify that!" I thought, "It's Time for another 'conversion' to the cause!" As usual I had my trusty little camera with me (I never leave home without it)! I asked Didier the restaurant owner if he would take a photo of us three. Always smiling and eager to oblige Didier, took this photo and just before he clicked the shutter, Kevin chanced to remark "Wouldn't it be funny if the two grandmothers showed up!" Kevin and Charlie's grandmothers to whom they were particularly close had both died relatively recently: Kevin's grandmother Anna in November 2007 and Charlie's quite soon after. Didier handed the camera back to me; I switched into 'review' mode and sure enough, there was a tiny orb sitting on the lapel of Kevin's

From left to right: Myself, Charlie and Kevin in April 2008 dining out in Cannes. The owner of the restaurant took this photo on my camera, and for once I'm on the other side of the shutter! The tiny orb which appeared here was sitting right over Kevin's heart. Was it the spirit of his recently deceased Grandmother?

jacket.

Admittedly it was a very small orb – but it was there never the less. I passed the camera across to Kevin: "Wow!" He exclaimed, " It's sitting right over my heart!" I must admit that deep down I secretly suspected that it just *might* be one of the grandmothers and decided that it was most likely to be Kevin's grandmother Anna, seeing that 'it' was so close to him. I felt a twinge of regret that there hadn't been two orbs in the picture which would have made it nice for Charlie too. I ran off a few more photos of Kevin and Charlie in the hope that I might be able to get a shot with at least two orbs in it but in typical 'Light Beings'

After the dinner one last photo with Didier – and an orb over Charlie's heart!

manner they went all camera shy and there was not the slightest sign of one. Too bad I thought. They're very capricious you know and they are not always there when you want them.

The meal over, the boys settled the bill and we left the restaurant with Didier who accompanied us out as far as the street. Such a good time had been had in a wonderful ambience that one or two last photos needed to be taken of the boys and Didier as a souvenir of a great evening. This time I was taking the photos. I didn't see it until I got back home and downloaded the photos onto my computer. There it was! A perfect small orb and this time it was sitting over

Charlie's heart! Stunned, and really pleased I remembered Kevin's remark: "Wow! It's sitting right over my heart!" and it seemed as though to prove that it was indeed The Grandmothers out with them in Cannes that night, the 'Light Being' had placed itself right over Charlie's heart too -- thus letting them know that both the American grandmothers had shown up. We need to learn how to interpret all the signs and to trust the 'information' that we are given.

Yuna And The Orb

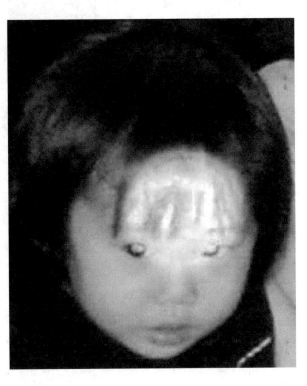

This amazing orb photograph shows my son John's Japanese niece, little Yuna who was not quite two years old at the time with a very large orb almost covering her forehead. It seems to be gazing deep into her eyes. The incredible thing about this photo is that the orb is clearly reflected in the child's eyes and making a bluish-white light in them. This is simply not a colour you would expect to see in the eyes of a Japanese.

Surely, if the orb is reflecting light into the child's eyes, it positively proves that it is there and that it is a luminous body -- a physical object -- that it is an actual presence and is occupying the space between the child and the camera but is much closer to the child to be casting a reflection of bright white light into her jet black eyes.

Dancing By The Light Of The Silvery -- Orb!

The spectacular photo on the next page, was taken at our friend Christopher's sixtieth birthday party in the South of France. It was a magnificent night, warm and balmy and the party was roaring at its fullest with loud disco music blaring, while all Christopher's friends boogied around the pool. I decided to take some photos. It seems that we humans were not the only ones enjoying the party that night!

Once again it proves to me that the louder the music and the bigger and noisier the party the more the 'Light Beings' seem to like it! It would appear that they can feed off the kind of energy generated by a loud crowd and grow -- rather like they do at rock concerts as we saw in Chapter ten. It has been amongst large crowds that I have captured the biggest orbs by far. This orb above Ashley and Jo must measure several metres across which can be judged by measuring it against the big house in the background.

I wonder how often it happens that anyone who is not an initiate of the

'Orb Phenomenon' and who might have taken a photo like this at a party, would look at it later and say "Gee Maud! Look at the moon! I don't remember seeing a moon that night – how much did I have to drink Dear?"

The Uninvited Wedding Guest

No it is not our friend Heather who was the uninvited wedding guest that day but the big golden orb sitting behind her head! This photo was taken at the wedding of friends in Brighton in England on March 17th 2002. There were orbs in many of the photos I took at the wedding that day, but the most dramatic and largest orb of all was the one which appeared behind Heather's head.

For the purposes of our research into the orb phenomenon, this is an extremely valuable photograph and I consider myself very lucky to have it, because the orb is actually *behind* Heather's head which gives us a definite spatial reference to the orb. The greatest difficulty with orb photography is estimating the distance of the orb from the camera's lens. When the orbs are placed behind one subject and in front of another it becomes very easy to estimate the distance between the orb and the photographer. By comparing it to the size of Heather's face, we can get an idea of the size of the orb – which is probably about the size of a smallish human head.

The celebratory atmosphere weddings and parties, big dinners etcetera, are all happy occasions, and they seem to attract the 'Light Beings' who really love gatherings of family and friends. They might even have a big social advantage over us! They seem to know who *we* are -- if only we knew who they were!

And Last But Not Least – Moi!

The photo here is of 'guess who' in the pink! Me at a dinner party and I'm nearly invisible because I'm almost entirely engulfed in two or three very large and very pink orbs! The photo was taken on my camera by a friend. She took three photos in quick succession. The flash was operating normally and the photo taken a few seconds before this one was completely normal and so too was the one taken immediately after. Close scrutiny of the photo convinces me that I was in fact engulfed in two or three very large pink orbs. I find this photo unbelievable! I am so completely enveloped in a dense pink light which is so opaque that I am only just visible and. The other dinner party guests who are dancing right behind me no more than three or four feet away and are almost obliterated. You might say that this is a total 'pink-out'!

The Friendly Poltergeist

This is Moi up on the Col de Vence at around 11.30 pm on June 28th 2008. It was just after the Summer Solstice of the 21st, and there were plenty of orbs around that night. I am striking what I call the 'Optimist Pose' and hoping an orb will land on my hand. No orbs -- but whose is the disembodied hand trying to find out what I have got in my pocket? Was he perhaps after the keys of my new car? Funnily enough I was passing through a phase at the time where different things had started disappearing and then reappearing mysteriously in my home. Could this be the hand of my roguish but friendly prankster of a domestic poltergeist?

CHAPTER FOURTEEN

How To Take Photographs Of Orbs

So fellow trail-blazer, here's the bit you've been waiting for and here you are all gung-ho and ready to go out into the field for a bit of serious scientific research and start photographing your own orbs. Let's go!

For several years I was truly the only person I ever encountered who had this phenomenon of orbs regularly showing up in photos until my son John suddenly started getting them too on a regular basis. It was beginning to look rather like a family trait. Like we were of some privileged, select blood-line that linked us back to the ancient Babylonians or Egyptians or something, avatars of ancient deities that bestowed upon us special hereditary gifts! Well you wouldn't necessarily *know* would you? No, no! Don't go calling the men in white coats, I'm only (half) joking! Seriously though, we did ask ourselves, what was this strange thing? Why us? Why me? Were we 'chosen' by *them* as a sort of advance guard, to whom they would first disclose themselves so that eventually through me/us and others like us their existence would be revealed and gradually accepted by the world population without causing mass panic? Who knows who they choose and why. We don't as yet know what any of this is all about, but I can tell you one thing for sure, that once you have started to take orb photos, the 'gift' will never go away. You're in it for life.

Photo Call For Dummies

As a photographer, I sure ain't no Lichfield or Snowdon. I know about as much about photography as could fit on the proverbial postage stamp. Just about all I know is how to turn on the camera, aim it at what I want to photograph and click. After all, isn't that what those ever-so-clever, user-friendly, fail-safe photography-for-dummies cameras of today are all about? I can just about manage my ASA settings, but that's pushing my little technical boat out to its furthest limits. My camera pretty well stays permanently on 'automatic' unless I want to suppress the flash for some reason or other, and even then I sometimes have trouble getting into 'manual' mode and have to reach for the hand-book to read up on how to do it. Truly! So just as long as you can accept that any technical questions asked will probably be met by me with an uncomprehending stare, we are going to get along just fine.

Fortunately the 'Light Beings' don't seem to be too fussy about what the photographer knows or doesn't know. In fact Lord Snowdon would certainly have an apoplectic fit if they kept showing up in his photographs and they are in all probability polite enough and smart enough to know that they'd get no welcome in that quarter and so it seems, they give the professionals a wide berth.

I know several professional photographers like Pat from New York, who have never seen an orb and neither have they ever heard of the phenomenon which is pretty strange considering the huge volume of photographic work they do. On the other hand, this 'dummy' with nothing more than a simple digital camera and zero technical competence attracts them like moths to the flame. Go figure!

Perhaps they like me and come to me because I like them and welcome them but I do nothing in particular to get my orb photos other than go out and start clicking away. And that's all you need to do too. That's honestly all there is to it. Nothing more, nothing less and don't listen to anyone who tries to get all technical and tell you otherwise. They are either there for you -- or they aren't but first, it's always a good idea to try to enter into some sort of psychic contact with them. This is easy and takes not much more than light meditation for a moment or two. However I have a sneaky suspicion that they are already with you in your immediate environs and that they are just waiting for the moment that you are ready for them to come in and reveal themselves to you. The very action that you are putting in right now by reading this book gives you a really big head start and puts you well and truly ahead of the game because you wouldn't be reading this if you weren't already interested in the subject and fascinated by them.

Operation Orbs

There's really no particular technique needed for photographing orbs but I'm going to give you some tips which might be helpful in getting the enterprise underway or at least to give it a good kick-start. Are you ready? I have found that through direct contact with me, many of my friends very soon begin to take their own photos of orbs and as I said, just reading this book will be opening the door

"Is it me you're looking for?"

into their world for you. Probably the most important and indispensable ingredient for photographing the 'Light Beings' is an intense and burning desire to do so. Even if you feel a little bit foolish doing so, during your meditation, say a little prayer in your heart and make a respectful request that they show up for you. They are very polite and need to be invited in. It's also a very good idea to reassure them that you're not nervous or afraid. They definitely seem to sense fear and will stay away if they think you might actually freak out if they show up in your pictures.

There's something else to remember; about them too: They're a law unto themselves and they tend to do exactly what they want to do, so be warned, they're cunning and they're just a mite mischievous but with a lot of patience and above all the absolute determination to succeed, there's absolutely no reason why you won't soon be photographing your very own Light Being friends like an old hand.

First Prepare The Camera

If you have opted to go orb hunting beyond your own home territory; e.g. in a cemetery, at a rock concert or out in the streets of your city, etc, preparing your camera before you leave home is extremely important so that you don't have to worry about it once you are out in the field. There are one or two essential routine things to do in order to have your camera ready for the session ahead.

To start with, get that battery fully charged. There's nothing more maddening than running out of juice in the battery -- especially at night when the constant use of the flash, checking the results on the LED screen and showing them to friends, uses up the camera battery very, very quickly. I've done it myself in the early days and even latterly come to think of it, so make sure that the battery is fully charged and too, if possible, take a fully charged spare with you as well. If by chance you also happen to have a second camera or you are able to borrow one, get it fully charged up too as a back-up in case anything goes wrong with the first.

As part of the routine before you leave home, check that your camera lens is fresh and clean and that there are no tiny specks or spots on it. This is for obvious reasons because any little specks on the lens could possibly show up looking a bit like orbs and we don't want to give those debunkers any fuel to stoke their fire with do we! Besides your colours will be fresher and brighter if the lens is clean.

Getting Those Camera Settings Right

If you are really into the serious business of orb photography, why not invest in a second memory-stick or even better, one with eight giga-bytes on it like I now have. I know that they're quite expensive, but this is a huge memory will more than see you through a night of intensive photography. It will really pay off too, if you take another minute or two before leaving home to get your camera settings right because believe me, it is seriously a real drag trying to change those camera settings out in the dark when you can't see properly.

Preset your camera to whatever setting you think that you will need for wherever it is that you plan to go and what you think the lighting conditions are likely to be. Once you've seen your first results, if the photos are coming out nice and clear, you shouldn't need to change it at all for the duration. 'Automatic' mode and a high resolution setting is probably generally best. Remember high resolution or 'super fine' will give you less photos but optimize the ability for enlargements later. It will be very frustrating when you get home if you got a great shot of an orb and want to bring it up bigger on the computer screen and then have it break up into pixels too early because the resolution was too low. Okay admittedly you get more shots with a low resolution setting but you can't go very far with them later. This is where taking the pictures in high resolution with a big memory-stick pays off a thousand-fold. I really want to emphasise that.

A low resolution setting on your camera is perfectly okay while you are in practice mode before you actually start getting orbs because it lets you take hundreds of pictures which you will want to discard once you know there's nothing there. But once the orbs start to come through, I truly recommend that you erase all your unproductive efforts from earlier and *immediately* go to the highest resolution that your camera permits because this allows you to make enlargements later. You will want to have a good close look at what the interior

structure of your orb looks like. Maybe you'll even find a face in there!

Not Going To Win You Any Prizes

The main thing to realize right from the outset is that by its very nature, orb photography is not going to win you any photographic competitions for quality. It is nearly always typified by rather low-grade photographs because we are usually operating in less than optimum conditions. Lighting is invariably poor in churches, night clubs and so on and we are often out in all weather conditions and in all sorts of strange places where we think that there might be orbs present, like cemeteries, on a moonless night. If it's very dark, the flash doesn't always have a very great reach and your photos will possibly be dark and grainy-looking as a result. Don't worry too much about the actual quality of your pictures – at least not at the beginning -- it's orbs you're after, not prize photos. What we are trying to do initially is to get you started actually taking photos of orbs. Once you can do that without any effort you can begin to afford to be a bit choosy about quality – but not at the beginning.

Patience and Perseverance Win The Day

The key words to bear in mind when trying to photograph orbs are patience and perseverance. Having frequent little mental or even better, audible chats with the 'Light Beings' is essential to the project. Tell them that you are looking for them and ask them to come in for you. Remember that by the law of averages, the more photos you take the more you are increasing your chances of capturing them. Remember too, that the orbs could be flying about almost anywhere so just keep on photographing in roughly the same area turning slightly to the left and to the right until finally an orb decides to fly into firing range and bingo you've got 'im! It is fairly important to stay in approximately the same place so as not to confuse them and it gives them time to 'find' you. If you keep moving around too much, they might have trouble keeping up with you. You may feel a little silly at first just standing there taking the same view over and over but that's how it's done and you do get used to it quite quickly!

Belinda as not too many of her fans are ever likely to see her, striking what I call the 'Optimist Pose'! She is hoping that an orb will land on her hand! Soon after this was taken, she would begin photographing orbs too.

Like Belinda, people now seem to be adopting what I call the 'Optimist's Pose' which consists of holding your hand up in the air and asking the 'Light Beings' to land on your hand. I've yet to see one actually land on someone's hand, but striking the 'Optimist Pose" really seems to 'work' believe it or not, because the 'Light Beings' come flying in to find out why you're standing there with your hand up in the air! (I told you they're very curious!)

Don't laugh or make silly jokes about the 'Light Beings'. They don't like that -- and always remember to let patience be your constant companion in the venture, and don't give up before they show up. And they will -- they always do -- err eventually!

Try Everything At Least Once!

Never be afraid to experiment in all conditions. This photo here is a long way from being my best orb photo but I take quite a perverse delight in it and want to include it because it is a debunker's dream scenario! It was taken in  the rain, in the dark, using a flash and then it was light-enhanced! That's pretty well just about everything you shouldn't do! This is what it produced. Do we have genuine orbs or do we have raindrops reflecting the flash? It's up to you to decided what you think. Personally, I believe that these are genuine orbs which have come out to drink in the rain. I do not believe that they can be confused with raindrops because raindrops do not measure twelve inches or more in diameter, are not round; never were and never will be! Orbs *are* round and can measure any size.

Video Cameras

Here I am writing a book about photographing orbs and I'm almost embarrassed to admit that I have never yet experimented with a video camera to photograph orbs. I keep promising to buy myself one, but as yet simply have never got around to doing it. Either I am too set on up-grading my existing camera to a bigger better model, or the budget is umm -- 'budgeted'. For whatever reason I have never yet owned a good video camera. Coming up I promise!

If you go on 'You Tube', there are many film sequences showing orbs on the move and I have no reason to think that those video clips are anything but genuine. It seems that with patience, orbs are just as easily captured on video as on still pictures. It is really well worth taking a look at some of these footages because you see the extraordinarily fast speed at which orbs can travel. We know that already, because an orb on the move leaves quite a trail behind it which you can see, even better in still pictures. Now that I know what I'm looking for, I have developed an eagle eye and have become very quick at spotting orbs on the move in TV programs and documentaries. For example:

'La Ferme' & Daniel

About three years ago there was a very popular TV reality show in France, called 'La Ferme' (The Farm). The scenario was this: A diverse group of nine or ten celebrities were put on a very isolated farm together and expected to run the farm, care for the animals and be entirely self-supporting through their own efforts. And of course at the end of each week someone was voted off by the others and by the public. We are all familiar with the reality show format aren't we!

Well I was addicted to 'La Ferme', not just because it was very funny and extremely entertaining, but mainly because of the enormous presence of orbs. I used to put in a video cassette and record the programme so that I could study the orbs later and I would play and replay frame-by-frame and examine those orbs in their every detail. I am convinced that for the most part, they were genuine orbs and not dust motes or insects as one could expect in the country (oops I almost forgot to include the seeds and pollen!) No, I was fairly convinced that I was seeing the genuine article and that these were real orbs.

The thing that had me convinced most of all was that there was a very popular personality in this particular series by the name of Daniel

Ducruet. Daniel happens to be the ex-husband of Princess Stéphanie of Monaco and is the father of her two children. Extremely good-looking, sweet-tempered, always smiling, always helpful, ready to mediate when arguments broke out and ever-willing to do the worst jobs on the farm, Daniel made it right to the last episode and not an episode did I miss! It was my daily soap opera and kept me up with the on-going doings in the daily lives of the 'Light Beings'!

The point of telling you about this is that all the orb activity in 'La Ferme', was invariably around Daniel – in fact when Daniel was there, the activity was not just sometimes there, it was *always* there. I am sure that he must have a very strong 'Soul Pool' of people who loved him and who are now passed over, who were enjoying the show as much as I was and actively participating in it as unpaid 'extras'! I was so impressed with this at the time that I wanted to write to Daniel and tell him about the presence of the 'Light Beings' around him. But then I thought that he would probably think that I was just some sort of crank -- and so I resisted the temptation. But maybe he'll read the French version of this book one day and if he does, he should go back and review the tapes of the show and he will easily see exactly what I am talking about.

What To Watch Out For

When you think you might have spotted an orb in a video or a DVD stop the tape (or DVD) rewind and replay in pause mode frame by frame.

The only thing that can truly be confused with orbs is lens refraction which is very common in movies, because very often the cameraman is filming into the sunlight or with the sun at right angles to the camera. These conditions almost always cause lens refraction so you need to watch out for that. It's fairly easy to diagnose because to start with, lens refraction is usually either hexagonal or octagonal (that is to say has six or eight sides) and the refracted light always travels at the same speed as the camera and in the same direction as the camera following its movement until it eventually disappears when the camera has left the lighting field that caused it in the first place.

Orbs have their own behaviour which is easy to spot once you know what you are looking at and they have their own unique high speed of locomotion. You will see a white ball of light speed from side to side of the image at such a high pace that you might even think you imagined it. Track back and check it out. Unlike light refraction or shafts of sunlight, orbs act completely independently of the camera and can be quite hard to follow as they often have a very erratic trajectory or flight path. The very best thing that can happen if you are trying to decide whether or not you have spotted a genuine orb is if it actually goes behind something like a pillar in a church or a person and then re-appears on the other side. Then you positively know that you have a genuine orb in your sights and you can quite rightly feel very excited about it.

I see them all the time nowadays and it is always exciting! I never get used to it. Before I wind up this chapter on photographing orbs I should mention something else for you to bear in mind when you go out with the specific purpose of photographing orbs. You don't need to focus on any particular subject or a person simply because it will make a nice picture. This is perhaps why genuine orb pictures have a strange beauty all of their own and take some getting used to before you really begin to appreciate them. They are almost an art form in their own right. The background subject is usually immaterial. The real subject is the orb. It is very easy to see the difference between photographs like mine which are typically those of someone who has deliberately set out to photograph orbs and someone else's photos who has deliberately set out to take a photo of (let's say for

example), a family group or a pretty view and then accidentally captured an orb in the picture. The backgrounds in my photos are often totally uninteresting -- the sort of thing you wouldn't dream of taking photographs of normally. So if you want to get pictures like mine, you just stand where ever you happen to be, whether it is in your own backyard, or out in the open countryside or even in a cemetery (if that's the kind of scary thing you fancy) and click away again and again aiming at nothing in particular, turning this way and that so as to cover the area. Aim fairly high too because they do seem to like a certain altitude, especially in churches and cathedrals etcetera, where they have a tendency to lurk up in rafters and organ lofts or even halfway up apartment buildings, outside people's un-shuttered windows as the photo on the previous page shows, which is why I call the group of orbs on the facing page the 'Peeping Toms'!

With orb photography it's only through experience, practice and by constantly experimenting that you will eventually learn how to determine the real McCoy from the fakes and 'posers' and by keeping good records you will come to understand their behaviour too -- and perhaps one day you will get to know what the 'Light Beings' are *really* up to, why they are here and what it is that they are trying to say.

Just About Any Old Camera Will Do -- As Long As It's Good!

As far as cameras go there's no real pre-requisite. My first photos of orbs were taken on an old-fashioned Nikon 35mm using ASA.200 film until I got my first generation digital camera of 2.5 mega-pixels. Some of those early photos are still quite good even today, as long as I don't try to enlarge them but the quality truly can't compare with the new generation cameras and I might as well mention here to emphasize the point I have just made, that unfortunately in my ignorance and inexperience, at some stage I resized all those early orb photos. I have learnt since and knowing what I know now -- every precious pixel counts!

I then progressed to a five mega-pixel camera and now I have a ten mega pixel which is fantastic. Not only does it take vastly better, more detailed photos than I ever got before, but I can achieve the highest possible resolution, plus I can enlarge the results repeatedly in order to really study the orbs before the pictures start to break up into pixels on the computer screen. Of course you can go on and on increasing the pixel power of your cameras until infinity. It's like an addiction.

Bigger-better-more-more-more! And there's no prize for guessing who's already planning her next big camera!

I also invested in an eight giga-byte memory-stick. With that huge memory

I can take photos ad-infinitum on high resolution, without worrying about running out of memory. This is a fairly important consideration, as it avoids the necessity of trying to free up memory space out there in the field where you could in fact be deleting something very interesting not immediately visible on the LED screen. As you will see in the next chapter where we will be discussing the advantages of light-enhancement in orb photography, there is often a lot more in the photos than at first meets the eye.

Before we move on, just let me say once more, that it is really important to have your camera set to the highest resolution for taking orb photos. This allows you to blow up the size of the photo on your computer so that you can examine the orb's structure without having the picture start to break up into pixels too early.

The reason why a digital camera is absolutely essential is that you can take dozens and dozens of photos without wasting film. You simply couldn't have done on a regular camera with a roll of film in it. It was cost prohibitive and we couldn't have afforded the cost of developing. I have taken hundreds of photos with orbs in them, but for every photo I have taken with an orb in it, I might sometimes have taken twenty or thirty without any results at all.

They've Always Been There

This brings me to another very important point. I believe that the orbs have always been here amongst us. They definitely didn't just happen to turn up on our planet at the exact same time as digital photography was conveniently invented and start showing up in our photos then. They have always been here, but the main reason why orbs didn't show up in any great numbers on the old 35mm cameras using the old traditional film of twelve, twenty-four or thirty-six frames, could well be because people quite simply were very careful and economical with the number of photographs they took. Each photograph really counted and had to be meaningful in order not to waste film and not to incur unnecessary development costs. With digital we can click away to our hearts' content and take hundreds of photos if we want, of nothing in particular just to capture one teensy little orb, at no cost whatsoever. Once the original cost of setting up for digital is met, the rest comes free.

Another valid reason why the orb phenomenon might not have been frequently reported in the old days with traditional cameras and film, could be that if there was ever an anomaly in a photograph, it would most likely have been written off as a development fault because of all the liquids and chemicals used in the process and discarded ending life torn in half and tossed into the trash can. On the other hand, with digital cameras we are faced with the 'fault' straight away because the orbs show up instantly on our LED screens so we therefore can't ignore them.

As I was nearing the end of writing the original draft of this book, I was going through several old shoe boxes of photos, not for any reason to do with the book, but because I was trying to whittle three boxes down to one to make some badly-needed room in my bookcase. Looking at the old photos I got quite lost down memory lane of times gone by and suddenly stopped dead in my tracks when I came across one taken on an island in the Thousand Islands group in Indonesia with a beautiful bright orb sitting up in a tree. I had either forgotten all about it or never noticed it, but knowing what I know now, it came as a real surprise to see this.

They have always been there. Now that you know what to look for, you too could well find that if you go through old photos you will find some with orbs in them. I'd like to hear about it if you do.

Just Like Family Photos

I keep all my orb photos – it's a form of deference for them and just as I wouldn't tear up or discard photos of friends or family, I don't throw out my orb photos either. It's partly just in case they are people -- and too if they have been good enough to turn up for a session then I feel I owe them that small respect!

To sum up the 'how to' on orb photography:

- The key words are patience and perseverance.
- Treat the 'Light Beings' with reverence and respect.
- Have frequent little mental chats with the 'Light Beings'. It's probably as reassuring for them as it is for you.
- Make sure that you camera is ready: Batteries charged, settings regulated, the lens is clean and you have enough free space on the memory stick.
- Don't be afraid to do lots of experimenting in all weather conditions, rain, hail, sun and snow and in all lighting conditions as well.

- Study what you get and if you really want to be serious about it, make notes and keep a record of dates, location, weather conditions etcetera. Very often I have not always done this only to regret it later. You think that you will remember – but invariably many orb photos later, weeks, months or even years down the line you will find that you have forgotten. Therefore keeping your data is an important part of your research into the Orb Phenomenon

- From time to time transfer your very precious photographs and the relative data off you PC and onto a CD so that it is safe in case of a hard-drive crash -- it also frees up space on your computer.

- Never give up!

If all else fails when calling in the 'Light Beings' you can always try a bit of Ritual Communing. The lop-sided orb which has come in for my friend looks very familiar! It seems to me that we have seen this very same lop-sided orb several times already.

CHAPTER FIFTEEN

Day Time Night Time -- Any Time's The Right Time!

I have read a couple of books recently written by other authors, who propose the theory that orb photography depends on the photon explosion of the camera's flash to light up the orbs causing them to fluoresce which is when they become visible and therefore photographable. I have been told that this notion is also promoted at lectures on the subject. And so presumably these people do all of their photography just after dusk or at night.

I am afraid that as this has not been my experience at all, I cannot agree with this hypothesis and if this book puts out one and only one big message, I would like it to be that my readers gets it firmly fixed in their heads that orbs do not *only* appear at night and do *not* rely on the flash to be photographable. This is why I have deliberately included as many daylight photos as possible in order to prove the point. Orbs are a constant around-the-clock presence amongst us and not merely night creatures like moths, that hide themselves away all day only coming out once the lights are lit.

From the very first moment that I started photographing orbs, I have been able to capture them in daylight even on the brightest of sunny days. In fact my very first ever orb appeared in a photograph taken on an island in the Thousand Islands group in Indonesia before the advent of digital photography. Not only was that orb, which was

floating high up in a tree, taken in broad daylight under a harsh tropical sun, but it was also taken on my old Nikon 35mm camera. This instantly sweeps aside two conventional theories about orbs. The first being that they are a recent phenomenon of uniquely digital photography and the second that they are un-photographable in the hours of daylight. You will remember won't you how I told you that after I had the spectacular shower of orbs the night of the fireworks, I went out first thing the next morning armed with my camera and the orbs *were still there*. This was of course in the daylight hours on a bright sunny morning in the South of France.

I cannot stress it often enough in order to impress it upon people's minds that orbs appear just as readily in broad daylight on a bright sunny day as they do at night, just as long as you manage to catch them with a reasonable contrast of tone in the background to throw them into silhouette as this photo here taken of an orb set against the garden shrubbery shows. They don't usually show up

This lovely day-time shot was taken up in the hills behind Nice on a bright sunny day with a blue sky with just a few clouds floating around up there. It is further absolute proof that a flash is absolutely not needed to photograph orbs. A genuine orb is a luminosity in its own right and does not depend on the flash of the camera to illuminate it.

against a sunny sky for instance – the camera needs the contrast of a coloured background to pick them up. But that of course is just plain logic.

It would seriously be a great pity to limit your photography of these beautiful creatures to night-time excursions only, because you believe, or you've been told that that's the only time to get them. You will be missing out on their glorious daytime luminosity. With patience you will definitely capture them during the day. They are out there just waiting for you. Just remember that orbs are luminous bodies in their own right, and as such have a radiance that certainly does not seem to be in any way diminished or dimmed by the sun. I have taken many daylight photographs of orbs where the morphological details are just as clear and as well-defined as any that I have taken at night using the flash, if not better. This is very rewarding to achieve so do keep trying.

Swinging In The Rain

I have a theory that orbs like rain. I think in fact that they need moisture in order to survive, and it is perhaps for that reason that they are often to be found in or near bodies of water and according to some photographer divers, even underwater.

It could very well be that water is a major part of their physical make-up and when it rains they come out of hiding like snails do, to drink and to re-hydrate. I have noticed that orbs when photographed in the rain, or just after it has rained, have a more opaque appearance and are white and slightly fuzzy at the edges. I have found that during a rain shower is a very good (read that as excellent) time to catch them and I recommend that when it rains you go out and try to take photos of them.

This can in fact be slightly 'touchy' territory and we have to be very, very careful here because the debunkers have this reasoning that if the flash chances to go off in the rain, it hits the raindrops which reflect the flash and thus creates false orbs. They might be right: but this is of course presuming that they are talking about night photography in the rain when using the flash. I've tried to prove the theory and it doesn't seem to work. Actually it's not even particularly logical for the debunkers to say that, because if the flash in the rain causes orbs, then after a hundred and fifty-odd years of photography, this would be such a common occurrence that everybody would know about it, and we'd all be moaning on a rainy day "Oh my, it's raining today, what a shame I won't be able to take any photographs all day long, I'll get those awful white blobs all through them!" I never got a white blob in a photo in my life because of the flash hitting a raindrop. Did you? Honestly, those debunkers will say anything to prove a point!

Try taking your photographs in the rain during the day time. You don't need to use the flash and I am sure that even if you are a rank beginner, you can

This photo gives us an excellent lesson in telling the difference between rain and orbs. It is raining extremely heavily and the streaks of rain are topped by tiny white balls. But there is also a beautiful and genuine orb in the picture which gives us a perfect comparison between the two. After seeing this photo, I am sure that you will agree that there can be no possible confusion.

tell the difference between an orb and a raindrop. It all boils down to common sense and of course, maintaining your own integrity.

Light drizzle or even quite heavy rain is extremely difficult to photograph and very rarely shows up in a photo, but rain can show up quite clearly if it is raining as heavily as it was when I took the above photograph. As you can see it was a positive deluge. My objective was to see if I could actually photograph rain and I deliberately set out to achieve exactly this. I was very pleased with the result because it settles a lot of contentious arguments. The bonus of course, was the orb showing up as well – like it had been reading my mind and knew exactly what I was trying to do!

Great care needs always to be taken, because the beginner could possibly confuse raindrops with orbs, because the raindrops can show up as white streaks (often falling obliquely when it is windy) which are usually topped by small white blobs which, to the inexperienced eye could be taken for tiny orbs. But as this photo shows, the white streaks caused by rain are always all angled in the same direction, something which orbs who operate independently of each other never do.

Since owning my ten mega-pixel camera, I have taken quite a few photos which show both raindrops and orbs and believe me, even the most ardent debunkers would have to reluctantly admit that there is no possible confusion between which are the raindrops and which are the orbs.

So I would absolutely advise the beginner to go out and try taking lots of photos in the rain, although with a strict warning to be extremely careful not to allow any rain whatsoever to get onto the lens because even the smallest water drop on the lens will very definitely look like an orb in your photos. Keep a running check on that and even try to have some sort of hood or protection for your camera so as not to run the risk of getting raindrops on the lens.

I always encourage people to try experimenting in all weather conditions. That way you will learn as you go, and you will gradually get to know when the orbs are likely to appear and you will also learn to tell the difference between anomalies and phenomena. An *anomaly* is something unusual which shows up in a photo and which shouldn't be there and which has it origin in natural causes and is explainable -- such a light refraction when photographing into the sun or a stray sunbeam streaking across a photo. A *phenomenon* is something unusual such as an orb which shows up in a photo and which cannot be explained away by natural causes.

Cheats Never Prosper

There is another even more important reason for being absolutely certain that there was no rain allowed to get onto the lens is that it boosts your confidence in what you are trying to do and also it removes all possible, lingering doubt from *yourself*. It's no fun saying to others later "Well – um, I think it's an orb; it could be an orb but it might have been a raindrop but I'm not really sure." Your friends won't take you and your new skills very seriously. And besides, there's absolutely no satisfaction in cheating, not even to yourself, because *you* know deep down how you obtained the photo and whether or not your methods were absolutely beyond reproach. Either it's the real McCoy or it ain't!

As for me, as far as photographing in the rain is concerned, I hardly ever go out in the actual rain, I'm much too much of a sissy to do that -- and besides my hair tends to go frizzy -- so I usually stand just inside the door of my apartment out of the wet, or point the camera out of an open window (not a closed one). By doing it that way, it also eliminates any possibility of rain drops hitting the lens and then the thorny question of 'did they or didn't they' never enters into the equation.

All orb photography has to be undertaken with nothing but the highest of integrity, as any cheating discredits the whole discipline not only for you but for everyone in the field. If I ever have any doubts about any single photo I prefer to discard it or file it away in a folder marked 'Dubious', than trot it out and try to pass it off as a genuine orb photo. So when in doubt don't! As I said it's as much for your own confidence and satisfaction that a policy of 'rigorous honesty' needs to be adhered to and please don't go posting stuff on the internet or 'YouTube' unless you know for a one hundred percent certainty that you're dealing with the real thing.

I'll be writing a whole chapter on those dubious photos near the end of the book and I'll be giving you some fine examples with plenty of great pictures which will make you think twice before you authenticate what I call 'False Friends' or 'Posers'.

Night Shots For Starters

I say this with some reluctance, because I certainly didn't start out photographing my orbs by depending on the flash but it is probably a fact that it is easier to capture orbs at night using the flash. It certainly would be true to say that as a beginner, you might get positive results sooner and in greater numbers which of course is encouraging. The reason for this is, that as opposed to a bright sunny sky, night-time conditions provide a dark sky and a dark background which shows up the orbs to better advantage when the flash goes off. I absolutely don't depend on this at all and I never did. I think it's a shame and a sort of limiting 'cop out' in the fine art of orb photography to only go for night time photos. I also feel that the beginner shouldn't get the fixed notion in his or her head that this is the only way to get photos of orbs. It isn't. It might be the easiest way to get them but it is definitely not the only way.

The orbs are always there, day or night and I do not believe that they depend on any particular lighting conditions to show them up or to enhance them. I believe that the orbs/'Light Beings' will reveal themselves to you when they choose to reveal their presence which will be when it suits them – and not because the light or weather conditions are right. Having just said that, this is not to say that I never go out at night with the express purpose of photographing orbs. I most certainly do and that very frequently, but I don't limit myself to night shots and I just as readily go for day-time shots and as you have seen already, I get plenty of them.

When I am out taking photos at night and orbs are present (and they very nearly always are), I get a split-second's instant when the flash goes off, during which I clearly see a tinsel-like glitter in the illuminated darkness. This shows me that they are around and if they are there, and I have captured them in a photo, they are clearly visible as a round whitish or blank area on the LED screen of the camera. So the beginner should look for those tell-tale glitters either in his own flash or in that of his companions and keep on taking photo after photo, moving the camera from side to side. You will eventually get something. Of that I'm positively certain. Once you have got your first orb, try to remember (in spite of all the excitement that you will feel), to immediately erase all your non-productive efforts too free up the memory stick and then set your camera in high definition mode. Once you have downloaded onto your computer, you will need to be able to blow your orb pictures up as big as possible to get a really good close look at your new friends!

I usually have the LED screen of my camera set to a viewing time of between five or six seconds, which gives me enough time to inspect the photo and decide whether or not the shot is worth keeping. This is of course one of the great advantages of digital photography. If there is nothing there, the photo can be immediately deleted, if you really need to free up space on the memory stick. But through long experience, I don't erase from the camera anymore, unless I am really, really desperate to free up space, as you'd be amazed at what shows up on the computer screen once you are back home, which you might not have spotted out there in the 'field'.

The Reason Why We Don't See Them Very Often In Daylight

We have already seen this pink orb in an earlier chapter when we were discussing orbs with injuries. I want to come back to it for a moment before we leave the topic of daylight photography. This photo is just about as good as it gets to illustrate why the camera very often doesn't pick

up orbs in full daylight. Take a close look at this picture. You can see that the orb is clearly visible in all the places where it is seen against a dark background -- in this case where it is silhouetted against the hedge and a small segment on the right hand side of it against the tree. You can even see the ragged continuation of the top of the untrimmed Cyprus hedge right through the body of the orb -- but after that, we suddenly lose sight of the orb entirely against the clear blue sky. So although I absolutely maintain that orb photography is possible in broad daylight, I should point out that this is as long as your orbs have a darkish backdrop like a tree, a hedge or a grey coloured house as a background which throws them into relief. As long as they've got that, then the camera can 'see' them -- but the camera is highly unlikely to be able to pick them up against a bright background such as a sunny sky or a plain white sunlit wall.

At night we don't encounter the same problem because the night sky is dark navy-blue to velvety black and by its very colour provides a background 'canvas' for them against which the camera has no difficulty at all in picking them up.

A really nice time to take orb photos is at sunset or at twilight just after the sun has set, but before it gets dark. There's still quite a lot of light in the sky to give the photo a certain luminosity and the flash often goes off. This is the time of the day when you get the best of both worlds and you are giving yourself every chance of getting orbs. I have had some amazing results at dusk especially up on the Col de Vence where the vistas at sunset are pure magic! I have found that the 'Light Beings' very often make an appearance at this time – rather like Moi! I've had my afternoon siesta and am all fresh and ready to go out in the cool of the evening!

Some spectacular orb activity caught from a window in the main downtown street of Cannes. There had been quite a heavy shower then suddenly the rays of the setting sun broke through and bathed the street in a beautiful golden glow which prompted me to capture the moment. I was rewarded for my efforts by this lovely picture. The shops were shut, the daytime shopping crowds had gone home and the orbs were out in force peeking into the windows of the exclusive boutiques. I call this picture the 'Window Shoppers'.

CHAPTER SIXTEEN

Lighten Up & See What Gives

Orbs which you didn't see on the LED screen out in the field, very often show up once they have been downloaded onto your computer screen, especially if you lighten the photo and play with the dark/light contrast button. I'm a bit of a purist and these days I'm more concerned with trying to get the perfect 'portrait' of one of my 'Light Beings'. I therefore very seldom bother to fiddle with the light adjustment feature at the computer level unless I have a specific reason for doing so but lightening up your photos will very often produce some really spectacular surprises for the beginner and 'professional' alike, and show that there's a heck'uva lot more out there than you ever suspected. After all it's not about the quality of the photos, especially when you're starting out, it's really more about 'investigation' and finding out what's there that we normally can't see. The example on the next page shows you what can be discovered when you lighten up a little. Out in the field you might have been tempted to trash the photo on the left which just looks like a black frame with no orbs in it, but back home on the computer when you add a bit of light to the picture, you can see that there were in fact a myriad of orbs in there which is a really nice surprise and proves yet again that there is more betwixt heaven and earth than meets the eye.

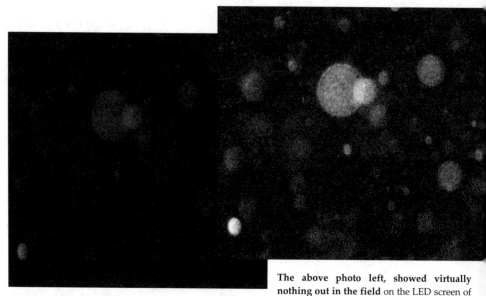

The above photo left, showed virtually nothing out in the field on the LED screen of the camera and not too much back at home on the computer screen either, but with a little light-enhancement which is available on all good photo imaging programs, you can see that there's much more in the photo that was at first apparent.

There's another very good argument for lightening the photos on the computer and bringing up the contrast etcetera. Don't forget (especially those of you who depend on the flash photons to blaze the orbs into life), that the maximum reach of the average flash is only about ten metres if that, and there will be orbs out there a long way beyond that range. So always try a bit of lightening of your photos and see what you get. You could be in for a real bonus. I don't consider light enhancement of photos to be cheating in any way. All this is about

These two versions of the same picture show quite dramatically what lightening your photos can do. The original photo which is not shown here, had at first sight an almost zero presence of orbs. After a 'medium' strength lightening process (photo above) you start to see plenty of orbs. The second example of the same photo after further lightening shows a myriad of orbs! So don't hesitate! Lighten up and see what gives!

a voyage of discovery and the more you investigate the more you will find out. Just before we leave the subject of light enhancing photos let me just say that there's a win/lose situation that operates here and usually what you gain on the light enhancement roundabouts you lose on the definition swings. When you lighten your photos you always lose detail and definition. So although you might get more of what you didn't know you had, you could see a lot less of what you've already got. Just like in real life! It's your choice!

Getting Creative

By occasionally dipping into the 'paint box' available on my photographic editing program I often fool around and take a look at my orbs in 'negative, in 'sepia' in 'relief' or I 'solarize' or 'pixelate' them and so on and so on. You too can do this. It's a lot of fun and very often it deepens your understanding of their structure and quite often viewing the orbs in different photo modes shows up their inner markings better.

To show you what I mean, I have reproduced here three versions of the same spectacular orb. The first picture on the left is the orb in its natural state. The second is in negative and I gave it a blue tint just for the fun of seeing what a blue orb looks like. And the third version is 'solarized'. This can't be taken seriously of course, but as you can see it does give the orbs a new perspective and very often brings out details which can be clearer than in the original photo. I think that the 'solarized' version here does just that. You can see the orb's rim much more clearly and some of its inner markings are easier to make out too. Sepia is another good colour mode to view an orb for a clearer picture. Sometimes the many different pixels of colour confuse the issue and a monotone can eliminate that.

There's no reason why you can't experiment like this. Orb photography doesn't always have to be a deadly serious business you know. Why not have fun too? Just as long as you don't *ever* try pass your 'special effects' off as the real McCoy – but then you wouldn't' dream of it would you!

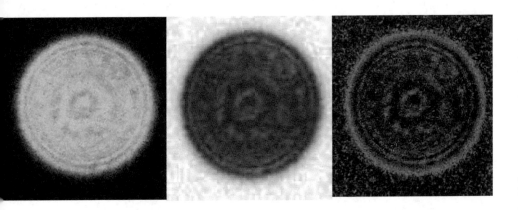

I don't usually save the results after playing around with my pictures in this way. It takes up unnecessary space on the computer and I just might look at them a few months down the line and think 'What the heck was *that!*" quite forgetting that I had only been experimenting. It truly is just for fun and strictly only ever for my own personal entertainment – and not meant to mislead you or anyone else!

Record-Keeping Pays Off

Whenever I have altered a photo, I *always* keep the original format and I then save the altered version in 'Save As' with the mention 'lightened' or 'light enhanced' or whatever I've done to it. The reason why I do this is so that I don't 'kid' myself later that the original photo was like this and also to remind myself what I did to it because as I said elsewhere in the book you think at the time that you will remember, but a year or two down the line you find that you don't. So it's a really good idea to systematically keep good records whenever you have altered an image in any way at all.

The other thing to watch out for is this business of resizing pictures. I can't tell you how often I have resized photos in the past and hit the 'save' button much to my bitter regret later. It is the worst feeling when you realise that your precious orb is now a silly, small thing, good for not much, and the action is irretrievable! I feel like writing this in capital letters but I don't want to look as though I am shouting at you. But please -- always but *always* keep a copy of your precious photos in their original size and rename your working copy by filling in the 'Save as' feature on your photo processing program. You never ever know when you will need them again -- like for example when the day comes when you too write your own book about orb photography! There's going to be nothing more maddening than finding you've only left yourself with a small resized version of your beautiful orb photo. There's not a lot that you can do with it after that.

So let's now take a nice long coffee break before we move on to bigger things like UFOs and Crop Circles! Coming up next.

PART TWO

Exploring Wider Horizons

CHAPTER SEVENTEEN

On Orbs & Crop Circles

The subject of crop circles is in fact not strictly within the scope of this book but I want to include something (quite a lot actually!) about my visit to the crop circles in Wiltshire, England and my experiences there, primarily because the circles are in themselves so fascinating and anything I might say even if it is inadvertently, you just never know, might add a small piece to this very large and perplexing puzzle.

Is there a connection between the crop circles and the orbs? I am not going to pretend that I *know*, neither am I going to try to put forward or make up some theory as to the whys and wherefores of it, but I am persuaded 'psychically' that there could well be a correlation between crop circles and the orbs. That somehow on some level they interconnect. There are too many anomalies that have been witnessed by serious observers which add up to a strong argument 'for'. There have been too many reports of 'balls of light' in and around the circles and too many photographs and videos of orbs and other light phenomena to be ignored. By the sheer weight of photographic and eye-witness evidence it is time that this is taken seriously by the world at large and a program of meaningful research is undertaken by governments who would start treating us like responsible, intelligent adults, and would keep us apprised of what is going on.

There is without a shadow of a doubt something happening out there that we do not as yet fully understand. If it is something that is *not* coming from the realms of human-kind, then logically it is coming from somewhere or someone else. Who or what then? One thing that it most certainly isn't, is a bunch of idiotic practical jokers in various places of the globe, going out in often miserable climatic conditions and freezing half to death in waist-high wheat just to perpetrate a massive hoax on the world in general. Frankly -- why bother? What would be the point? This has the distinct whiff of a double debunk to me!

I am just a beginner at this game and have only been out to the crop circles once. That was in June 2007 shortly after the activity for the 2007 'season' had started. My friend Belinda who has had a long and very successful career as a rock singer, had just finished a gig in London the night before and was having to go to France a couple of days later. She is right into anything that has anything to do with the supernatural and has been making an annual pilgrimage out to the crop circles in the past few years and 2007 was not going to be an exception. She was going to see the latest circles or bust! And I was going to go with her or bust!

Belinda is a 'seeker' and very much in touch with things of a spiritual nature. But let me get this straight right from the outset, she is in no way wacky either in her outlook or in any of her beliefs. As I said she is a seeker and by that I mean she is a serious seeker of the truth. She is a fountain of knowledge on certain esoteric subjects and she, and her whole family are all extremely well-informed on a wide variety of current issues. She keeps herself up to date and has an open and critically objective mind on most questions, until she has decided for herself what's what. I have never found her to be wrong or off balance in any of her final conclusions on anything that we have discussed in depth -- and that has been many.

Limousines, Mud-Caked Shoes & Belinda Makes A Discovery

Divas are accustomed to traveling in style, and Belinda being no exception, ordered us a limousine with a chauffeur for the day. We took off early that morning heading for the Wiltshire Plains and the crop circles in the leather-cushioned comfort of a big black Mercedes with tinted windows. It was the day of the Summer Solstice, 21st June. It was also a really foul, wet and windy day -- but did we allow that to daunt us? We certainly did not! We only had one day at our disposal and raining or not we were going to make the most of it. We were also accompanied by a young mutual friend, Heidi, who had never done anything like this in her life and she, like me was all agog with excitement and breathless wonder at the adventure!

Once we arrived in Wiltshire, Belinda the veteran crop circle hunter who knows the score and knows how to scan the landscape for the presence of a crop circle, asked our chauffeur to drive at a slow cruising speed while she looked for the tell-tale signs. Much to my immense surprise, she very quickly spotted one small and very simple circle for us. The driver parked the once-pristine Mercedes up a rough dirt trail off the main road, and leaving its dry and cozy interior, we

Belinda and Heidi in the crop circle Belinda spotted from afar. It was very fresh and had possibly been made during the previous night. Later on in the day we reported it at the esoteric shop the 'Silent Circle' and were told that we were possibly the first to discover it and to set foot it. The girls by the way they are posing, certainly look as though they, in the manner of explorers of vast unknown continents, are staking the territorial claim for King and Country!

braved the foul weather and the driving rain and trekked out along the muddy 'tractor tracks' to the circle. We took our photos and trekked back again to the limo and the waiting chauffeur who, on seeing the squelchy, mud-caked shoes which were about to board his immaculate limousine, registered utter dismay. He had to get used to it there and then. This was the way his day was going to go!

At this point there was nothing in any of our photos which gave even the slightest hint of the presence of orbs. This was disappointing but just as we were about to get back into the car muddy shoes and all, I suddenly noticed that some cows in the next field were behaving very oddly. They were running in a kind of

Belinda is making her way across the field to try to determine what had frightened the cows. She could see nothing but this strange fog appeared in one of my photos. The 'fog' was roughly round, grayish-white, very blurred and dense enough to block out the light and the view behind it. It probably measured about 1½ -- 2 meters across and was quite close Belinda but even closer to me come to think of it! Two whitish objects can be seen streaking sky-wards in front of Belinda. The cows at this stage had completely vanished, and had gone into hiding in the copse of trees. They obviously didn't like whatever it was. (This photo has been light-enhanced in the two areas concerned to show you better -- the original was very dark).

disorderly, panicky way towards a copse of trees as though something had suddenly frightened them and as though they wanted to hide or seek shelter in the trees. Belinda made her way over to the fence in the field to see if she could work out why the cows were behaving in this way while I snapped photo after photo in the general direction of the cows. No orbs, but there was a mystifying sort of ground fog in one of the photos which according to Belinda is a typical phenomenon out there at the crop circles. She was certainly very excited about it. And I figured she should know.

In the same photo when I got it back home and light-enhanced it on my computer, I saw that there were two quite wide streaks of white light which appeared to be zooming upwards as though leaving the ground and heading at great speed into the sky. I have since found out that lights speeding skywards from the land is also a typical phenomenon out at the crop circles. Whatever the fog and the streaks of light were, the cows were obviously sensitive to the ambiance they created there and seemed to be agitated by it. Animals and the way they behave if it's in any way unusual, are always a good gauge that there's something happening that is not quite normal. It's always a good idea to ask yourself why and to take time to check it out.

Fish & Chips & The Chalk Horse

We drove around fairly aimlessly for the rest of the morning, eyes scanning the endless expanses of wheat and barley fields with no success. There wasn't another crop circle anywhere to be seen. It was still quite early in the season after all. We hoped not *too* early, because our expedition was, at that time, our one and only bite at the cherry. We were all going to France the next day.

After stopping at Pewsey and lunching on fish and chips at the famous old pub on the canal 'The Barge Inn', we briefly admired the nearby Chalk Horse which is supposed to be 3000 years old -- but we had specifically come for something else so we cut short any time spent appreciating the 3000 year-old World Heritage marvel and continued our search for a circle which might have been made yesterday! (Talk about a weird sense of cultural perspective!) After an hour or more we were still having no luck in the crop circle department. It was beginning to be somewhat less than pleasant driving aimlessly around the

Wiltshire plains in the pouring rain looking for something that didn't seem to be there.

Eventually we found a likely-looking 'pit-stop', the 'Silent Circle', where we thought we could make enquiries. The 'Silent Circle' is an esoteric shop on the roadside out by one of the chalk horses and so we pulled in and stopped there a while. There I bought a couple of DVDs on crop circles, one of which would later turn out to have huge significance, while Belinda chatted to the owners and to one or two other people who seemed to be in the 'know' and who gave her directions to a new crop circle in a field at Yatesbury -- right by the local landing-strip. Following the directions we had been given, we drove on out there and found the circle with no trouble at all -- it was right by the road.

Belinda and Heidi jumped out of the car, clambered under the fence and went into the circle. I was feeling tired and cold and had lost more than just some of my enthusiasm at this stage -- but not for long. Not one to be ever left out of anything, I soon joined them. We were amazed to see that although it had rained extremely heavily all day, bizarrely the interior of the circle was bone dry, the blackish/grey soil being almost of a sandy, dusty consistency. It was as though it had been micro-waved. How could this be? The term 'scorched earth' came to mind.

Belinda suddenly announced that she was going to test the circle's energy by lying down in it and, feeling instantly nauseous and headachy, she declared that it was "Very powerful!" I, on the other hand declined to actually lie down in the circle but on moving through the formation, I felt a strange sensation of elation come over me. Gone was the tiredness and dispiritedness of earlier. Suddenly I felt as though I wanted to dance and sing. It was as though all my batteries had

The Yatesbury Circle: 57 circles all linked together by a vast spiral within a circle make up this massive crop circle estimated at 300 feet (92meters) across, which appeared overnight at Yatesbury on May 30th 2007. This was the crop circle we visited. The design has been connected to the Kundalini serpent of the chakras. It is coiled into three and a half turns. Naturally, I made a connection between the 57 circles and 57 orbs strung out like pearls on a necklace. (Picture by courtesy of Lucy Pringle, www.lucypringle.co.uk.)

been recharged and I felt strong surge of new energy flood through me. It was a great feeling -- a natural high.

The overriding impression that I got in the Yatesbury Circle was that by the sheer size of it and by its complexity, when you stand inside it you know -- you positively *know* -- that it was not made by human hand. It's immediate proximity to the road and to the airport in the adjoining field completely rules out the possibility of creating it artificially without someone seeing the activity and knowing that fraud was a-foot! And it certainly was not made by two old codgers jumping around in the dead of the night on a board attached to a piece of string. (Of all the possible hoaxes out at the crop circles, that would surely rate as the greatest of them all!)

Not An Orb In Sight

Disappointingly there had been no orbs in any of our photos all day. There's no real explanation for it. They just weren't there. Yet all the elements which The 'Light Beings' usually love, and which should have made for their appearance were present. We were out at the crop circles; it was the day of the Summer Solstice and The 'Light Beings' usually love rain. The only appearance of an orb or 'Light Being' in all of our photos that day was in one that Heidi took of Belinda and me with matching umbrellas from our London hotel, braving what was a veritable deluge out there on the Wiltshire Plains. In Heidi's picture you can clearly see that the rain is slanting down with a real force and dripping off our umbrellas. But there tucked under Belinda's umbrella as though trying to take shelter from the downpour is a small milky orb. Heidi's first orb photo ever! There are one or two other very small orbs in the photo but the rest is rain, easily

Belinda and me with matching umbrellas from our London hotel, out seeking crop circles on the day of the Summer Solstice, 21st June 2007. The rain is pelting down and there is no way that I would normally have opted for this as a pleasant way to spend a day. But in fact we had a great time. Are we mad or what! (Photo by Heidi Cook)

discernable as it is all slanting in the same direction driven by the wind. (You've all learnt how to read this sort of photo by now haven't you!)

Back To Civilization & A Soak In A Hot Tub!

After thoroughly investigating the Yatesbury circle we decided to call it a day. We were all tired and very cold; our clothing, especially footwear, was soaked through and Belinda was still feeling off-color after lying down in the circle. I mean to say, on the normal scale of nice things to do on a rainy day, you have to be *mad* to be doing this sort of thing don't you! But it had been great fun and as we got back into the car for home, we were in a semi-dazed state of wonder and awe at the hugeness and the mystery of it all.

By the end of the day I couldn't believe that I hadn't captured any orbs at all that day. For years I had been convinced that I was going to be *The One* who, with a few easy clicks of the shutter would prove conclusively that there was a definite connection between orbs and the crop circles. My discoveries would make headlines all over the world! But alas-alack, it would seem that it takes more than just one day's outing to get world-shaking revelations out at the mystical crop circles. Better qualified people than I have tried for years and not as yet succeeded and I guess that ultimately, any revelations will be in the Crop Maker's and the Light Being's own sweet time – not mine or anyone else's!

Once back at the hotel after the long drive back to London, we farewelled our long-suffering chauffeur who was muttering something about now having to take his mud-caked limo to be 'groomed' before he could go home. (Grooming *cars*? I thought that was for horses!) I did actually feel seriously sorry for him when I thought of the pristine limo that had met us that morning and compared it to the sorry sight that a day out with us had left him with!

After long soaks in hot tubs we gathered back in my room, ordered room-service club sandwiches and all wrapped up in warm, cuddly blankets, we tucked our feet up and watched the DVDs we had bought at the 'Silent Circle'. The subject of the DVDs? The Wiltshire crop circles of course. What else? What a great day it had been!

CHAPTER EIGHTEEN

More On Orbs & Crop Circles

I became convinced some years ago that there was a real connection between orbs and crop circles when I stumbled upon a photograph on the internet of a three-circle formation which although nothing like as beautiful and creative as many of the other more spectacular circles, was of a detailed complexity that was mind-blowing. It showed three identical circles with a maze-like pattern of seven interconnecting concentric circles interspersed by numerous 'wheel-spokes' radiating from the circle's centre to its periphery, and looking very like the cross-section of a tree trunk. This at the time corresponded *exactly* to the structure that a good orb would show in my photos. It just couldn't be a co-incidence. The Circle Makers were surely trying to tell us something and waiting for someone to make the co-relation between the two. Well I'm doing it now – slightly belatedly maybe, but I'm doing it here and now in this book, and better late than never. I wonder if there's anyone else out there who has ever made the same connection between crop circles and orbs as I am doing right here.

The inset photo here is one of my own orb photos and I truly can hardly make a distinction between the design of the three 'orbs' in the crop circle and my orb. All the elements are there: The strong resemblance to a cross-section of a tree trunk with seven concentric circles; the multi segments radiating out like spokes of a wheel from the centre to the outside edge and in the crop circle 'orbs' and the real orb, there is a definite nucleus and also a definite border. The co-incidence is

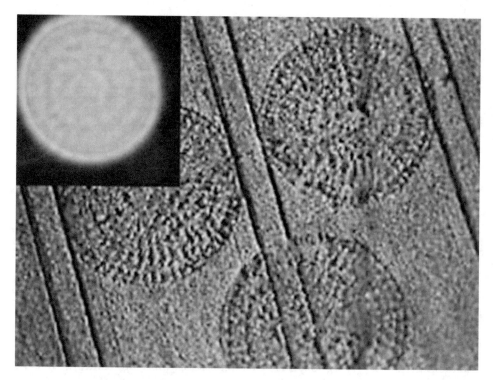

Is it just my imagination or do these three crop circles shown from the air resemble something we are becoming more than slightly familiar with? Could someone from somewhere be trying to tell us something? Could there be some sort of Cosmic Secret encoded in these orbicular designs that we should know about? Are the circle makers actually depicting a group of orbs so that we can make a connection? (Photo from Internet: author unknown)

too great to be ignored -- there's no doubt that the crop circles in this formation here, look exactly like any typical group of orbs. Beyond doubt, I believe that the Crop Makers are drawing our attention to the orb phenomenon for some reason and trying to tell us something about it that we should know. But what? The conclusion here is inescapable. If the Crop Makers need to tell us something about orbs, that means that orbs have a truly big significance and the message could be important. I hope that they will continue to draw our attention to it.

The E.T. Of Crabtree Farm

There are some very bright people out there who have been working on decoding the crop circle known as the 'Crabtree Farm E.T.' with the stunning portrait of the Alien which is shown on the following page. They have discovered that by a code-breaker of a series of 001001s that they can actually decrypt a decipherable and coherent, message encoded in the orb-like disc beside the E.T. Fortunately for us, those considerate Crop-Makers from another galaxy left us the coded message in English which was very thoughtful of them. (Thanks chaps, otherwise we might have missed the point entirely!) The decipherers divulged that the message encoded in the disc beside the 'Crabtree Farm E.T.' reads: *"Beware the bearers of false gifts & their broken promises. Much pain but still time. There is good out there. We oppose deception."* The message apparently then signs off with the 'ting' of a bell. (I wonder how they translated that bit!)

I can't say that I personally find this message is particularly illuminating. It doesn't seem to say anything of sufficiently great significance to justify all the hard work involved in both the making of the circle and the hours and days and weeks of painstaking deciphering – but then I tend to be rather 'high' on

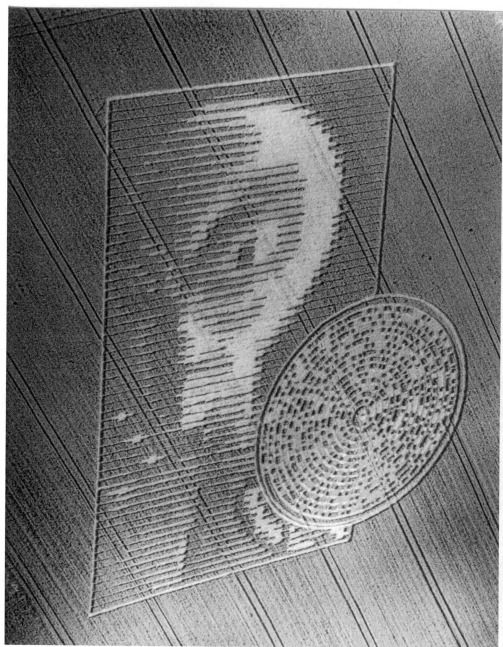

This beautiful aerial photo of the 'Crabtree Farm E.T.' is by courtesy of Lucy Pringle. www.lucypringle.co.uk.

By a very strange synchronicity of Cosmic timing and design which most assuredly means nothing of any real significance except that it's a weird co-incidence, my photo of an orb shown here by the statue in my garden has strange echoes of the 'Crabtree Farm E.T.' Crop Circle depiction of an Alien with an orb beside him pictured on the previous page. The 2002 date coincides too. Could the pattern in the orb be deciphered too?

material and worldly values so therefore on a New-Age Spirituality Scale from one-to-ten, in all probability I rate really low! I probably don't have the kind of concentration needed to meditate long and hard on whatever it is that has to be meditated on in order to grasp the full deep meaning here. There are times when I definitely need things to be spelt out to me very clearly phrase-by-phrase as one would to a child (I never do get the punch-line of a joke), and this is one of those times! Perhaps with more time, more will be revealed and it will all fall into place and make perfect sense. Meanwhile I'll just keep on with taking the photos!

Nevertheless the 'Crabtree Farm E.T.' is an extraordinary crop circle and to my mind, far too large and complex to be 'man-made'. And, into the bargain, there's the presence of that discus-shaped, orb-like motif that so closely resembles an orb. It's almost uncomfortably uncanny.

Note too how those clever crop-makers haven't lined up the square which frames the E.T. with the tractor tracks in the field but have got it at exactly the right angle so that from the air it looks as though it is standing upright in the field in a sort of 3D effect! That can't have been by accident and to my mind takes a great intelligence to figure that out in advance. I'm sure that human logic would have thought to use the tractor tracks as the frame and line the picture up with them. Would have made the job much easier too.

A Consciousness Inherent In Nature?

The following excellent 'essay' is an eyewitness report written by an investigator into crop circles who had a lot of success photographing orbs inside crop circles. I found this on the internet many years ago and was so intrigued by it that I kept it never for a moment imagining that I would one day write a book on the subject. Unfortunately the reference to its authorship is long lost, so I therefore cannot give any credits to it, but should the author be reading this book, and recognize his/her writing please accept my grateful thanks and get in touch with me. You have eloquently into words exactly what I always suspected and hoped to find out for myself. I hope that through your seeking and with the passage of Time you and Robert have found the answers to some of your questions.

"For years Robert has been taking flash photos at night inside crop circles which, when developed, show single or multiple strange semi-opaque orbs and other light phenomena not usually visible to the naked eye. He has found that such experiments are most productive in new crop circles, but that-in some cases unusual lights/orbs can be photographed even weeks or months after the initial event. More recently he has discovered that he can actually see quite a few of these light objects before they are photographed and has also noted that many of the objects now being caught on film are not only much brighter and more dense but are much more complex in structure. I, too, seem to have become more sensitive to the presence of the objects, often seeing brief flashes of light which when I can get off a shot or two in their direction quickly enough-result in the objects apparently being caught on film. What are the light objects? Are they in fact becoming more complex too, perhaps mirroring the evolution in design of the flattened plants? (The wheat in crop circles) Are Robert and I (and, apparently many other people) victims of our imaginations? Or is it possible that human faculties are capable, at least in some situations, of recognizing external consciousness and/or purpose in energy-forms or life-forms currently unknown to us and unnamed? Was there a consciousness in those lights? Or, was there a consciousness directing them? Was it our sub or unconscious? If not ours, was it Jung's collective unconscious? Was it a consciousness inherent in Nature? Or was it from another dimension, galaxy or, perhaps, directly from the Almighty? Robert and I don't know. What we suspect is that the answers to these questions-in fact the actual pursuit of these answers will greatly affect human awareness. What we *hope is that 21st Century humanity will recognize this possibility soon and join in the effort to uncover new aspects of reality we may currently only faintly imagine."*

With the dawning of the Age of Aquarius, the endeavor to uncover those new aspects of Cosmic reality that up until now we only faintly imagined is on the march and gathering momentum. There is a new consciousness surfacing today and I believe that we are soon to be rocketed into a dimension which will consist of a new reality.

Aye, Circles Everywhere -- But Ne'er An Orb!

One day in September 2007 there were newspaper reports of a strange circle which appeared overnight up on the Col de Vence in a field of wild grasses and measured 32 meters in diameter. It was extremely impressive, very cleanly and clearly defined and I took many photos of it for my records. But there was not a sign of even the most miniscule orb in any of the photos which I thought was rather odd, given the correlation with The Col de Vence and the mysterious 'crop circle'. I somehow expected that there would be orbs galore around this manifestation so evocative of alien energy, mystery and other-world-ness. This absence of orbs combined with my total failure to capture any orbs at Wiltshire was disappointing. Was I going to have to consider the possibility that perhaps orbs are not in fact connected to UFOs after all? That the oft-reported lights witnessed out at the crop circles which seem to be busily working with purpose around the crop formations, are not necessarily orbs? Only time and more study will tell. Fact is that the crop circles appear on the earth's energy grid or along Ley-Lines. So too it is proven, does intense orb activity. They have a decided penchant for old places of worship and major monuments such as the Pyramids which are built along the earth's magnetic grid. The strength of the energy field could well be the one and perhaps the only common denominator between the two and could be what links them in terms of locality and frequency of manifestation. The two phenomena themselves though, may not be even related and could come from quite different cosmic dimensions. There's a lot of painstaking work to be done in this field and while I love a good puzzle, there are people out there with a lot more of the convoluted, way-out variety of lateral thinking brain-power and patience needed than I will ever possess, who are dedicated to figuring all this out. I'm just happy to keep on taking the photos.

Several months after the appearance of the big 'crop circle' up on the Col de Vence, I was talking to one of the group of G.E.E.S.A the UFO phenomena researchers who study such things. He happened to say that he had been up there recently and that the soil where the circle was burned into it was blackish/grey and had a dry, sandy, dusty consistency, almost as though it had been micro-waved. I was really stuck by this, because his description of the soil was almost word-for-word how I described the dry soil at the Yatesbury crop circle in England.

CHAPTER NINETEEN

The Col de Vence

The Col de Vence merits a book in itself. As the dictum says, "there's a book in everybody", and as this might be *my* one and only, I'm going to grasp the opportunity right here and now and include the Col de Vence. It is perfectly appropriate to do so as the Col de Vence is highly relevant to the story but before we go any further; first a translation for you of the French word *'col'* -- it means mountain pass in English.

It's extraordinary, but having lived here for nearly 30 years and despite knowing the region extremely well, somehow the Col de Vence had entirely escaped me. I had explored every mountain pass and old village in the hinterland almost everywhere in the Alpes Maritimes and beyond -- *except* the Col de Vence and I can't explain why. I have an artist friend who lives near the town of Vence and I had visited him there often but somehow had never gone on through the town and out the other side onto the road which leads to the Col itself. It's as though it was blinkered from my awareness and I was blindfolded to it until the right moment came to discover it.

That moment for discovery came during the visit with Belinda and Heidi to the crop circles in Wiltshire in England when we stopped at the mystical shop 'The Silent Circle'. I was browsing through the DVDs on sale there and saw one entitled 'UFOs & Crop Circles: Col de Vence, France'. "This looks interesting", I thought, "this is right in my area back home!" I bought the DVD which was a documentary of an investigation by a group of Frenchmen into increasing paranormal activity up on the Col de Vence where UFO sightings and many other unexplained phenomena repeatedly take place.

This was enough enticement for me and my curiosity was thoroughly aroused, so one Saturday afternoon I got into my car and drove the 50-odd kilometers separating Cannes from The Col de Vence. Once I had traversed the town of Vence itself, I sort of followed my nose and suddenly I saw the sign post pointing to The Col de Vence. Something about that sign had an instant effect on my adrenalin levels and I knew that I was on a road to new discovery from which there was going to be no return. I was right.

Once clear of the town and its houses, the road climbs suddenly, steeply winding uphill and civilization quickly gives way to a wild, untamed lunar landscape where the predominant color is the beige of desiccated grasses interspersed with the drab grey of the rocky outcrops so characteristic of the area. There are spectacular views down to the Mediterranean far below where the sea blends with the sky and adjoins the lost horizon to the mystical ambience on 'The Col'. Everywhere there is profound silence and the only significant movement is an occasional buzzard gliding on thermal currents seeking signs of life below, on which to prey.

I was very aware of being alone up there and I felt slightly afraid although of what exactly I do not know. What I did know, is that I would not be stopping the car and getting out of it to take photos. No way! If there were any photos to be taken it would be by stopping the car, leaving the engine running and winding down the window, while remaining at the ready to take off like a shot out of a gun if needs be. I vowed that the next time I came up here, I would most certainly not be coming alone. As it turned out I did not have very long to wait before I had some willing candidates in my friend Mike from Nice, his son John and Belinda.

Just Your Average Bit Of UFO Spotting

Belinda wanted to come because if it had anything to do with UFOs, crop circles and aliens she was definitely on for it. Mike wanted to come because he had heard that there was a 12th century Templar chapel up there at Saint Barnabé and anything to do with the Templars was more than enough lure for him and John wanted to come simply because everyone else was going. But basically I think that we all wanted to go because it felt like a big adventure and so we decided to make it for the following Saturday just to see what would eventuate.

Nothing like a bit of good old-fashioned UFO spotting on a Saturday night, especially in good company. What could be more normal?

I got together a substantial picnic of chicken pie, French bread, cheese and boiled eggs plus a couple thermos flasks of good, strong coffee and just in case it might get cold later, I also amassed a large pile of assorted rugs, scarves, warm jackets, gloves etcetera to take with us, even though it was still technically late summer. After all we were going UFO spotting up on the Col de Vence and anything can happen on a mountain. As the Boy Scout motto says, "Be Prepared". Belinda picked me up and we set off from Cannes in her car. By an incredible stroke of synchronicity, considering that we all came from completely different directions, we managed a chance rendez-vous with Mike and John on the main road just outside the town of Vence, and fell into convoy there. Our big adventure was about to begin!

The Templar Chapel

First we drove into the little hamlet of Saint Barnabé, to find the Templar Chapel. This presented us with no difficulty whatsoever as the chapel is just one of no more than half a dozen buildings in the entire community and the only edifice even vaguely resembling a church. Saint Barnabé has a population of 80 souls -- real living ones not ghostly ones. Our timing could not have been better as judging by the puddles on the ground, we had just missed a passing rain shower. The sky was now clear of any clouds, and as it was still well before sunset and there was plenty of light for photography. The leaves on the large Hazel tree next to the chapel were already slightly tinged with autumn yellow, well ahead of it's relatives at lower altitudes, for up here on the Col de Vence, at just under 1000 meters, the season was considerably more advanced than at sea level. Even though it was still late afternoon there was already a definite nip in the air not as yet felt down on the coast. 1000 meters is a very respectable altitude indeed, a fact that we would fully appreciate much later in the evening but for the moment our full attention and our cameras were focused on the strange little chapel.

From the very first click of my camera there they were! Orbs a-go-go! They were right on time for the rendez-vous with me that is, but not for the others which further proves to me that they will line themselves up with the camera of the person that they know and who they have chosen to let photograph them while staying clear of those people they don't yet know and trust. It's very possible that they are shy. I believe they are. Otherwise how else can you explain that they were *there* -- physically present -- I was getting them but Belinda and Mike weren't -- at least not yet?

Souls In Mourning?

Of all the photos I took of the chapel that evening, in which just about every single one was peopled by orbs, the one on the next page is my favourite. It shows the little chapel with three big, bright orbs marching in single file up to the door of the chapel as though going in to worship, with two baby orbs in the procession as well. One or two other orbs are hovering watchfully in the vicinity. It is very tempting to tell oneself that perhaps on that night so close to the anniversary of the massacre of the Templars seven hundred years before, these orbs were the Templars' mourning souls returning to commemorate the demise of their Order, and that of their comrades. Who knows? I certainly don't discount the notion. There is a very heavy residual pain-body associated with the disbanding of the Templars and echoes of it linger in the environment to this day.

A Mecca For Mike

Mike had certainly found his Mecca! The Templar Chapel fascinates: It is tiny, and it is old – very old. It was built by the Templar Knights whose elite order was drawn from the crème-de-la-crème of European aristocracy and was so treacherously attacked and disbanded in the year 1307 by the Philippe 'Le Bel', King of France, known to English speakers as Philip 'The Fair'; so named presumably, because he was stunningly good-looking. Good-looking he may have been, but oh what a wicked, and avaricious heart had he Philip the Fair, acting initially alone but later with the cowardly complicity of that turncoat and traitor to the Templar Order, Pope Clement V, managed to bring to its knees the greatest multinational business and banking conglomerate so far known to mankind in its day. Besides banking and business, the Templar Knights were also a superbly trained and disciplined fighting machine. It was as cruel and inglorious a stroke of treachery ever devised by any king. This was on Friday 13th October 1307 and to this day we still superstitiously stay in bed, mind our step or buy lottery tickets on Black Friday. That's where it originated -- honestly!

The 13th October also happens to be Mike's birthday -- so perhaps it's from there that he gets his fascination for anything and everything to do with the Templars. Maybe he is a born again Templar. It wouldn't surprise me.

The Templars' presence up on the Col de Vence and at Saint Barnabé would not have been without forethought of purpose. The Templars never did Anything unless it had a very solid raison-d'être. Usually their choice of sites

Facing Page: **The Templar Chapel** in the tiny hamlet of Saint Barnabé on the Cold de Vence. This photo was taken just a few days before the 700th Anniversary of the cruel suppression of the Knights Templar Order. There are five orbs which seem to be marching in perfect single file up to the Chapel door as though going into pray. Are they mourning souls returning to commemorate the demise of their Order, and that of their fellows? A close look at one of the orbs on the ground shows that it seems to be casting a shadow.

allowed them between a half to a full day's ride to the next Commanderie. Saint Barnabé is situated at a high altitude slightly to the north west of Nice where, at convenient proximity to the port, there was also a major Commanderie in rue de la Prefecture. It would have been considerably more than a day's ride off the mountain down to the coast and then making the often perilous crossing from bank-to-bank of the unpredictable River Var, before crossing the last open stretch of country leading into the bustling township of Nice.

On the lower slopes of the Col de Vence at a rough halfway point between Saint Barnabé and Nice, lies the town of Vence itself where, on the northern outskirts was yet another Templar Commanderie which was of considerably greater importance than the small outpost at Saint Barnabé. The ruins of this Commanderie, now incorporated into the beautiful hotel/restaurant the 'Chateau Saint Martin', can still be seen today.

A Medieval Chapel With An Enigmatic Past

Saint Barnabé was most probably an 'outpost' for the Commanderie at Saint Martin, and today the hamlet is still tiny, counting as it does approximately eighty inhabitants. It is highly likely, given the inhospitable nature of the Col de Vence area, that the outpost at Saint Barnabé would have been established there to serve as a place to break a journey, or as a mountain refuge for the traveler in times of inclement weather. A hostel with its little chapel and its own small farm providing just enough simple produce for food would have provided a single night's stop-over for the journeyer from points north who needed only to reach the Mediterranean and had no reason to tarry there for more than a single night; just time enough to rest, eat a hearty meal, offer prayers of thanks for having brought him safely thus far, and to feed and refresh his most valuable asset and faithful travel companion -- his horse.

Without knowing the full and precise history of this little chapel -- nobody

Interior of Templar chapel at Saint Barnabé: There is a large orb in the photo circled in red.

does -- we do know however that it predates that inauspicious date of Friday 13th October in 1307. It appears to be hastily built without any thought given to the esthetics of architectural refinement. It is built of local undressed stone which is still to be found strewn about the entire area in limitless quantities.

The chapel looks as though in its day it was possibly thrown together as a temporary place of worship for travelers and transient occupants of the harsh land, and yet miraculously it is still standing all these centuries later having defied earthquake, harsh climate and diverse occupancy undoubtedly by a long succession of sundry tenants from flocks of goats, sheep, squatters, vagabonds, back-packers and so on down through its existence, until its current use today as a private chapel by someone in the hamlet.

It is squat and ugly but it is a brave little edifice bearing silent testimony to those ancient builders who even for the most humble of structures, knew how to build to endure. Yes it still stands. And there we were just a week or two short of the 700th anniversary of that, murderous, fateful date contemplating this little church and trying psychically to penetrate its enigmatic past. It felt like a pilgrimage.

CHAPTER TWENTY

The Black Villages

There is something particularly awesome about the high plateau of Saint Barnabé, where the thousands upon thousands of sun-bleached stones and rocks strewn about the countryside makes one wonder what insanely enraged giant hand flung those rocks across that vast inhospitable lunar landscape.

Here nothing much grows save wild grasses, wild dog-rose and stunted oak and beech trees, twisted and tortured by the constant wind and harsh climate. I had heard that by venturing a kilometer or two off the beaten path, you come across a geological oddity that the locals call the 'Villages Negres' – the Black Villages. Do not ask me why they are called so, I do not know. Perhaps the origin was forgotten long ago and no one knows today. These are not villages at all, but extraordinary areas of stone formations fashioned by millennia of water and gas action which has resulted in a fine example of 'karstic' landscape, so bizarrely sculpted that with very little stretch of the imagination needed, one can clearly see forms of animals, humans wearing hats, sphinx, tombs, pyramids and dolmens. There's even a lifelike camel there modeled in stone.

Seeing this extravagant creativity of nature, one feels vaguely disturbed and can't help asking oneself the slightly uncomfortable question "What if?" "What if these shapes weren't the result of water action? What if they were made by primitive man or even by aliens?" On the Col de Vence nothing seems normal, anything is possible and many questions remain unanswered.

After investigating the Templar chapel to Mike's satisfaction, we got talking to some locals, a young mother and her two children who we met on the road by

A general view of one of the smaller of the 'Villages Negres' (Black Villages) on the Plateau de St Barnabé: The strange thing about this is, that it looks as though all the stones were at some time meticulously cleared from the flat part of the land and neatly stacked in tidy piles off to one side. Clearing an area perhaps for UFO landings? Anything is possible on the Col de Vence. Note the power pylon on the horizon. I'll be talking about power lines later.

the chapel. We mentioned that we had heard about the 'Villages Negres' and another locality up on the Col de Vence, the enigmatically-named 'Plateau of the Idols'. The woman told us that 'The Plateau of the Idols' was too far to try to get to at that late stage of the day, but that there was still enough daylight left to visit the nearest -- albeit the smallest of the 'Villages Negres'.

Matthieu (Matthew in English), the woman's son, a sandy-haired, freckle-faced boy of about nine or ten, who was obviously looking for any excuse to go for a good ride on the mountain bike he was doing wheelies on in the middle of the road, pleaded with his mother to let him show us the way to the 'village'. With some hesitation his mother finally agreed once she was assured by eager Matthew that he had already done his homework that night and so we left on foot with Matthew leading the way, while putting the bike through its paces for our benefit.

Green Men & Landing Sites

Once Matthew was satisfied that we had been given an adequate demonstration of the full range and diversity of the bike's maneuvers, he fell into step beside me and I was surprised by his opening question.

"So are you looking for the Green Men?" he asked without preamble.

"Err no ….. not exactly", I replied. Then, "Yes! In fact yes. Do you believe in the Green Men Matthew?" I asked him, thinking to myself, hey, this kid's a local, he might know something.

"Well", he said, "I've never actually seen one ….. but I know they exist."

"Do you indeed?" I said "and what makes you think that?"

"I've seen lights." he said enigmatically.

"What sort of lights?'

"Moving lights in the sky and in the bushes. I've seen a pink light too"

"Goodness" I said, "that's very interesting ..... what else do you know?"

"I know where they land ..... I can show you if you like."

"Ooh yes, please do!"

I translated this conversation to the others and saw Belinda's eyes light up instantly. Moving lights and alien landing sites were exactly the sort of things she had come for.

Matthew took off again on the mountain bike with renewed vigor, leading the way along the rough track until we came to a large oval grassy pitch of about

Matthew's landing site for the Green Men: A perfectly oval-shaped crater in the landscape, resembling an arena. It has been cleared of all rocks and stones. But by whom? Mike is pacing it out to measure the diameter while Belinda looks on.

70 meters in diameter, a sort of sunken arena protected on all sides by natural rock formation while an uneven stony path led down to it from where we approached.

The extraordinary thing about this crater-like formation in the wild stone-strewn landscape, was that there was not a single stone visible anywhere inside all of its vast circumference. The land was perfectly clear of anything that might impede the landing of ..... a spacecraft! Bizarre, but I say it yet again; this is the Col de Vence where the bizarre is commonplace!

Mike and Belinda scrambled down the stony path into the arena while Matthew, John and I lingered up on the rim of the crater. Mike started to pace it out to measure the diameter, while Belinda, who, as we have already seen, likes to 'scientifically' test the 'Earth's Magnetic Energy' in places like this by lying down in them, promptly lay flat on her back and made out like she was making 'snow angels' and before long declared "Wow! This is *really* powerful! I can tell already, I'm getting a headache and feeling nauseous!" I was instantly reminded of her testing the power of the crop circles in Wiltshire by lying down in them and I remembered how ill she got there! So much for Belinda's scientific methods and of course I couldn't help asking myself, why does she keep putting herself through this?

All the while that Mike and Belinda were carrying out their 'investigative research', I took photograph after photograph, trying to capture some sort of orb or other activity in this strange place. Not a thing. It was disappointing.

Finally Mike and Belinda emerged from the crater, and we continued to follow our trusty guide Matthew towards our destination, the 'Black Village'. Eventually we came to a very steep rise in the land which not even Matthew's marvelous mountain bike could tackle. Half scrambling and half pulling ourselves up by tree roots, we clambered up the short but steep slope, slipping and sliding on the loose stones, causing minor avalanches. We finally emerged in yet another surreal and breathtaking vista. Spread before us was the 'Black Village'.

The 'Black Village'

At this point the change in the character of the scene surprises. From the rock-strewn chaos of the plateau, this new landscape gives the appearance of being altogether more structured. The stones were suddenly much larger more like dolmens or standing stones and could easily by squinting up the eyes a bit and with no great stretch of the imagination be taken for a village or a stone-age settlement of some sort.

Someone else at some time had evidently thought so too, for joining up with the big natural fortress-like stones were, constructed by a relatively modern human hand (as opposed to an ancient or an alien one), stone walls with doorways making what they perhaps hoped would be a house free of all overheads, lost up there in the vast wilderness where they could come with a sleeping bag, set up camp and commune with nature while watching out for UFOs.

It all looked quite cozy, and there were the remains of a campfire in one of the 'rooms', the roof of which was formed by huge living Ivy vines with their large glossy leaves providing a luxuriant green canopy. It was all very strange especially as the 'owner' had thought it necessary to underpin his claim to his makeshift dwelling by posting a sign of unambiguous warning which read 'Proprieté Privé': Private Property. Belinda, Mike and John nosed around this strange habitation while I clicked away with the camera, becoming ever more bemused by the fact that I was still having absolutely no success whatsoever in capturing any orbs.

The Black Village: Belinda inspecting the makeshift abode up on the Col de Vence in one of the 'Village Negres' or 'Black Villages'. Man-made stone walls and big natural fortress-like stones join together to form a 'stone-age' type house, while a very modern-age sign warns us keep out: 'Private Property'. It all looked rather cozy.

There had been nothing at all since the Templar Chapel. Very strange: Clearly the 'Light Beings' weren't too interested in hanging out at the 'Black Village'.

Soon Matthew's mother and sister came to find him and fetch him home for supper and after a gentle reminder telling us that the remaining daylight was now running short and warning us not to linger up there for too long, they left, with us following on their trail soon after. It would not be at all funny to be caught off the beaten track up there on the Col de Vence after nightfall. A fall, a sprained ankle or broken leg could prove fatal. The temperatures after sunset, as Matthew's mother had told us, were already touching zero and the nights bitterly cold. We were soon to find that out for ourselves.

No orbs in this picture but this shows the ruins of another man-made structure near the Black Village. It has once been quite solid and was probably used as a shelter for a shepherd for his goats or sheep. The inclement weather has done its work over the centuries. I also wanted an excuse to put this photo in because as you can see it captures the extreme beauty of the area. Perhaps you can just see the 'Black Village' dimly in the left background.

TWENTY-ONE

The UFO Spotters & A Picnic

We arrived back in the little hamlet where we had left the cars by the Templar Chapel just as dusk was falling, and set off in convoy to find a suitable place to provide us with a vast uninterrupted stretch of sky for our big night out UFO spotting. We soon found a place where we could get both cars off the narrow, single-lane road and where we were provided with the added bonus of a couple of large flat-topped stones, one of which would serve perfectly as a table for our picnic, and the other as a seat. Night-life up there on the Col de Vence was looking promising. All our needs were being catered for; even down to the table and chairs.

The sun had only just set behind the mountain ridges and the sky was turning a soft orangey pink melded with dark navy blue. It was a good time, with an excellent quality of light to start photographing for orbs. I didn't have to wait for long. After a few non-productive shots, suddenly there they were again bigger and better and more numerous than ever. It was intriguing I thought, that they were back in such force after the worrying dearth most of the afternoon and I couldn't help wondering if it had something to do with the fact that we were once again not all that far from Saint Barnabé and the Templar Chapel where I had

Col de Vence: The sun had set and the sky was turning a soft orangey pink melded with dark navy blue in the latter stages of sunset. A perfect light for orb photography and the orbs were back again in force.

captured the orbs when we first arrived. As the crow flies we were probably no more than three kilometers away. I wondered if the 'Light Beings' favored the Templar connection.

I was reassured to see that they were back again and was keeping a close eye on Mike and Belinda who were clicking away in earnest. I found myself saying a little mental prayer to the 'Light Beings' that went something like: "Please let Mike and Belinda get photos of you. Please reveal yourselves to them too." I think they heard.

Orbs-a-Go-Go For Belinda And Mike

Suddenly there was an ear-splitting, earth-shattering scream from Belinda, and that girl who can belt out a rock number like no one else can, sure knows how to use her voice. "I've got one! I've got one! Look! Look! I've just taken a photo of an *orb*!" I never saw anyone so excited in all my life! Sure enough, she had just photographed her very first orb, a beautiful bright sphere with a strange structure which I up until that point had not seen before. It looked rather like an eyeball! A bit gruesome to look at admittedly but there it was – an eye in the sky. Were we being observed? The orbs were taking on a new pattern.

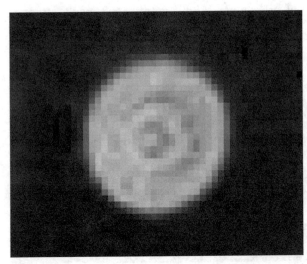

After the excitement of Belinda's first orb photo had died down, tranquility temporarily returned to the Col de Vence. But not for long. Within a minute or two another loud and triumphant cry rent what otherwise might have been the still night air up there on

Belinda's first orb photo: There were actually several orbs in the picture which were only visible with light enhancement. The main one looks rather like an eyeball or a glass eye! Are we being observed? Spoo-ooky! (Photo by Belinda Carlisle)

the Col de Vence. This time it was Mike. "Hey! I've got one too!"

Well let me tell you, did I ever laugh at that! For it was Mike who had always been one of the great skeptics and who was the leading protagonist of the 'faulty camera' theory and it was Mike who had constantly nagged at me these last five or six years to write those letters to the camera companies. Now he had just photographed his own orb on his own camera. "Ooh," I said with malicious glee, "Got a faulty camera have we Mike?"

One orb photo followed another. We had struck the proverbial pot of gold of the celestial kind. With all the hilarity and excitement, the ooh-ing and ahh-ing and the squeals of delight going on up there that night. I'd not have been at all surprised the orbs hadn't taken flight out of sheer fright, disappeared and gone into semi- permanent hiding until things quietened down again. But no, they obligingly stayed around, giving us full permission to take some really amazing photos not all of which were of orbs either. Along with an extremely strange-looking butterfly which probably *was* a butterfly but might have been an orb in disguise because it cast a very round, suspiciously orb-like, shadow, I also took

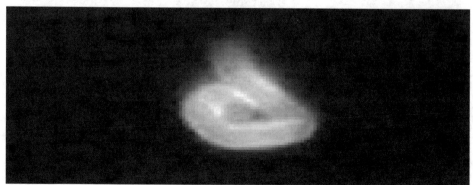

Col de Vence: Ullo-ullo what 'ave we here? Is it a floating doughnut high up in the sky or is it a stray piece of spaghetti spinning out there in space? Someone suggested that it could be an orb in motion doing a complicated high-speed maneuver. It's a weird one indeed.

pictures of several strange lights in the grass, a couple of orbs in motion, a 'doughnut' in the sky plus several other strange celestial luminaries of a kind that I had never captured before. One could say that had been a very good and productive night's work -- but I must say that I am still wondering about that butterfly. Can they survive at 1000 meters and zero degrees temperature?

CHAPTER TWENTY-TWO

Strange Sightings

If anyone ever needs a reminder as to how good food can *really* taste, I can thoroughly recommend trying a picnic in the open air on a freezing cold hillside at night. A simple chicken pie eaten with the fingers and a hot coffee out of a plastic mug becomes a feast for a king. And plain old bread and cheese with a hard-boiled egg never tasted so good. But the air was becoming decidedly nippy and one by one the assorted rugs, scarves, jackets and so on were finding their way out of the trunk of Belinda's car and being wrapped around chilly shoulders.

In spite of the encroaching cold, the general mood was still riding high and we all agreed that of all the odd-ball things we could be doing for entertainment on a Saturday night, this took some beating. However by about 9.30 we were definitely starting to feel the harsh reality of Matthew's mother's warning about the cold up there at night on the Col de Vence. It was all-invasive and could no longer be ignored. Everyone was beginning to feel as though they were freezing half to death in spite of the rugs and jackets. By10.15 pm we reluctantly admitted that we were forced to call it a night, abandon the mission and go home. Slightly disappointed at having to pack it in so early, but beaten by the cold, we agreed that we had seriously underestimated the mountain at night but vowed to come back again soon and when we did, be better prepared.

Peculiar Photographic Distortions

There is another oft-reported and well-documented phenomenon which occurs on the Col de Vence which is weird distortions in photos which mostly take the form of inexplicable disruptions in the focus. I took one such photo that afternoon while we still had plenty of daylight. It was of a small copse of trees. The foreground was in perfect focus. In the middle distance were the trees and the tops of the trees, the branches and leaves were completely out of focus and looked rather as though a hurricane or a giant broom was sweeping them all to the right. There were several very pale orbs in the picture too. Needless to say there was not a puff of wind. I can't find a logical explanation for this puzzling distortion.

A Couple Of Strange Sightings

'Aliens' and UFOs were the original order of the day (or night) for us but as it happened the orbs turned out to be the main attraction. However as far as UFO

sightings went, all was not quite lost. John and Belinda saw something very strange which unfortunately Mike and I both only just missed as we happened to be looking in the wrong direction at the very moment when this

'thing' blazed briefly across the sky. They both described it as being like a shooting star but bigger and slower with a long sparkling tail, like when the fairy 'Tinkerbell' in the Disney cartoons waves her magic wand. It was an iridescent silvery-turquoise-greeny-blue color and it simply faded or died out.

Then just as we were about to leave, I too saw a strange light. It was very similar to a satellite but much, much bigger and less star-like than a satellite. It was traveling in the wrong direction to have been either an airplane or a satellite. It was extremely high in the sky moving very swiftly and steadily in a straight line from east to west. It stopped for a few seconds in mid-flight, continued its trajectory and then seemed to merge and become one with the biggest star just above the horizon of the hill opposite us and never re-appeared. It had a smaller

Above: The strange light which sped across the sky just as we were packing up to go home: Could it be a UFO? It has another small object below it which seems to be keeping a-pace with it..

object beneath it which seemed to be traveling with it and seemed to be keeping pace with it.

The Whirly-Gig Thing-a-me-bob

This strange 'whirly-gig' thingy showed up in a photo taken that night. It was hovering just above the ground quite close to the wheel of Belinda's car. It looked not much more than a strange white smudge in the photo. It was intriguing, so I brought it up as high as possible and this was the result. Anyone ever seen anything like this before? Maybe it's the butterfly's cousin in chrysalis! Just joking!

Yes, it was a great night out up there on the Col de Vence but for me the best part was that Belinda 'The Seeker' and Mike 'The Skeptic' had become initiates to the 'cause' and had now joined the select club of photographers of cosmic 'Light Beings'. Moreover, through the person of Mike, whose conversion transformed a doubter into a 'believer', albeit an ever so slightly reluctant one, another debunker bit the dust that night. Brilliant!

I've not since had any reports back from Mike of further orb photos which

Col de Vence: Mike, John and Belinda studying Mike's orb photos.

is not really surprising as he is not a particularly great camera enthusiast, but Belinda, much to her immense delight has gone on to take several fine orb photos from the time of the night of the UFO Spotters' picnic up on the Col de Vence. And more than that, she has passed on 'The Gift' to a friend with whom she later traveled around India. This friend had never heard of orbs and became obsessed with them after Belinda showed her the pictures of the ones she had taken. The friend's obsession took the form of an intense desire to capture her own and the desire very quickly became a reality and she went on to take orb photos fairly consistently all through India.

Belinda also seems to have passed on 'The Gift' to her son's sixteen year-old school friend Damien, who has taken many orb photos – especially of Belinda at her shows – and in them she is always surrounded by orbs.

In all seriousness I'm telling you this; once you've been given 'The Gift' it's yours for keeps. Once the 'Light Beings' have adopted you they will stay with you through thick and thin and that is probably going to be for the rest of your life. They're loyal to say the very least and starting from the very moment when they first find you, you will never be alone again. I suspect that all they ask in return is that you don't laugh at them and carry the word of their existence to others.

As for me, following the night of the UFO Spotters' Picnic, I was to continue my adventures up on the Col de Vence for the next few weeks until winter snows closed the road to cars like mine. But more about that in the next chapter.

CHAPTER TWENTY-THREE

A Growing Obsession

During the week that followed the UFO Spotter's picnic, I was beginning to be consumed by a growing obsession with the Col de Vence. It would not let me rest. It was haunting me day and night and beginning to severely interfere with my powers of concentration. My mind seemed to be set in some sort of one-way track and kept harking back unbidden to the irresistible, magnetic, mysterious pull of 'The Col'. I had to go back and it had to be soon; just as soon as I could find someone to go with because although since the picnic I was much more familiar with it, I still didn't feel that it was a place where it would be particularly advisable or safe for a woman to be venturing alone in the dead of night.

Time and time again I replayed the DVD that I had bought at the crop circles in Wiltshire, studying every copse of trees, bend in the road and other land features until I felt I knew what was what and exactly where to find it. I visited the website of the guys who had made the video and left several messages for them to contact me which went unanswered. I would have like to have shown them the photos and the anomalies in them that I had taken on the night of the UFO Spotter's picnic, and to report our UFO 'sightings' up there. I thought that they might have found them significant following, as they did, so soon after the appearance only a couple of weeks earlier of the crop circle in the wild grass in the field. Evidently I was wrong.

Too bad I thought. After all these guys are the acknowledged experts, the 'gurus' of all things to do with alien activity on the Col de Vence and I guess they wouldn't be interested in hearing from a newcomer to the game. They are probably constantly inundated with all sorts of wacky people. Nevertheless the disregard of my messages stung and had not earned them any 'Brownie Points' in my personal hand-book of 'Best Etiquette', but perhaps it was perfectly understandable. So I resigned myself to going this thing on my own.

Then, right out of the blue with an unbelievably incredible turn of synchronicity, friends from overseas were visiting Cannes and mentioned that they had been invited to join people that very next Saturday night at a fancy restaurant called the 'Château Saint Martin' (that same restaurant of the Templar ruins I've already mentioned) and did I happen to know where that was? With an instant adrenalin rush at the very mention of the name, I told them. "It's on the road that leads to the Col de Vence!" Did I by chance know how best could they get there they asked. They'd been told that it was pretty remote and that they would have to make their own way there. I couldn't believe my ears; "I'll take you," I said without even thinking twice and crossing my fingers behind my back against the white lie that I was about to utter, "I'm going up that way myself on

Saturday night. I can drop you off at the restaurant if you like and pick you up later – no problem!"

Wow! I couldn't believe it. I had actually been presented with a possibility; nay it was more than that, it was a *legitimate* reason to visit yet again the new object of my all-consuming obsession and it had come less than one week after the UFO Spotters' picnic. There was a force operating here that could not be denied. I had to grasp the opportunity. I had to answer the clarion call.

Saturday finally came and when I dropped my friends off at the Château Saint Martin, had they seen the contents of the trunk of my car they would have been truly perplexed. There was an assortment of roll-necked sweaters, big scarves, wooly hats, ski jackets, rugs and even a long fur coat in the trunk of the car -- enough to suggest to a casual observer that I might be about to embark on an Arctic expedition; but having learnt the lesson of the biting cold on the mountain the weekend before, and not wanting to be forced to abandon the 'excursion' because of it, I was well and truly prepared. In addition to all that, I had already donned under my cotton blouse before leaving home, a sweltering layer of thermal underwear!

As well as all the thermal prerequisites, there were two digital cameras, binoculars, a picnic for one, a thermos of coffee, a high-powered flash-light and a roll of 'loo-paper': I was prepared for any eventuality. And just in case I ended up being forced to fill in time down in the town Vence until the midnight pickup back at the Château Saint Martin, I had with me a bit of your everyday light reading – my friend Tim Wallace-Murphy's latest book, 'The Knights of the Holy Grail' – it seemed highly appropriate for the Col de Vence because the book is all about the Knights Templar and as you know, the Knights Templar positively colonized the Col de Vence in centuries gone by. (You will remember Tim -- he is Chief Skeptic in my entourage and is constantly telling me that I need to get my camera checked!)

No Moon At All -- What A Night

I had no idea how the night was going to pan out. I had four hours to fill in until midnight. It was a deliciously long stretch of time to be up on the Col de Vence, but not such a delicious stretch of time if being there was not going to work out as hoped. Maybe it was going to be just too scary, in which case I had a 'Plan B' formulated which was to go back down to the safety of Vence and install myself in a café somewhere and read Tim's book while waiting until midnight to go back for my friends who were living-it-up in the high style to which I was much better adapted and I might say -- thoroughly accustomed! I was definitely beginning to have some serious moments of doubt tinged with regret. It would teach me to keep my big mouth shut in future before recklessly offering to drive people all over the countryside on a Saturday night!

I dropped my friends off and drove out through the majestic wrought-iron gates of the Château de Saint-Martin but instead of turning right and driving on down to the town as right-minded folk would do, I turned left and with my heart in my mouth and the now familiar adrenalin surge which seemed to be brought on these days by anything to do with the Col de Vence, I took the road leading to The Col. There must have been a moon somewhere that night as it was only one week before Full Moon but wherever it was, it certainly wasn't up there on the Col de Vence shining for me. No sooner had I embarked upon the mountain road, than the car seemed to be swallowed up in an all-encompassing cocoon of blackness so dense that not even the Xenon headlights on high-beam were able to penetrate it. The next uncomfortable sensation I was aware of with just a prickle of fear, was that of being utterly and entirely alone. There was not another car on the road nor the presence of a house or of a living being of any description anywhere around. Then came yet another nasty realization which was that in the total darkness out there on the narrow road on that mountain pass, there was no possibility anywhere of safely turning the car around and going back, without the very real and fatal possibility of disappearing forever over the side of a steep cliff into a bottomless ravine below. There was absolutely no way of scuttling back to the warm safety and comfort of a café in a well-lit town. I was committed. I felt like a sardine on a conveyor-belt. I couldn't get off and was forced to go on to the canning station.

In that moment I decided that I was definitely stark, staring and raving mad. This was the last – repeat *last*-time I would do anything like this. But wasn't it just a teensy bit fun – actually? What was the title of Susan Jeefers' book? "Feel the Fear and do it Anyway!" Looked like I was doing just that.

Once More Into The Breach

Like a homing pigeon that instinctively knows exactly where it is heading, I followed the direction which led to the relative 'security' of what was at least partly familiar, the spot on the road with the two big stones where we had had the UFO Spotters' picnic the week before. Although it seemed a lot further than I remembered it, I found the place easily enough, backed the car off the narrow road and got out to inspect the scene. Same place, same view but somehow being alone up there held nothing like the same appeal of being up there the other night in the hilarious, zany company of my loony friends. It seemed hostile, much darker and even colder. It was just plain spooky. I donned a few more layers of warm clothing from the supply in the trunk of the car, and then saw the headlights of an approaching car tracing a beam along the road. Dark thoughts of axe murders and serial rapists passed through my head, so I quickly jumped back into the flimsy safety of my car and locked the door. This was *not* going to be a fun night! The car went on by.

The U.F.O Researchers

As I sat there debating what to do, yet another car came along, this one with foreign registration plates. "Strange", I thought -- for this was a tiny road, the one that eventually lead to the little hamlet of Saint Barnabé. "There seems to be a lot of traffic out here tonight for such an isolated part of the world." I decided that maybe the best policy was to drive on into Saint Barnabé, and see what if anything, was going on.

I hadn't gone more than a couple of kilometers, when I suddenly saw that there was an open gate on the left with a rough track leading into an open field. There were cars parked in there and lights and people. Quite a lot of people in fact. Maybe this was where it was all happening I told myself, and drove cautiously in through the gates scanning the scene to see what I could make of it. It looked interesting. There were several cars, a Range Rover plus a 4-wheel-drive a camper van and one or two high-sided vehicles. People were sitting or standing around camp tables laid with French bread, cheese, salami sausage, and wine and

Col de Vence: G.E.E.S.A. A French UFO phenomenon research organization. I ran off a few photos of orbs by way of an introduction to them. They were very serious and professional with telescopes and computers etc, set up on the site.

a hurricane lamp was burning, giving off that eerie blue-white light of theirs and too, there were telescopes set up in the field. The occasional explosion of light from a camera flash briefly pierced the dark night. It looked all very friendly and convivial.

I parked my car and like any 'new kid on the block' I kept a respectful distance but approached tentatively nevertheless, smiling and throwing polite 'bon soir's to left and right. These people all seemed to know each other well. I thought that maybe they were some sort of UFO Watchers' Club. Maybe they were the 'Gurus' from the website who hadn't answered my emails.

Faithful Friends On Standby

Feeling a mite too shy to break into the group by just bowling up brazenly and introducing myself, I decided that it might be a good idea to make my entrée by an 'oblique route' (I'm a Cancerian you know -- and crabs always approach the object of their desire by scuttling sideways), and so I opted to pull a 'rabbit' or two out of my little hat of tricks by running off a few photos of orbs by way of an introduction. My 'little friends' were faithfully on standby and with a click or two of the camera within less than a minute, I had several really good bright shots of orbs to show. I went over to the nearest person in the group, who as it later turned out would become my friend and teacher Laurent, and said with a feigned air of total innocence, "Look what I just photographed! What do you think this is?"

He looked slightly stunned "How did she do that? I saw her go over there just a minute ago, take some photos -- and now she's back with some magnificent orbs!" Everyone crowded around to see. My camera was promptly hooked up to a lap-top lying on the back shelf of the Range-Rover and my photos and I became the centre of centre of attention for a glorious moment.

"Where did you take those photos?" someone asked. "Oh just over there by that tree." I said with a nonchalant wave of my hand. Several people picked up their cameras and went over to the tree and before long everyone was clicking away and having varying degrees of success in getting photos of orbs.

That was it! I had earned my badge of admission. It looked like this was going to be a fun evening after all.

My 'little friends' were faithfully on standby and within less than a minute and a click or two of the camera I had several really good bright shots of orbs to show. Through them, I earned my badge of admission to the French UFO research group!

CHAPTER TWENTY-FOUR

Orbs, Ectoplasm & 'Lentil Soup'

My initial assessment of the group in the field had been correct. This was indeed a UFO Watcher's Group but had nothing to do with the 'Gurus'. With all the equipment they had set up out there that night I could tell that they were very serious about their work and of course they were extremely interested in the Col de Vence because of the recent 'crop circle' found up there. Some of them had come from quite distant places in France. Their leaders seemed to be Jean Noel and Laurent and thanks to my orb photographs, within no time I had exchanged e-mail addresses with them both, promising to send them copies of my photos the next day. Apparently I had 'The Gift' and they wanted me to join them.

There was a woman there that night, a breeder of dogs whose name was Michelle. Michelle informed me that apart from breeding dogs, she was able to make contact with the 'Light Beings'. She said that she had started like me, by photographing orbs but that the orbs had become so invasive that they had in fact become something of a nuisance. She said that she had had to ask them to stop as they were constantly getting in the way. They stopped. She said that there followed a long interlude when all went quiet and she was getting nothing at all in her photographs and she became quite worried about it. She was afraid that she might have 'broken the spell' -- that precious line of communication between her and the orbs by telling them to go away and that they had permanently taken away 'The Gift'.

Then suddenly it started: She noticed that she was getting wisps of smoky, misty white areas in her pictures which she took to be ectoplasm. This new phenomenon continued to intensify especially, in (wait for it) a Templar Church near where she lives which was not far from a village called Trigance, in the Verdon -- a mountainous area where the Templars had been particularly operational up behind Draguinon in the south east of France.

Michelle then took a CD from her bag and put it into the CD-Rom drive of the laptop on the back shelf of the Range-Rover. We all gathered around to watch and when a page of thumbnail photos came up, she made a selection and filed through the most amazing pictures of this ectoplasm surrounding a young woman in the Templar Church. It was extraordinary. At one point the young woman was so heavily enveloped in the ectoplasm, that she was just about totally obliterated by it. According to Michelle, the ectoplasm is a natural evolution of and a stage further in the orbs' physical manifestation and that soon they would be able to 'complete' the process and appear to us in an almost solid and recognisable form as they were when they were living. She said that she firmly believes the orbs to be the spirits of the departed. Another thing that Michelle said that night was that she (like me), was convinced that animals could see the orbs. She, as a dog breeder said that frequently when her 20–odd dogs were on the lawn at home or out on long walks across the hills where she lives, they would suddenly begin to bounce and play and leap into the air as though someone was throwing balls for them. They would go into doggie 'mad-mode' like my Cocker Spaniel, Tinkerbell used to. Michelle said that when her dogs did that, there were always orbs present and that she had hundreds of photos to prove it.

Philippe, Me & 'Lentil Soup'

I stayed in contact with Laurent and Philippe from the UFO Watchers' Club and exchanged photos and e-mails with them all the following week. We arranged to meet up on the Col de Vence for a photography session on Saturday night of the 29th September. It was a perfectly clear and cloudless night. It was just past the full moon, and there was no fog or mist of any kind to explain the very strange phenomenon that Philippe and I would photograph that night. It was an extraordinary photographic feat that proved to me for once and for all that the camera sees and records what is *really* and truly there and that if one camera is good – then two are even better!

To explain: Oh, but first a word of warning! I'm pretty sure that the debunkers are going to have a field day with what's coming, so put your fingers in your ears now everyone because they're going to have plenty to say about these particular photos. I can hear them now! "Dust!" they'll scream; "Pollen!" they'll shout; "Seeds!" they'll roar; "Fakes!" they'll positively bellow! Well go for it you guys, you can scream until you are blue in the face because I can tell you that these are photos of a genuine phenomenon.

To fill you in on the background details: There were basically only three of us up on the Col that night; Philippe, myself and Laurent. The only other people who came up there during the entire evening were Jackie the park ranger with three 'clients' a man and two women who were out checking on the roaring stags who were rutting at the time (cute huh?) and they had well and truly been and gone by the time Philippe and I took our extraordinary photos. The total traffic tally all night was three cars (crawling at snail's pace over the rocky terrain) and seven humans with a whole great mountain range all to themselves standing around quietly talking and occasionally walking as far as the nearest car to get a cup of coffee from a Thermos. That's all and this was spread out over four or five hours; hardly your classic, fair-ground crowd, milling around kicking up cloud after cloud of dust.

'Lentil Soup' On The Wing

Once Jackie and his clients moved off into the night to track down the stags (sooner them than me by the way, judging by all the roaring that was going on out there in the impenetrable blackness of the night), that left only Philippe, Laurent and myself. So no dust chaps. The season was slightly autumnal. No pollen either at that time of year. There was no mist or fog, and no seeds. You have to see the scrubby grasses and mountain plants at that high altitude to know that it's not lush grasslands that we're dealing with here. Mother Nature was not exactly bursting forth that night 'neath the full moon with an explosive shower of fat, burgeoning seed buds distributing munificence and fecundity to the four winds. Oh no. It's barren, it's sparse it's bare. It's the Col de Vence. Okay so I think that I have disposed of the obvious scenarios that the debunkers will try to come up with to disparage these two photos. All I can tell you is that there were no environmental conditions known that I can think of that could account for the extraordinary phenomenon which came to pass that night.

Philippe and I were standing shoulder-to-shoulder on the edge of a small cliff and chatting idly while photographing into the dark abyss beyond, focusing on nothing in particular as you do when you are trying to get orbs. Although it was just past full moon, there was no moonlight, the moon not yet having risen above the high horizon of the mountains forming the rim of the plateau.

Standing there side-by-side, taking shot after shot, Philippe and I suddenly realised that we had both photographed a strange phenomenon and what's more, we had both photographed the *same* strange phenomenon at exactly the *same* time. It looked like 'Lentil Soup', composed of multiple orbs all crowded together in a gooey-looking brown mass. This was absolutely amazing! We compared the pictures on the LED screens of our cameras uncomprehending but very excited. After all, this was exactly the sort of thing that we had come up to the Col de Vence for. Martyrs to the cause, we were prepared to suffer considerable discomfort by enduring the cold night air on a mountain until the wee small hours in order to capture the rare and unusual! Now we really did have something to write home about. But what on earth was it?

Evidently it was some sort of passing cloud of a mass of *something*. But a mass of what? A mass of orbs? There are countless orbs present but they are in fact quite small and not showing a great deal of morphological detail. The mass is dense the colour is brownish-grey. We were photographing into empty space in the black night where there was nothing happening in particular and suddenly this 'cloud-like thing' appeared. Shortly after that it was gone just about as fast as

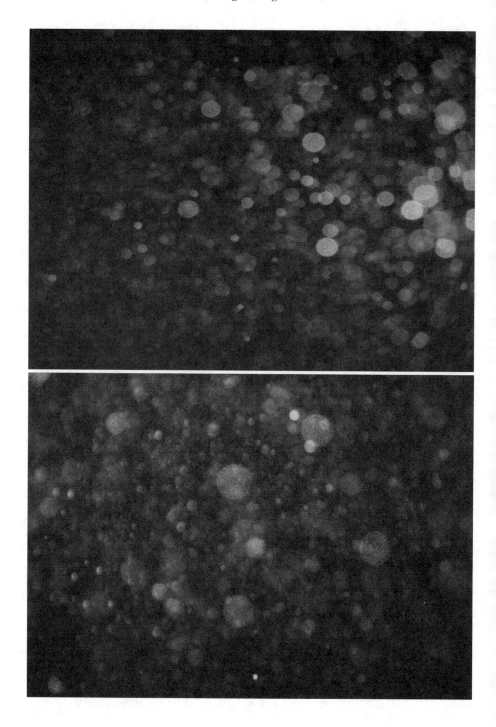

it came. Strange ideas came to me. Was it a 'Soul Pool'? Was it a nursery for baby orbs? Well, why not? My guess is as good as any. It was all very bizarre. It reminded me of a school sardines or of herring and the way they cluster together and wheel and swim as one single entity as though driven or ordered by one commanding consciousness; or like a massive flock of tens of thousands of Starlings, wheeling and speeding through the autumn skies in an immense black cloud, never once colliding one with another, until they settle as one body on a particular tree which as one mind they have selected as the perch for the night.

There's a sort of highly sophisticated radar system at operation in all this -- a sort of universal blending where hundreds or even thousands of individual entities merge in perfect unison and move as one amalgamated body. It's fascinating and it occurred to me that the cloud of 'Lentil Soup' which looked as though it was made up of a mass of thousands of orbs comes into this category. We have yet a lot to learn my friends. It comes back to René Descartes again. "I think therefore I am", or in the case of the 'Lentil Soup', it is visible to the camera therefore it exists therefore it *is*. Absolutely no-one can deny the presence of that strange brown cloud of bubbles because *two* cameras independently saw the *same* thing at the *same* time. Like I already said, the camera never lies – and the *two* cameras provide endorsement for each other! That's the beginning and the end of the argument as far as I am concerned. This is incontrovertible proof that a formation of something phenomenal was passing through the neighbourhood at that time. It was physically beyond the frequency of the wave-length accessible to

Opposite Page: Philippe's photo (top) and mine (below) taken at the identical moment up on the Col de Vence. There was an invisible cloud of something passing through the area and both cameras 'saw' it. What could explain such a phenomenon? (Top photo Courtesy of Philippe Vincintelli.)

the human eye but it was perfectly visible to a digital camera.

Needles to say, neither Philippe's nor my photos have been touched or enhanced in any way whatsoever. The originals are on my computer and they still carry their original 'tag' numbers which 'proves' that they have come off two different cameras. Even better, my original photo is still locked and write-protected on my camera. That is to say that it cannot possibly have been touched or altered in any way. Annoyingly, earlier that night I had already used up all the battery power on my 10xmega-pixel camera through recording and replaying several times "Le Bruit" (see next chapter) and so I was using my old five mega-pixel camera which I had brought with me as a back-up. It was very fortunate that I had the backup camera but unfortunate that the quality of my photo is slightly inferior to Philippe's as I am sure that my 10xmega-pixel camera would have optimised the picture. Never mind the most important thing is that I *have* the photo regardless of its quality and for that I am really grateful.

Of Fogs That Go Past In The Night

And before we leave the subject of the bizarre multiple groupings of orbs up on the Col de Vence, let me show you two more spectacular pictures.

The picture on the facing page shows a foggy effect which looks like a dense mist or cloud of some sort. But it was a perfectly mist-free, fog-free, starry, clear night. Like the cloud of orbs in the Lentil Soup pictures, this is another one of those mysterious Col de Vence phenomena which I am unable to explain. We get an excellent sense of perspective in this picture because of the foreground of grass and rocks. The 'fog' is well and truly behind them and appears to be at quite some distance from the camera lens. Because of that foreground giving us a definite

depth perspective , the possibility of it being condensation of my breath on the night air can be ruled out because it is much too far away.

The photo over the page is another spectacular photo taken just after the Summer Solstice on June 28th 2008, and shows more multiple orb activity. Once again we have a excellent guide to the perspective because the foreground composed of grass, wild flowers and the small shrub shows us indisputably that *all* the orbs without exception are well behind the shrub and foreground grass and are therefore not against the camera lens.

A Footnote For Any Remaining Doubters Out There!

Just let me assure any lingering debunkers out there that there is no way that I'm interested in playing some idiotic and senseless hoax on the world at large. What would be the point? And what would be the point of writing this book only to have it be shot down in flames because I have distorted the verity of any of the information I have given just for the sake of creating a sensation? One small distortion of the truth will discredit everything. No thanks!

Another extremely beautiful Col de Vence photograph which shows a unique multiple orb activity where thousands of orbs have formed a dense mass very like the 'Lentil Soup' phenomenon. They are keeping a slight distance from me which is easy to judge because they are all behind the foreground of grass, wild flowers and the small shrub on the right. This gives us an undeniable depth perspective and positively proves that the orbs are not dust, pollen, or seeds floating in front of the camera lens. I estimate that they must be at least 12 feet away but they are still within reasonable reach of the camera flash.

CHAPTER TWENTY-FIVE

'LE BRUIT' ('The Noise')

My new friend Laurent of G.E.E.S.A, the French UFO research organization, happens to live in a small town very close to Cannes, and rather than take two cars up to the Col de Vence on the night of 29th September, we agreed on a pick-up point and so we went together in my car. It was good to have the company for the long drive. Philippe came up under his own steam. On the way there, Laurent told me about yet another mysterious phenomenon up on the Col de Vence which the French call 'Le Bruit' -- 'The Noise' in English. He described it as a mechanical sound which can be heard from a certain spot on the main road just a few kilometres short of the little mountain village, Les Coursegoules. He suggested going to see if it was there that night before keeping the appointed rendez-vous with Philippe up in Saint Barnabé. The detour would cost us not much more than half an hour and what is mere time when you have the whole night ahead of you on a mountain top?

Laurent was dubious that we would hear 'Le Bruit' that night though, because according to him, it was too soon after the full moon and apparently "Le Bruit" for some reason or another is never heard around the full moon. But you never know until you investigate and so we decided that it was definitely worth going to have a look-see.

We arrived at a certain spot on the winding road where there was just room to pull over and stop a car and Laurent told me to pull in there. We got out and before I could even get my bearings, there was a triumphant shout from Laurent. "Il est là! 'Le Bruit' est là!" -- "It's there! 'The Noise' is there!"

Machinery Chugging Away Where Nothing Exists

Sure enough there it was. Quite clearly and loudly audible; a strange, extremely rhythmical mechanical noise like machinery grinding away, somewhere up there in the mountains at more than 1000 meters of altitude. What on earth could it be? The Col de Vence had by no means exhausted its supply of tricks and surprises!

The odd thing about 'The Noise' was that it was very difficult to tell exactly where it was coming from. At first I thought it was coming from somewhere higher up on the hillside by the road and then I was sure it was coming from way down in the valley below. And then both Laurent and I agreed that it sounded as though it was coming from both those places simultaneously. Perhaps there were two sources of 'The Noise'. It seemed to fill the night air. It was everywhere. It was difficult to identify yet it had echoes of something vaguely familiar but what? Did it sound like an electricity generator? Did it sound like a dairy milking machine? Did it sound like a pump of some sort? Could there be a top-secret military base and a system of tunnels hidden deep inside the mountain? Something to do with mining came to mind but that was probably because Laurent had told me in the car on the way up that there used to be an old lignite mine in the valley below, now long since disused. So could it be the 'ghosts' of the lignite miners setting the old machinery to work? Could aliens be using lignite as a power source? Could the aliens have their own machinery and be extracting the mineral in the dead of night? Have any other lignite mines had UFO activity in their proximity? Crazy ideas for a crazy phenomenon.

By setting the camera on 'video' mode I stood and recorded 'The Noise' for a long moment, even though there was absolutely nothing in the vicinity that made a picture. Once again the night was that cocoon-like, all-enveloping black so typical of the Col de Vence. Does the moon ever shine up there?

As I was recording, suddenly a small white ball of light zoomed into the camera's line of vision at an enormous speed from 'stage-right'. It stopped dead-still almost in the centre of the image and hovered for several seconds. At that point in the video you hear me say in a hushed, slightly scared voice to Laurent "I've got a light!" and just as I said it, the light zoomed off to the left at high speed and all the time 'The Noise' kept on grinding away not missing a beat.

If you want to have some idea of how 'The Noise' sounds, the best description that I can give is this: Put your finger in your ear and wiggle it in a very steady but quite fast rhythmic way in the following pattern: 1,2,3,**1** pause1,2,3,**1** pause 1,2,3,**1** pause and so on. The final '**1**s' I have put in bold as this is where the emphasis comes in the rhythm. Add to that a slightly metallic sound and you pretty well have 'The Noise'.

While writing this, I have just taken another look at the photos I took in the vicinity of 'The Noise' and I see that with light enhancement, there was quite a strong presence of orbs in the environs although the quality is very poor and extremely grainy because of the deep darkness of the night so the photos are not worth reproducing here. The flash had a reach that night of about two meters, or so it seemed, before it was swallowed up in the void of dense inkiness and nothing was visible to the human eye in that impenetrable darkness.

Lignite & High Tension Wires

There is just one other thing that I should mention about 'The Noise' and the area in which it is. There are two things in fact. One is that it is very close to the new 'crop circle' up there in the field of wild grass. Probably no more than a kilometre. And the other thing which I think is very important to mention is that about three hundred metres away, there is a corridor of high tension wires which runs right down the valley, up and over the hills and branches off in all sorts of directions. There is a major electrical grid system up there on the Col de Vence spoiling unfortunately the aesthetic beauty of the whole area.

Here, I must add that there is no way that there is any confusion between 'The Noise' and the singing of the high-tension wires. It was my first question to Laurent and he assured me that the possibility of that was long ago ruled out by serious investigators who have made a profound study of 'The Noise' and who still don't know how to explain it. It is a very real mystery.

To get my little non-scientific penny's-worth in, I am intrigued by the following 'facts' and it mightn't be a bad idea to list them so that anyone who is interested could make a study of them and see if they can find a correlation between what's going on up there on the Col de Vence in comparison to other areas elsewhere in the world with a similar 'profile'.

- The area is known for its UFO activity which is unusually high.
- There is the presence of an old lignite mine which is a low-grade fossil fuel and could therefore be a possible source of power or energy.
- There is a very high concentration of high-tension wires channelling through the whole area which could provide a source of energy.
- High mountainous terrain with many plateau areas which are wide open to the sky, providing ready-made 'landing places' for space vehicles or for helicopters for that matter.
- Extremely sparsely populated area.

I have an interesting little post-script to writing the preceding description of events of that night in September when Laurent and I heard 'The Noise'.

We Found the Crop Circle & The Noise

In February 2008 once the roads were clear of the winter's snow and ice, my cousin Juliette who was visiting from New Zealand, and I went up to the Col de Vence. I wanted to show her something of what I had been writing about as she had just finished reading the draft copy of my book and she was now totally fascinated by the whole subject and especially intrigued by the Col de Vence.

I showed her the Templar Church at Saint Barnabé, the 'crop circle' in the uncultivated field which we found with no trouble at all, and then with absolutely no real hope of finding it, I suggested that we could at least *try* to find 'The Noise'.

I parked the car at approximately the place where I thought it was. (You will remember that when I went there with Laurent, it was on a moonless night and we were in pitch darkness, with no visible landmarks to distinguish the location from anywhere else along that long and winding road in the middle of nowhere.) It was not going to be easy to find, so where I stopped this day, was definitely guesswork, but surprise, surprise, no sooner had we got out of the car than we heard it! That eerie mechanical noise was grinding away up there high in the mountains with not the slightest feature anywhere in that bleak landscape that could account for it.

If it had been baffling at night, it was doubly mysterious by day as we could truly see that there was definitely nothing there up there! Just rocks, some sparse vegetation and a sheer rock face about fifty metres along the road from where I had parked the car. The only unusual thing worthy of note in the immediate vicinity, was that at some time during the winter there had been quite a serious avalanche or landslide which had left a massive scar on the mountainside which reached right down to the road. The landslide was right next to 'Le Bruit' but apparently hadn't affected it because this day my old friend 'Le Bruit' was resoundingly audible. I was especially surprised to hear it because it was in the middle of the day -- about 1.30pm. I suppose I had always imagined that it would only be heard at night. Even Laurent later said that as far as he knew no one had ever heard it in the middle of the day before. (But then, perhaps no one had ever gone seeking it during the day before -- as most of the G.E.E.S.A sorties up on the Col de Vence were at night for UFO spotting.)

Juliette and I walked a small distance along the road to see if we could pin-point its source more precisely. Juliette dropped slightly behind me to take photos while I continued walking along the road in a Northerly direction.

It seemed that 'Le Bruit' was definitely getting louder which meant that I must have been getting nearer to its source. I kept on walking until I found myself beside the sheer and

very solid rock-face which formed the upper side of the road, while on the 'down' side there was a very steep drop into the ravine below where the old lignite mine had once been.

As I walked along the road, I had the slightly uncomfortable sensation that I was being observed by an unseen something or someone. (Juliette said later that she had felt exactly the same thing too). I approached the solid wall of rock and was just about to press my ear against it to see if the noise was coming from inside

That's me walking along the road at the locality of 'Le Bruit', trying to identify its source. As you can see there is absolutely nothing there that could account for it. A little further along the road I came to a sheer rock face and was about to press my ear to it when 'The Noise' abruptly stopped. Was I getting too close? Had I been observed? (Photo by Juliette Clark)

the mountain itself when all of a sudden, almost as though alarmed that I was getting too close to making a discovery, 'it' or 'someone', flicked a switch and turned it off. The noise abruptly ceased. There was only an eerie silence after that! It was most strange. 'Le Bruit' needs a lot more investigation. Something is causing it – but what?

Juliette took this photo looking down into the deep gully on the other side of the road where we thought the possible source of "Le Bruit' might be. But it is a complete wilderness and an extremely bleak one at that! There is nothing here that could possibly explain the strange phenomenon. (Photo by Juliette Clark)

CHAPTER TWENTY-SIX

Orbs & Their Power-Up Sources

A great deal of serious study is needed to understand the correlation between the appearance of the orbs and the prevailing climatic and electrical conditions. I can only put forward my observations which may help get the show on the road, but this book is beyond the scope of anything scientific – I'm just the photographer.

Hydro-Power

As I said in an earlier chapter, I noticed many years ago that orbs take on an opaque, milky appearance during a rain shower and stay that way for some time afterwards. I believe that they have a need to re-hydrate themselves from time to time and so it follows that they probably have a considerable water content in their composition and need to keep that level topped-up within an certain range in order not to die.

After or during a rain shower I have not noticed any appreciable increase in the actual size of the orbs. In fact it tends to be the opposite – they appear to get smaller. It is as though their opacity is caused by the fact that they close up and shrink inwards on themselves rather in the manner of a sea-anemone digesting its prey. It is extremely likely that the orb does this in order to maximize the absorption of available moisture and stays that way until it has finished the process. This makes perfect sense, for if the orb was to swell and therefore increase its surface area, moisture loss would be dramatically more rapid with a larger surface area. After the absorption process, the orb gradually returns to its optimum size and this is when the internal pattern of the orb is at its most distinct.

Floating riverboat restaurants on 'The Creek' in Dubai. The orbs were out in full force that night hovering over the water. They were always there in such profusion that I wondered if they traveled to the source of water from the nearby desert to re-hydrate. It was like this every night.

Conversely I have observed that the weak transparent orbs (Type 7), generally occur after a long dry spell which further proves their need to hydrate from time to time. In areas like the Col de Vence where there are very few sources of water such as lakes, ponds, rivers etcetera the hydration process could be problematic for them. Not only is this an area with a serious shortage of natural water sources, but it is also an area with a very low rain fall. The orbs therefore need to travel to seek out distant places where there is a supply of water.

An in-depth study of orbs should also include data on the incidence of manifestations in hot dry desert areas. It could well be that these areas are not favorable to their ability to thrive or even to survive. Conversely, it would be interesting to discover if they live near an oasis where there is an abundance of water. They definitely live in great profusion near coastal areas in the Middle East as many of my photos taken in and around Dubai prove. Here I had orbs in great profusion. Anyone ready for a camel ride?

By Jove! Bring On The Thunder!

I have also noticed a marked increase in orb activity and in their numbers immediately before and just after a thunderstorm. This could well mean that they need to recharge electrically as well which should not surprise us as they have the capability to travel at enormously high speed and in order to do that they must essentially find an energy source from somewhere. It could be that a thunderstorm puts a sufficient electrical charge or 'free-radical' type electrons in the atmosphere which they can absorb in a 'refueling' process and thus obtain the energy and power needed to whiz around the way they do.

I have long been convinced, that they tend to congregate around high-tension electric power lines and pylons as a source of power or energy. It is only relatively recently through going up to the Col de Vence that I myself have ever been in really close proximity to high-tension power lines and their pylons. As this spectacular photo shows there was an extremely high concentration of orbs up there one night after sunset and also it was during the week of the Summer Solstice. Could power lines provide a source of 'fuel' for orbs?

Photo taken after sunset on the Col de Vence in June 2008 just after the Summer Solstice. These orbs are all very pale and lack luminosity after a long period of drought – they urgently need to find a source of water.

They Have An Inner Source Of Luminosity

A healthy orb also has an intense luminosity especially around the outer edge or mantle. This appears to resemble a sort of aura which usually glows in a color other than that of the main body-color. Blue, orange, yellow and intense silver have been the most common aura colors I have observed. While the orb's luminosity is beautifully visible at night against a backdrop of a black night sky, it is in no way diminished by sunlight. This probably indicates that the orbs can draw upon a source of energy from within themselves which could indicate the presence of stored electrons. It has been written recently by an observer that they have the capability to release a wide, detectable spectrum of electromagnetic radiation. Presumably this means that this electromagnetic radiation can actually be measured. Fascinating. First catch your orb!

People Power

After years of observation, I now believe that there is every indication as well that orbs can refuel by drawing from the massive energy which is released when a large group of people are gathered together for big public events such as political rallies or a rock concert. I have gone into this in some detail in Chapter Ten where I talk about their presence at rock concerts, so I won't repeat myself here except to emphasize that the biggest orbs I have ever taken photos of have been at rock concerts. Here they gather in vast numbers and positively seem to grow to gargantuan sizes, measuring in some instances several meters across. Their inner markings become much better defined than usual and they take on a great luminosity as well. So apparently there is something in collective human energy which suits them.

On the other hand, if it's not collective human energy that suits them and if we put aside for a moment the 'scientific' approach, could it be that orbs are in fact, spirits of the dead and they absolutely adore loud music and the close contact with humans just as they did when they were living in their old environment in the three dimensional world which we live in now and so they simply come along to join the party and be in on the fun? You'd do just the same wouldn't you? Yes -- let us not forget – orbs just might be people too.

Turn Up That Volume!

As I was writing the above, it occurred to that loud music could also provide a source of energy? That's perfectly possible too. Maybe the orbs like vibrational turbulence in the air-waves. There could be a very powerful source of energy in 'Harmonic Resonance'. Wasn't that how they levitated the stones that they used to build the Pyramids and how the walls of Jericho came tumbling down because of the resonance Joshua was able to create with all those trumpets blaring away? And isn't that how sopranos can shatter glass? Harmonic Reson-

We have already seen massive orb concentration at Rock Concerts and here we have a gathering of associates at a post-congress dinner dance in the old Pope's Palace in Avignon. Not only are there two enormous orbs and many smaller ones present but there is a high presence of ectoplasm as well. This is one of the rare times when I have captured ectoplasm. It wasn't cigarette smoke because the Pope's Palace is a national monument and smoking inside was not allowed!

ance can dematerialize matter and alter its structure. Are there any scientists out there who would like to develop that theory?

As a conclusion to this chapter, I want to put forward just one more theory relating to orbs and their energy sources. Let's allow ourselves to accept just for a moment that orbs are the spirits of our loved ones (and who can say at this stage that they are not?) The souls of the departed have passed over into that other dimension which vibrates at a rate which is out of sync with ours. Maybe it's faster, maybe slower -- just like that radio station that David Icke wrote about that is out there merrily broadcasting, unheard by you and me, because it's on a wavelength which is not the wavelength that we're tuned into.

Could it be possible that by drawing on and using one or several or all of the above energy sources, the spirits of the departed are able to transmute (shape-shift in other words) and take on, maintain and sustain a *specific form* that has the physical ability to break through that invisible barrier that separates our two worlds, and come within very, very close range of penetrating our three-dimensional reality?

Could it be possible that there exists a *one-and-only specific shape that has the capacity to dwell in all dimensions?* A kind of Universal, inter-dimensional Master-Key that can fit every lock. If these things were possible, then The Spirit of the departed by transmuting into this *one-and-only specific form,* can now just about infiltrate and hijack our three dimensional frequency and through so doing become visible – if not quite as yet visible to the physical human eye -- visible to the eye of the camera. If this were so, then that *one-and-only specific shape,* that Universal, inter-dimensional Master-Key, can only be nature's simplest, most basic structure and its most perfect creation. That perfect creation is The Sphere.

The Sphere is the shape of all things great and small. It is the shape of the smallest cell from which all life springs. It is the shape of our planet Earth, the sun, the moon and the stars. It is the shape of the orb.

Perhaps it is a secret truth that the sphere is nature's perfected creation and we, poor, complex, imperfect, multi-formed, multi-coloured creatures, are but nature's mutants.

CHAPTER TWENTY-SEVEN

The Night the Lights Went Out

In the summer of 2007, my old school friend Cloudy was making one of her annual trips from New Zealand to Europe and as usual, a trip to Cannes to see me was included on her itinerary.

Whenever Cloudy comes to stay we try to find an 'adventure'; that is to say, a major car journey into the wild blue yonder to take what comes and to explore new territory. This year we decided on Corsica – that mysterious Mediterranean island a hundred miles or so off the south coast of Provençal France. It had been many years since I had been there and Cloudy had never been, so it seemed like an excellent idea and more or less on the spur of the moment, we packed up the car, put it on the Corsica ferry boat and spent a fantastic week touring around the island, and I might modestly say, having a lot of success with the locals! I think the spectacle of two 'old girls' beetling around like a pair of thirty year-olds in a sporty little convertible number with the top down, warmed the cockles of the Corsican hearts. We made friends everywhere we went -- from tour bus drivers who always waved and gave a blast of the bus horn, to fierce-looking clan chiefs toting serious looking firearms while guarding their territories by the roadside, and who also always waved, but fortunately for us didn't give a blast of the rifles!

We loved it and I can thoroughly recommend Corsica as a place to go. The views are to die for and each and every bend in the road brings a new surprise with an even more beautiful vista. It was a veritable feast of scenic beauty comparable only with New Zealand (and France) of course! *And* the U.S and Canada – Okay and the rest of the world!

One of our notable stop-over points was a very picturesque town on the west coast of Corsica – L'Isle Rousse (the Red Island) -- notable for its pinkish-apricot rocks which in certain lights can take on a soft russet red tinge. We found a reasonably good hotel quite quickly. It was practically empty because the main season had finished a couple of weeks earlier and the hotel had no difficulty in giving us two adjacent rooms with adjoining terraces which offered a magnificent view out over the strange apricot-coloured rocks and to a small ancient sea tower.

We threw our cases into our rooms and set off to explore the rocks and the tower and then walked into the village and the lure of its many colourful and tempting boutiques until the first hunger pangs hit. We quickly found an authentic seafood restaurant in the old town, which overlooked the beach and promptly ordered a positively decadent feast of giant prawns and (excuse the expression), pigged-out on them using fingers and all! I tell you I have never been

Cloudy and the famous Giant Prawns

able to face a prawn giant or otherwise since that night!

All the way through Corsica from the moment we arrived, up until that day, there had been a complete dearth of orbs. Try as hard as I might, I had not managed to capture an orb since the time we landed in Bastia two or three days earlier.

Suddenly half way through the meal I felt the familiar 'telepathic call' of the 'Light Beings'. I promptly picked up my camera and began taking photos over the balustrades of the restaurant, aiming in the general direction of the beach and out to sea. There they were! Orbs a-plenty. The dearth was over and the 'Light Beings' had tracked me down in Corsica at last! The pretty apricot/rose-coloured orb pictured on the next page, was just one of the many taken from the restaurant. There are many smaller orbs in this picture too, which would be visible through lightening it but I wanted to show you the original rose coloured orb, and this beautiful colour would have been lost through light-enhancement. The extraordinary thing about the colour of this particular orb that it is exactly (repeat *exactly*) the colour of the famous pinkish-orangey shade of the indigenous rocks in the area which give the place its name 'L'Isle Rousse' or Red Island!

What could this possibly mean? I read it as yet another sign from the 'Light Beings' telling us that they are intelligent little critters and know precisely how to get their message across -- as long as we learn how to read it.

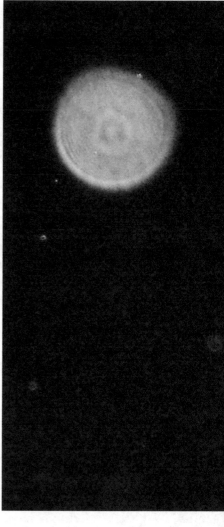

Cloudy & The 'Light Beings'.

After the dinner Cloudy and I walked the couple of kilometres back to the hotel, and as it was a still and balmy evening we sat out on the terrace enjoying a quiet night-cap before turning in for the night. We were talking about orbs and I was idly taking photos and having some minor success and I happened to say to Cloudy something like "They're here right now -- so why don't you get your camera and see if you can capture some as well?"

Cloudy came back with her camera and was soon getting orbs right alongside me! More and more orbs were flooding in and Cloudy who is a very 'in touch' person spiritually was actually whispering in hushed awe at the presence of the 'Light Beings' as though they might go away if she spoke in a normal voice! She said that she could really feel the atmosphere change. I'm more used to it so didn't pick up on the atmosphere like Cloudy did, but there was definitely something 'electric' in the air that night as you will soon see!

Perhaps at this point I should fill you in a little on Cloudy and her background and we will come back to what happened that night in a moment.

As twelve year-olds, Cloudy and I started boarding school on the same day back sometime in the early fifties. She was from a high-country sheep-farming family and was horse crazy as was I. She was also the naughtiest girl at school and I, probably egged on by her, was perhaps the second naughtiest girl at school. We both always seemed to be in trouble. The only difference between us was that I took my school studies fairly seriously -- Cloudy didn't. She was usually away on another planet, either acting mysteriously or being naughty. Even at that young age Cloudy was showing the early signs of the mystic that she was to become.

'Cloudy' By Name – Cloudy By Nature

The reason why she is called Cloudy by me to this very day, has nothing to do with the fact that she is normally to be found dwelling in higher realms -- some might say up in the clouds -- but because her maiden name was Anne McLeod (she like myself was of good old Scottish immigrant stock), and it doesn't take any great leap of imagination to see why someone named McLeod was quickly nicknamed 'Cloudy' by the other girls at school. And it suits her -- 'Cloudy' by name -- cloudy by nature!

Cloudy was never of the same world as either her family or the most part of her friends. Somehow she was just born different. She seemed to have come from another dimension. She was/is a real 'daughter of the Universe', always a seeker, always very mystical, seeming to talk in riddles half the time and she was constantly reading up on alternative religions. From as far back as I can remember she was very strongly attracted to the Himalayan region and countries such as Nepal and Tibet and so on.

Her artist husband John Harrison was first and foremost a mountaineer and had climbed in the Himalayas with the late Sir Edmond Hillary and Peter Mulgrew ('Pete of the Bees' who I mentioned earlier in this book). Theirs was a vertiginous world of towering mountains, Tibetan Sherpas, pony-trekking, back-packing, skiing and travelling to the most distant and inaccessible places of the globe. All of this was for the most part way beyond reach of mere housebound mortals like myself because at this stage of my life I was a struggling solo mum fighting to keep the proverbial crust of bread on the table and Cloudy seemed to be leading a life which embraced people and cultures which had barely entered my consciousness -- much less the realms of my small, narrow existence. Baby-sitting Cloudy' infants was just about as close as I got to that world. On the surface what did we have in common? Not a lot. Yet, whatever it was between us, there was always that indestructible thread of deep friendship that began the day we arrived at our new boarding school and bounced up and down on our beds, testing to see whether or not they were going to be comfortable enough!

Cloudy seemed to have everything: She was very pretty with smoky grey eyes and brown curly hair, had a tall, dark and handsome husband who was a well-known figure in the international world of mountaineering and who was also an accomplished water-colourist and made beautiful pictorial records of his climbing expeditions in the Himalayas with Ed Hillary. They owned a beautiful old rambling Colonial-style home in a semi-rural area just outside Christchurch, with lots of cats, dogs and horses and two lovely little girls Sue and Wendy. What could possibly go wrong?

No one could ever have foreseen that Cloudy's life was soon to be tragically overcome by a dark tidal wave of terrible loss. One afternoon like any other while spending a weekend with her parents in their high-country sheep-station homestead, John was called out on a mountain rescue operation in the Arthur's Pass in the New Zealand alps to search for a team of missing climbers. John's tent was engulfed in an avalanche while he was sleeping inside. He never returned home to his wife and two little daughters.

Gradually Cloudy picked up the broken pieces of her life and bravely got on with her new sad role as a widow and solo mother of two. She must only have been about twenty-four or twenty-five at the time. We were close neighbours and we always saw a lot of each other throughout those years and even though our lives eventually took completely different paths both geographically and in terms of destiny, we never lost touch and so that is how we came to be beetling around the tortured roads of Corsica together in the last days of an Indian Summer in 2007!

Not only is Cloudy a psychic with mediumistic abilities, but she is also a fully trained counsellor and a Past-Life Regression Therapist with many years of experience. The reason why I have filled you in on her and her background is because it is going to be very important that you believe what follows here. Cloudy is fully 'in touch' with the Universe and she just 'knows' things and if she says something about something -- then you'd better sit up and listen because after more than fifty years of close friendship, I've never known her to be wrong in arcane matters. (Yes it's maddening isn't it!)

The Culprit? Is this the orb or the Light Being who answered Cloud's request for 'a sign' and blew the lights?

So let's get back to the main story and our hotel in L'Isle Rousse after the giant prawn dinner. As I said, we were sitting out in the balmy Corsican night air idly photographing for orbs when suddenly Cloudy started photographing them too. (This as I've already told you, usually happens to people who are around me and I would have been very surprised if she hadn't). Cloudy being Cloudy, once she began photographing the 'Light Beings' immediately started communicating with them in a trance-like way saying that she was absolutely certain that they were trying to make contact and using her as a medium. After a few moments she broke her concentration, lifted her head and announced that she was going to ask *'Them'* to give us a sign that they were on our wave-length. She half-closed her eyes and once again went into trance mode. Within seconds there was an abrupt, slightly muted, but clearly audible static crackle in the air rather similar to dry lightening or the crack of a stockman's whip and without warning the lights of the hotel flickered and went out leaving us suddenly enveloped in total darkness. So much for asking the 'Light Beings' to give us a sign!

"Oh my God! We did that!" said Cloudy in a hushed voice tinged with awe (did I detect a teensy note of fear?) Now if Cloudy says "We did that", I really have to believe her. I have never known her to be wrong when it comes to psychic and mystical matters, remember!

Completely disoriented, we fumbled around in the pitch darkness trying to get our bearings, and by using the lights of our mobile telephones as torches, we managed to find our way to the hotel reception to report the power failure. Stupefaction! It was only our sector of the hotel that had blown. The rest of the hotel; reception, restaurant and so on was perfectly fine and a-blaze with lights! It *was* just us!

As far as the puzzled hotel owner was concerned, a blown fuse in his hotel was not a common event. So uncommon in fact, that he had difficulty finding the main fuse box in our sector of the hotel and had to ask Cloudy to hold the torch for him while he found the right fuse!

Cloudy's hushed declaration "We did that!" echoed hauntingly in my ears. Indeed, it certainly seemed that we *had* done it. Yet it hardly seemed possible that we could create an electrical malfunction and blow a fuse with just two digital cameras taking flash photographs into the dark night. Or was there something else?

Could it have been that the real culprit was the magnificent 'Light Being' whose photo is pictured on page 280, had heard and was answering Cloudy's telepathic request for 'a sign'?

Who can ever say for certain -- but it sure makes a great mystery story!

CHAPTER TWENTY-EIGHT

The Sacred & The Slightly Profane

Near the border between France and Italy, in a small alpine village about sixty kilometers from Nice there is a 12th century Church which was built by the Templar Knights. This particular edifice is extremely rare in that it is still in near-perfect, original condition and never suffered the indignity if being 'Baroque-ified' which sadly, in the prevailing fashion of the time, was the 16th to 17th century fate of so many lovely old churches.

By 'Baroque-ified', I mean that the purity and simplicity of the architectural lines of many, if not nearly all, of these early church structures were forever suppressed and suffocated beneath a frothy layering of frenzied, meringue-like plaster ornamentation, slathered on with such density that no semblance of the original church remained. There are some who like Baroque – I happen not to and fortunately 'my' church had escaped this disastrous fate or any other indignities of 'modernization' throughout the centuries, probably due to chronic lack of local funds and may the heavens be blessed for that today.

I call it 'my' church, because in a way I feel as though it was very much my discovery. Or I should say Cloudy's and my discovery. It happened a few years ago during one of Cloudy's annual visits to the South of France and we were off on one of our traditional 'adventures'. This particular adventure took us up into pre-alps between Italy and Nice and we were simply driving from village to village to see what we could discover.

Suddenly we rounded a bend in the road and down below us on what I could see was the banks of a mountain river flowing through a small town, I spotted the very distinctive tower of a church. But not just any old tower of any old church. This was the Templar tower of a Templar Church!

"Templar Church down there!" I near-shouted at Cloudy in my excitement "Let's go on down to investigate!"

A Templar Church & A Recumbent Corpse

We took a sharp left-hand bend in the road and wound down the hill and very soon arrived at the church. Disappointingly it was securely locked and we were about to leave when Cloudy spotted a notice near the big entrance doors. "Hang on a moment -- what does this say?" I went over to do translation duty and read out "To view the church, ring at the doorbell of the house opposite."

We rang at the doorbell and a very small female person with apple cheeks and an impossible 'mountain accent' (impossible for *me* to understand that is!) opened the door. We asked if we could see inside the church to which she promptly agreed. She ducked back into her house and reappeared with an

enormous iron key and told us that her name was Madeleine -- 'Mado' for short --
which struck me as being amazingly appropriate as the Patron Lady Saint for the
Templars was none other than Mary Magdalene; or as the French call her, 'La
Madeleine'.

'Our' latter-day Madeleine opened the church door with the big iron key,
all the time chatting away about the history of the church and the Templars but so
strong was her mountain accent, that I was only understanding every second
word. No matter! What I saw in the interior of the church was what I had come to
see! A real Templar Church – pure and unadulterated -- as the Templars had built
it eight centuries earlier. It was a perfect marvel!

This gem of a church almost merits a book of its own so I shall reluctantly
spare you any further description of it here and tell you about '*Le Gisant*'.

The word '*gisant*' in French implies 'lying' as in lying down, but in this case
should literally be translated as the 'Recumbent Christ'. That is to say, recumbent
as in a corpse. For a corpse it was and a very gruesome-looking corpse too,
girded in a loincloth and all painted up to look like Christ lying in state!
Mado with great relish told us that in fact 'Le Gisant' was a real human skeleton
encased in plaster! (Yikes!) She said that the person had suffered rheumatism and
you could see that by the fact that all his wrist, knee and ankle joints were
swollen! (Yes indeed I could!) She further told us that the main reason why she
suspected that under the plaster was a real human skeleton, was that the 'floating
ribs' were clearly visible. (Yes that was true -- they were!) And furthermore, she
said that floating ribs were unknown in medieval times ('Le Gisant' evidently
dated from medieval times.) Huh! That was interesting. I immediately supposed
that a simple modern x-ray would quickly determine for once and for all whether

or not 'Le Gisant' really was a human skeleton embalmed in plaster of Paris, but refrained from saying so to Mado, as sometimes the myth is best left intact -- for it is very often in the fantasy of myths that those echoes and emotions of childhood magic and wonder linger, and for some reason, at that moment I had a real need to believe that there was an actual human body in there and to take a perverse delight in the gruesomeness of this macabre relic from so long ago.

I gazed fascinated – riveted by this ghastly artifact, taking in every detail from the blood of Christ's stigmata painted on his hands and feet and also on his side where the Roman centurion's spear had pierced him. The crown of real thorns that he was wearing had caused (painted) droplets of blood on his brow and he was draped around the waist in a grubby-looking loincloth while someone (possibly Mado) had entwined a Catholic rosary around the fingers of his hands.

I felt sorry for him lying there so solitary and alone in Spartan splendor in his rudimentary wooden box, and asked Mado if it would be alright to take a photo of him. She said "Yes of course – go ahead" And here is the result. It seems that 'Le Gisant' was not alone after all. A magnificent orb was sitting just above his right shoulder.

There is a little post-script to this story about 'Le Gisant', and although it is rather personal, I am going to tell it all the same. Here it is: Mado told us that 'Le Gisant' had magical properties. Curative abilities and that he had performed many, many healing miracles. I pricked up my ears at this. Maybe he could do something for me! I had for some time been quite worried because I had found a lump in a place where every woman dreads finding a lump. I had put off seeing a

Facing Page. 'Le Gisant' in the Templar Church in the alps behind Nice in the South of France. This grisly relic evidently dates from Medieval times and it is believed that it is the skeleton of a real person which has been embalmed in plaster. He has a very nice orb to keep him company.

doctor about it mainly out of fear which I fully realize is ridiculous and irresponsible but I had decided that I definitely would do something about it at the end of Cloudy's visit --- but somehow deep down I knew that I probably wouldn't go see a doctor because I kind of knew that I had already left it far too long and it was most probably already too late. I had been worrying day and night about it for weeks and had done nothing. But now, here in this strange church in the back of beyond, was Mado talking about healing miracles from a grisly recumbent corpse!

I knelt beside 'Le Gisant' and placed my right hand on his brow and said a silent prayer about the lump and asked him to please take it away. I swear, I absolutely swear to it that for a brief instant I saw him smile. Maybe he did and maybe he didn't, but several days later I suddenly realized that the lump was gone!

I have been back to that church many times since and always make a point of saying a big hello and a huge thank you to 'Le Gisant'.

I will never know if the lump would have disappeared of its own accord or not -- it will have to remain a mystery, but I certainly don't want to start an international stampede up to that little mountain village of 'lumpy ladies' looking for a cure, so please treat that little episode as just a 'story'!

A Sister Church All Decked Out Like A Bride

There was a great templar presence in all through the Mediterranean area for the duration of their long two-hundred year history which lasted from the generally alleged time of their formation in the year 1118 until the cruel suppression of their order in 1307. Their stated objective was Jerusalem and the protection of pilgrims making their pilgrimages to the Holy Land and the shrines of Christ. The Mediterranean shores of Nice and its hinterlands were a springboard from points far to the North for the long land and sea-crossing to Jerusalem and this is why there is such a rich heritage of Templar churches, chapels and other Templar sites such as farms, castles, commanderies and/or preceptories in this area.

Topographical conditions throughout all history invariably determined where castles and strongholds were built. This was usually on the highest point in a region or on a hill-top (all the better to see the approach of your enemy). In the hilly back country behind Nice there are a great number of picturesque hilltop villages (les villages perchés – or perched villages) dating back many hundreds of years. These villages clustered and grew around the foot of the castle walls and

always originated because of the need to provide the castle with goods and services. Today we do not go to high ground to build our defenses and the butcher, baker and candlestick maker do not open up their businesses for our convenience at the gates of our homes, but these old villages have left us with a charming legacy and not too far from the Templar Church watched over by our friend Mado is another extremely picturesque hilltop village where there is an identical Templar church. Its sister.

As you can see in the picture on the previous page, very sadly this church has suffered extreme disfiguration by a heavy overlay of the Baroque style. Some may think it is beautiful but it hurts me, because I know how it really should look. For anyone who understands 11th and 12th century architecture there are still certain remaining features which are visible to the trained eye which have escaped the plasterer's trowel; such as the style of the vaulted ceiling and the beautiful pillar in the left foreground of the picture, which is pure Templar. The almost identical pillars can be seen in its sister church not too many miles away, wherein lies 'Le Gisant'. But this book is about orbs and not a lesson in Medieval architecture so I guess that the real point of showing you this picture is that yes, there was a strong presence of orbs in this church too.

Facing Page: A Templar-built Church in the Maritime Alps behind Nice. Not much of the original architecture remains visible under the heavy Baroque decoration. Yet for the 'initiated' eye some vestiges are still there such as the style of the vaulted ceiling and the magnificent granite pillar with the rope girdle carved in its circumference. A sure sign of Templar influence and origins. And a beautiful orb is floating aloft!

CHAPTER TWENTY-NINE

False Friends, Fakes And Posers

In this chapter I am going to show you some suspect photos which look like amazing anomalies but which cannot be attributed to anything other than your everyday environmental conditions such as cigarette smoke, lighting conditions, or breath on the night air. Sometimes it is extremely hard to make the decision to send such exciting photos to the 'dubious' folder and to not circulate them, but it has to be done if there is the slightest suspicion that they are in any way 'dodgy' and not genuine photos of phenomena.

The whole point of this is that anyone who wants to seriously take up photography of the paranormal has to adopt a policy of rigorous honesty, because the believability of this business of taking photos of orbs, ectoplasm and other anomalies, depends on the integrity of the individual not to try to pass as genuine anything that might be in any way dubious.

The field of the orb phenomenon needs to be taken seriously and if fakes are widely circulated on the internet and in publications, eventually people will just shrug off the whole subject and say "Well, you know in this age of digital imaging, anything is possible." So with a drum-roll here we go. Tara-tara! Enter the great exposé of False Friends, Fakes and Posers.

Fake Photo Scenario №1

'The Moon's a Kidney Bean' This beautiful luminosity caused great excitement when I saw it on the LED screen I thought I had a genuine UFO. And then I realized that the moon was very much in the vicinity and so tried the shot again. Sure enough I got the same result and it was definitely the moon.

I was on a boat that was rocking gently hence the almost triple image of the moon looking like a giant kidney bean. Out you go – into the trash can!

Fake Photo Scenario №2

The lovely slim young thing here who is posing on the couch is me many years ago. This photo was taken in Hong-Kong by a friend. I was really excited about it as I was sure that the spirits of

Venerable Chinese Ones had called in to bestow blessings upon me. I really believed this for many years until I gained more experience. While I was a heavy smoker back then (for once I am not smoking here), the person who took this photo was also a big-time smoker and always had a cigarette dangling from the corner of his mouth (it was considered sexy in those days). I have to reluctantly concede that this could very easily be cigarette smoke as I cannot absolutely swear that he was not smoking at the time of taking the photo. Unfortunately in the interests of verity this photo has to be discounted. By the way this photo was taken on a classic 35mm camera well before digital cameras were invented.

Fake Photo Scenario №3

This photo comes into the same questionable category as the one above. I took it in my garden and once again I got very excited about it when I first saw it. But heavy smoker that I was at the time, I more often than not had a cigarette going without even realizing it, and could well have just exhaled cigarette smoke into the environment at the very moment that I clicked the shutter. Therefore there is no way that I can guarantee that this is not cigarette smoke. It's a great shame because it'd be a fantastic shot – if it was genuine. But as there is a shadow of doubt, into the bin it goes. Someone, who claimed to be a medium, on seeing this photo said that she could see in it the image of a dog with long ears. My 'Mad Mode' Tinkerbell, the Cocker Spaniel had recently passed over and the cremation urn containing her ashes was buried right behind the tree in this corner of the garden but I have to admit that study this picture as hard as I might, I was quite unable to see a 'dog with long ears'. Nice as it would be to think that it was my Tinkerbell, I still have to treat this particular photo with extreme caution. It could very well be cigarette smoke.

Fake Photos Scenario №4

These two photos are definitely fake. I took them deliberately to test what cigarette smoke would look like when you actually set out to photograph it. So there's no way that I can pass the effect off as orbs in motion or ectoplasm about to materialize into a human form. We can see many photos like this on the internet and I am afraid that I am very skeptical about them and before accepting something like this, I'd need to positively know that no-one was smoking anywhere near the camera. This kind of fake is sadly all too easy to produce and could risk the integrity of the whole domain of spirit photography unless people are honest.

Fake Photo Scenario №5

This very strange photo was taken at the same time as the one on the next page. You can see the same golden street light in both pictures. But what is the golden object above the street lamp? It has a very clear and well defined form with a definite edge to it looking rather like an inverted Phrygian helmet. I have no idea what these lovely golden shapes are. I took a whole series of photos of this particular effect and none of them were the same. But with the proximity of the bright light in the background which is a strong halogen street light, I have to be extremely guarded and say this could be lens flare of some sort. Lens refraction normally shows a hexagonal or an

octagonal shape which is not the case here, but still we can't be too careful. This could be a reflection of light on the lens. The jury is still out on these photos and I am as just as baffled today by them as I was the night when I took the photos. I cannot write off these two photos as absolute fakes. If only it wasn't for that orange street light! Alas one has to reluctantly put it down to some sort of aberration of lens flare due to the lamps. A great pity. Objects of this type in fact are well documented and have been frequently photographed up on the Col de Vence. Maybe that is what I got that night but have never succeeded to capture anything like it since – not even up on the Col de Vence. Yes -- if only it wasn't for that orange streetlight! Bye-bye beautiful babies -- into the trash can with you too!

Fake Photo Scenario №6

This one is a classic and it almost had me fooled. I thought that I was photographing a series of the most amazing orbs ever yet seen! But I became rather suspicious when I noticed that the 'orbs' were appearing in exactly the same spot in the very centre of the image in each picture. Orbs simply don't do that because they move around too much. Could it possibly be? Yes I'm afraid so – a droplet of water on the camera lens! The glorious colors are caused by light refraction producing all the colors of the rainbow. Another dead give-away is probably the presence of the garden hose which you can see in the background. Into the bin with you too!

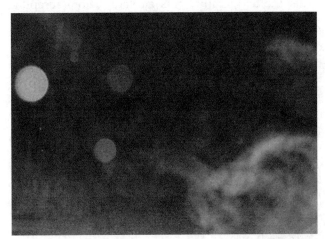

Fake Photo Scenario №7

This photo on was taken up on the Col de Vence and is an extremely important one in terms of demonstrating how easy it is to be fooled into making a genuine mistake and innocently passing off a photo as an authentic phenomenon when indeed it is nothing of the sort. It shows a beautiful orb with clear physical markings. But what I got really excited about, was the vaporous form of 'ectoplasm' down in the right hand corner. I thought that I was at last beginning to photograph 'spirit' like Michelle the medium: that is until Laurent, who belongs to the UFO research group G.E.E.S.A, and who has a lot of experience with this sort of photography, said without hesitation "It's your breath Antonia. Try taking another photo while breathing out into the night air." It was very cold up there – probably around zero but it never occurred to me that my breath was clouding on the cold night air. I tried again and sure enough the 'ectoplasm' was my breath on the zero degree night air, although the orbs are beautiful -- and genuine. It was extremely disappointing but it just goes to show how careful you have to be. Even when the air is relatively warm, and you think there can be no possibility of breath condensation, double check and take another shot using the breath test – just to make sure. Having learnt that lesson, I will always be a bit skeptical about other people's photos of 'ectoplasm'. I'd want to know the all the details of the prevailing conditions and what the temperature was etcetera, before accepting any shot of 'ectoplasm' as genuine.

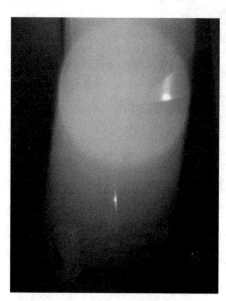

Fake Photo Scenario №8

This amazing photo looking like an orb beaming up, is unfortunately no such thing. It is one single hair which I painfully plucked from my head in the interest of conducting a scientific experiment. I then deliberately placed it in front of the camera lens and took the shot using the flash which gave a bounce-back effect off the shiny hair and created an artificial orb.

The Great Exposé

So now you know all! As I mentioned earlier in the book, I have never had any luck photographing dust and producing false orbs with it -- but when I do, I will let you know how I did it. Neither have I ever had any false orbs produced by taking photos when it's raining, bit I am sure that that is probably very easy to simulate by allowing rain get on the camera lens. And I've never been in the right place at the right time to photograph pollen which is apparently another contentious source of fake orbs. To tell you the truth, I've never actually physically seen pollen floating in the air except as puffs of yellow cloud out from the Cyprus hedges in the South of France when the wind gusts at a certain time of year. Next time (if ever) I see it, I will try photographing it to see what I can get. Also the next time I see a seed pod bursting forth, I shall help it along and catch the moment with the seeds floating in the air.

In fact these cases are really quite extreme and truthfully, I imagine that you'd have to be a fantastically good photographer to seize the exact moment when microscopic pollen flies by, and seed pods burst and tiny seeds are on the wing and get photos of it, but they do need to be mentioned here as these things are the basis on which the debunkers rest their case.

And while we don't need to be hard-nosed debunkers ourselves, and automatically cry out loud and clear that every orb photo must be a fake which has a natural and logical explanation, we must nevertheless be alert and constantly aware that what you see is not always what you are getting.

The moral of the story is, do not always be taken in by first appearances. When in doubt do not hesitate to ask the questions and even better get out there into the field and start taking your own photographs. Then when you have succeeded in getting your own orbs, try creating your own fakes. It is only through experience and experimenting that you will learn to tell the difference between false friends, fakes and posers and the genuine article.

CHAPTER THIRTY

Other Kinds Of Orbs

As we are nearing the end of this book, let's before we get there, take a brief look at other symbolic spherical structures such as for example the Cabala, that have had spiritual and religious significance to mankind throughout all of history. I have listed only a few here, but no doubt you can come up with plenty of others.

The Winged Disk

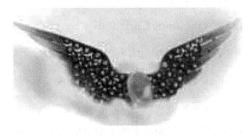

One of the oldest and best-known symbols which has come down to us from the ancient worlds of Egypt, Sumer, Assyria and Babylon is the Winged Disk, a circle or sphere, to which two outstretched wings are attached. To the ancients, this symbol represented the supreme god of the sky and because it dwelt in the sky, it necessarily needed, like birds, wings with which to fly or at least to pictorially speaking, to be seen to have the ability to fly. The beautiful piece of 19th century jewelry in diamonds embracing a pearl, shown on the previous page, demonstrates how through the millennia, the symbol of the winged disc has continued to be venerated. Why has it survived for so many thousands of years?

Could it be that the ancients knew that God in spirit form was indeed able to take on the nature of an orb? Or could it be that the ancients already knew all about orbs as we are beginning to know them today? In order to show that they flew -- or were air-born creatures of the heavens, were they adorned by the ancients with a symbolic pair of wings?

The Halo

A halo is a circle of light that surrounds the head or sits behind the head of a person who it is believed has godlike or saintly qualities. It originally represented the sun and could even be the origin of the golden circlet or crown worn to indicate kingship.

The halo is commonly used in Christian religious works of art to define the holy or sacred status of the personages although it would be totally erroneous to believe that the halo is a Christian invention. It predates Christianity by millennia and was depicted in Greek, Roman and Buddhist sacred art. Gods, emperors and various holy persons were represented with a golden, yellow or white circular aura around the head. Round solar discs above the head are seen in depictions of many deities of Ancient Egypt, including Ra, Hathor and Isis and are also found in many other ancient religions connected with sun worship.

Bhudda in 2nd and 3rd century art was represented with a halo. The circle is symbolic of eternity -- an existence without beginning without end and also represents the concept of reincarnation. This is an extremely ancient symbol associated with divinity and kingship and could even have had its origins in the spheres which we know today as orbs.

I really like this picture. **Even the lion has a halo.** A sacred lion? The lion is also a symbol of kingship.

Scepter & Orb – Symbols Of Kingship

The scepter and orb are ultimate symbols of kingship and still in use today. From ancient times, the Priest-King represented the embodiment or incarnation on earth of a god who depending on the religion was very often the Sun God. The

king or priest-king was depicted with a golden halo or aura of the Sun behind his head and holding the scepter in one hand and an orb in the other. The scepter represents authority and the orb carries a clear message of world dominion or of things temporal.

There exists a 2nd century coin from the reign of Emperor Hadrian showing a Roman God with his foot planted frmly upon a globe. In England, the Sovereign's Orb symbolises both the state and Church of England under the protection and dominion of the crown.

Most people today if asked, would probably tell you that the Orb of kingship represents the Globe the Temporal World – and they would be right , although I find it intriguing that it was only until relatively recent times that everyone thought the world was flat. It's those ancients again. They knew their stuff alright! They must have known the world was round, because if they thought the world was flat, the king would be shown to be holding a dinner plate ….. wouldn't he? Or could this representation come from a tradition much more ancient, associated with gods, kingship and the sphere of spiritual perfection? The orb pictured here was the orb made for the Stuart King Charles II. The golden orb itself is held captive in a jewel encrusted band and set atop by a bejeweled cross which achieves the purpose of 'Christianizing' the ancient 'pagan' orb symbol.

Mazes & Labyrinths

A labyrinth nearly always takes the form of a circle with a complex and very ordered design incorporated within it. It is an ancient symbol that relates to spiritual wholeness. The ancient ritual of walking or dancing the labyrinth can be considered an initiatory journey into our own spiritual non-material center and back again into the world. Making the journey into a labyrinth and the return journey out again, also encapsulates the death of the old and the renewal and rebirth of a journey in and out of an incarnation. Labyrinths have long been used as tools for meditation and prayer and by reaching beyond the temporal world, the presence of a cosmic order and the subtler realms of higher consciousness can be revealed.

Mazes or labyrinths have always been closely associated in myth with gods and kings. In Crete the legend of Theseus who, with the help of Ariadne, the daughter of King Minos, killed the Minotaur at the centre of the labyrinth is well-known and although this legend for all we know, might have some basis in fact, it is certainly symbolic of the timeless theme of the triumph of good over evil.

Many of my photos of orbs show an unmistakable maze-like design which is why I make this association between orbs and labyrinths. Labyrinths are as old as mankind and there are many examples of third millennium BC mazes-dating as far back as the Neolithic age which are as close to home as Glastonbury in England.

As late as the 12th and 13th centuries, mazes were also accorded considerable

significance by the Gothic cathedral builders and were often incorporated into religious buildings; the most famous example of this being in Chatres Cathedral near Paris.

Note here the amusing pictorial representations of the Four Winds. Is this perhaps implying that mazes were originally floating in the air as do orbs and can be borne upon the winds? The internal design of many orbs which I have photographed is entirely reminiscent of this basic design with six to seven main concentric circles divided by segments looking very similar to a cross-section of a tree trunk showing age rings.

The Flaming Pearl In Chinese Mythology

The flaming pearl in Chinese Taoist symbolism represents wisdom and spiritual perfection. It is the spirit of 'The Way', bringing about eternal changes. The dragon represents kingship or the emperor and he is nearly always shown with his long sinuous body coiling among the clouds, in quest of the 'Flaming Pearl' which is always just slightly beyond his reach. It is symbolic of mankind's

striving towards spiritual perfection with the implied message that the dragon (or the emperor) is the guardian of the Flaming Pearl of wisdom and spiritual perfection.

The 'Flaming Pearl' is also recognized by both Buddhists and Hindus as the incarnation of light, of inspirational wisdom, and of transcendent spiritual consciousness. It is the spiritual essence of The Universe. It is known too as the third eye of both Buddha and Shiva while Christian writings frequently make a simile between the Kingdom of God and a 'priceless pearl'. The Chinese drawing pictured here is of a five-toed dragon romping in the skies playing with a flaming pearl. Take a closer look at the pearl. Does it or does it not look exactly like an orb? Did the Chinese know something we have long ago forgotten and lost? This motive is extremely commonly repeated again and again in all Chinese art forms from paintings to decoration on porcelain to being woven in silk. The five-toed dragon is representative of the Emperor and is to the Chinese, a sacred symbolic of kingship and royalty.

Oysters Of The World Unite!

There is a romantic tradition which says that pearls are formed by the merging of water and moonlight, or that they are the frozen teardrops of the gods, while yet another says that pearls are created by a union between the masculine element Fire and the feminine element Water.

"Oi there! Wait a minute! What about us?" I can hear the Oysters of the world cry out in distress! "Don't we get some credit here in your book Antonia for all our hard work and suffering just so that you ladies can have something pretty to hang around your necks?"

"Yes of course you do my clever darlings -- next to diamonds, you are a girl's best friends!"

The Phaistos Disc

According to Wikipedia, the Phaistos disk is a disc of fired clay from the Minoan palace of Phaistos, most likely dating to the middle or late Minoan Bronze Age (two thousand BC). It is about 15 cm in diameter and covered on both sides with a spiral of stamped symbols or pictograms. Its purpose and meaning, and even its original geographical place of manufacture, remain disputed, making it one of the most famous mysteries of archaeology. The Phaistos disc is on display at the archaeological museum of Herakleion in Crete, Greece. But where on earth did it originally come from and what could it possibly say?

The mysterious Phaistos disc showing both sides. Just at a glance does it remind you of anything? And in case you need reminding take another quick look on page 194 at the Crabtree Farm E.T crop circle and the disc which accompanies him in the chapter on Orbs and Crop Cirlces. This is also very reminiscent of a typical orb structure reminding us of a cross-section of a tree. (Photograph Wikipedia.)

I find all these examples of 'other orbs' very exciting. Whichever way you look at it, through all these symbolic representations of things Heavenly and Temporal, from the Flaming Pearl of the Chinese, to the bejeweled Orb of European royalty, there is a common Universal thread reaching out to us down through the millennia, which like Ariadne's silken yarn, winds through the labyrinth of spiritual truths to arrive at its centre. We discover that they all relate to gods kingship, temporal and spiritual power and above all, without exception, they speak of the eternal quest for the attainment of spiritual perfection. They can all, with a very small stretch of the imagination, be likened to 'our orbs , the 'Light

Beings' -- Maybe it just so happens that, like so much else that we seem to have lost throughout the ages, the Ancients knew all about it.

Hathor & Isis Of Egyptian Mythology

Hathor (left) the Egyptian Queen of the Milky Way or Sacred Cow Deity wearing her head dress representing the solar disc (or is it an orb?) held between the horns of a cow. She dates back to at least 2,700 BC. On the right we have Isis wearing Hathor's head dress: There was a merger in Egypt mythologhy and Hathor and Isis became as one, Hathor-Isis. When one sees the familiar Madonna and child pose of Isis with Horus on her knee, one is closely reminded of the Virgin and Child of Christianity (albeit a little less modestly represented)! It does not take a great leap of imagination to transport the solar disc a little lower down and place it behind the heads of the ladies. All we need to do next, is to take away the cow horns and hey presto -- a halo!

CHAPTER THIRTY-ONE

Beyond The Curtain

It would have been enough for me / To stand beyond the Court / To view Your beauty from afar / A glance, but nothing more / But it was not enough for You / The distance far too great / You tore the Curtain with Your love / And called me through the Gate.

(Dallas Holm)

'Beyond the Curtain' was the original title which I wanted to give to this book but as we know, there is nothing new under the sun and I discovered that there is already a beautiful song by Dallas Holm carrying that name. When I checked out the words of the song I found that by strange co-incidence there were haunting echoes evocative of my relationship with the 'Light Beings'; especially in those last two lines: *'You tore the curtain with your love, and called me through the gate'.* If someone had asked me to write a poem eliciting my relationship with the 'Light

Beings', I could not have come up with anything as wonderfully appropriate as 'Beyond The Curtain'.

When I started writing this book I truly had absolutely no idea what I was going to say, how I was going to say it or indeed what the orbs really were. My main purpose was to get all my lovely photos collected in one safe place and tell anyone who cared to listen about my experience with this rather strange photographic phenomenon. But as the book went on something else happened: it seemed to take on a life and an energy of its own and it was almost as though it started to write itself. It seems that I began at page one, fingers flying over the keyboard, and went on straight through to the end, almost without lifting my head. Considering the size of the book, it got written in record time and I feel that the 'Light Beings' were there at my shoulder with every line and with every page, telling me to tell you everything that they want you to know about them. I have heard of people writing books and saying later that they don't know how the book got written; this book comes into that category as it just seems to have written itself. I really do believe that 'Their' presence has been with me all the way through and so with the greatest humility I take little or no credit for what's written here, or for any success that the book might enjoy.

Even though I have been photographing orbs and thinking about them for many years, to the point of being positively obsessed by them, the more I thought about them the more perplexed I was as to what they actually are and what is their true purpose if any. However through writing this book I think that I have begun to gain a bit of clarity – I could almost literally say I'm beginning to see the light. In chapter four 'First Define Your Orb', I made a list in more or less the order of my inclination (at the time) of all the possibilities I thought that these orbs could be. About a third of the way down the list one of the possibilities was that they were the disembodied souls of family and loved ones who have passed on. Having finished the book and having thought about it all the way through, I have in fact a steadily growing preference for that idea and would quite like to promote it to the top of the list. But I will leave the list in the order in which I originally wrote it, because otherwise I'd probably be tempted to change it every five minutes and it's high time for me to get this off to the publisher!

Fireworks from the terrace: Back to where the story started -- with a fireworks display and Old Flatface.

I believe that there is great merit in the idea of a 'soul-pool' to which all of us belong in spirit until we are required to continue our journey of learning and are sent to live an incarnation in the physical realm. I think it is perfectly possible that the orbs which visit us could be attached to the soul-pool to which we each and individually belong, and that they occasionally break away and come to visit us most especially at those critical times of our lives when we reach certain milestones such as graduation, engagements, marriages, birth of babies and so on or suffer the loss of a loved one through death. I believe that they are probably with us every step along the way as we navigate the course of life through our triumphs and our not-so-brilliant moments until the time comes for our own ultimate curtain call when we make the return journey 'Home' and rejoin the 'Source of the Light'.

CHAPTER THIRTY-TWO

The Last Word

"Most People don't believe in ghosts, until they actually have an encounter with one."

This the quote with which I have chosen to end this book, and ties in nicely with the quote which opened it, because basically it says just about the same thing. In other words, don't scoff or hold in contempt any concept or new idea that confronts you until you have thoroughly investigated it or until you have had some personal experience of it.

To Thine Own Self Be True!

All through this book, I have tried to be faithful to my own unique experiences which although they have been considerable and have taken place over many years, I am none the less painfully aware that I have only scratched the surface of this vast new territory. I only hope that something that I have written here can give someone somewhere a small clue or add a single piece of the jigsaw to the great puzzle as to what is really going on out there. We are still dealing in the realms of total mystery, the veils of which will only be lifted one by one , and that very slowly over many more years yet to come.

As I have already said, I have tried to stay strictly within the boundaries of my own personal encounters with the 'Light Beings', and apart from one or two special exceptions, I have avoided passing on to you experiences belonging to other people or anything that I consider to be hearsay.

Apart from tracking down photos of one or two specific crop circles, I made the internet more or less out-of-bounds during the writing of the book so that I would not be tempted to quote other sources or to start being influenced by theories and ideas that had nothing to do with my personal experience and understanding of the 'Incredible 'Light Beings' of the Cosmos'.

I had read two books on the subject before I started setting down my own view point of the subject. Despite an occasional overwhelming temptation to refer back to them to see what their authors had said about this or that, those books remained firmly closed for the duration of the writing of this. I did not want to be guilty of plagiarism, even unconsciously.

This is why there I have given no references to other books or to any websites in the book. Anyone who wants to further investigate the subject only needs to 'Google It' and they will find a multitude of choice of every type and description on the 'net'.

I made an exception to my 'exclusivity' rule with some of the photos, because it suited my purpose to illustrate a point, and therefore I have included several photographs in the book taken by people other than myself but almost without exception, I was actually with those people when they took the photos and saw them on the LED screens so I can vouch for their authenticity. Therefore unless otherwise specifically credited to someone else, all the photos in the book were taken by myself.

One of the most important photos taken by others was Philippe Vincintelli's photo of the "Lentil Soup" and I was standing beside Philippe when he took it, and I concurrently took my own "Lentil Soup" photo.

Two of the photos were taken by my son John. Although I was not with John when he took the photo of Michiyuki-san and the Wombat in the Sydney zoo, I would lay down my life in defense of John's honesty and integrity. I was there however the night when he took the photo of little Yuna the Japanese girl with the orb gazing into her eyes.

Two of the photographs of the crop circles which have I have included come from an impeccable and reputable source. They are professional photos from a private library owned by Lucy Pringle who is a force majeur in the world of aerial crop circle photography. The third crop circle photo was one I downloaded from the internet many years ago I have unsuccessfully searched for hours to find it again so as to ask permission to use it and give credit to the owner. I just have to ask that that person understands and if he or she happens to read this book, he/she is invited to contact me if they wish to do so that they can be given credit in subsequent printings of this book. That for me is a major photo and demonstrated one of the most important points in the whole book. By using that very important photo, we are advancing 'The Cause' my friend!

My cousins Margaret and Juliette Clark contributed some photos too, so it could almost be said that this book has been something of a family affair! Margaret's extraordinary photo of the Ghost of Muness Castle so stretches the imagination beyond the boundaries of believability that had I not been standing beside Margaret when she took the photo I would probably not have believed it myself. But you have to know my cousin Margaret: She is totally incapable of any form of deception. I wanted to use Juliette's photo of the 'crop circle' on the Col de Vence because it was quite simply better that any of the ones I took that day.

I believe that there is a yet lot of study in the field of real photography of the 'unreal' and that we are on the brink of discovering amazing new worlds as long as we can keep our minds and spirits open to these frontiers of hitherto unsuspected phenomena and not close the doors until we have spent some time exploring all the rooms of this exciting new mansion.

If all of these manifestations, orbs, crop circles, UFO sightings, abductions and so on, add up to an encounter of the third kind, and aliens from another galaxy are visiting us, then it is my firm conviction that whoever 'they' are, they mean us no harm. It may be that as we are now on the brink of the 'Age of Aquarius', they are here to reveal and to teach those amongst us who wish to be taught whatever it is that we need to know. There is more than ample evidence that this process has already started and is now well under way.

We have among us today many highly enlightened persons some of whom are politicians quietly plugging away for truth, and there are many brave souls out there, not at all popular with 'The Establishment' who, often at the risk of their own lives, have had and *continue* to have, the enormous courage to put their necks on the chopping block in order to get their message across.

There is a new race of 'Children of the Light' re-incarnating now who are easily recognizable because they are born with their eyes wide open and with a knowing and wise expression on their tiny faces. When they arrive in the world, they look about them with a calm and serene expression as if to say "Hello World – I'm back again. What have you been doing in my absence?" Treasure these children, for they are special. They are our messengers of the future and it is their mission here to bring forth and reveal all that has been hitherto hidden. I sense a great optimism in the wind, and hopefully in a small way this book is my contribution to the movement.

Perhaps A Source Of Protective Power In Our Lives

There have been many times when I am convinced that the orbs which I photograph 'belong' to me personally. They seem to travel with me wherever I go and I do believe that I am beginning to recognize individuals such as dear old 'Flatface' who we saw in several pictures throughout the book -- so it is not difficult to suppose them to be my protectors both in The Now and during those lost years of my life when I took many foolish risks and my drinking led me down some potentially dangerous paths. It always seemed that I had enormous protection which brought me safely through and that this protection was coming from a source which was simply not of this world.

That same protection continues to this day and leads me safe and sound through the highways and byways of this crazy world and makes child's play of just about every difficulty encountered along the way even if it's something as banal but as nasty and as frustrating bureaucratic red-tape!

I believe that someone or something watches over ach and every one of us and walks with us along every step of the way as we travel through this physical phase of our on-going existence which we call 'Our Earthly Life'. I believe that someone or something is hovering in the background of our lives to guide us through our difficulties and to pick us up and carry us when we stumble and fall along the way.

Maybe you call them 'Angels', maybe some call them 'Guardian Angels" while yet others might call them 'Spirit Guides'. Some might even call them a 'Higher Power' while others may simply say 'God'. It doesn't matter what you choose to call them, the fact is that they are here living amongst us now -- and I think that from here on, I shall always call them 'The Incredible Light Beings of the Cosmos'.

Seek and you shall find. The ongoing quest for truth and for knowledge is your responsibility. Maybe it is *you* dear reader who holds the key which will open the door to that world which lies just within our reach beyond the curtain. Use it and enter without fear.

God bless and happy hunting.

Antonia.

This is Not The End!

STOP PRESS!

How could I not have known when I wrote what I thought was that rather clever little line "This is not the End", that that particular wording was going to be entirely prophetic. It certainly was *not* - repeat not -- the end!

Also, I should have known better when I entitled the final chapter of this book 'The Last Word', that it would not be *me* the mere author of this book who would be allowed to have the 'last word' on the subject of the 'Light Beings'! Oh dear me no! No way in the world were *'They'* going to let me get away with that! Rather foolishly it has taken me all these months spent in the writing of this book, to finally realise -- only now -- that it was not me who has been in control: it's *them* who have been calling the shots all along! We must respectively remember that we are dealing with the 'Light Beings' and therefore if anyone was going to get in the last word then it was definitely going to be *them* and this they seem to have managed to do -- quite literally!

The book was finished and about to go to print when I suddenly started taking orb photos of such an extraordinary nature that they absolutely had to be included. I hastily called my publisher. "Was there still time to add a few pages at the end?" "Yes," he said, "we can still do it and yes, it can go in right at the end."

These orb photos are probably the most astonishing yet and they tell me that there is still much more to be revealed by the 'Light Beings'! These photos also tell me that they haven't finished with us yet! Maybe they are only just getting started!

This is how it happened: I was visiting the Camargue area in the South of France to research my next book on the subject of Provence and its many esoteric mysteries and travelling with me was a cousin from New Zealand. We had spent all day with yet another cousin who lives in the countryside outside Nimes. We had a great day catching up on a decade or two of family happenings as families do, and after a very nice lunch in the country, cousin Rose and I farewelled cousin Barbara and drove to Aigues-Mortes the town where we planned on staying for the night and booked into our hotel.

Although we were both tired, it was still quite early and so we decided to wander along the canal and take a look at the historic little town to see what we could see and also try to find somewhere nice to get a pizza. We were visiting the 12th century church 'Notre Dames des Sablons' (Our Lady of the Sands), when I took this photo of the interior of the church. I saw instantly on the camera screen that there was something about the orb that was unusual and was stupefied to see that there was a pattern in it which closely resembled writing!

Mystified, Rose and I went right around the church looking high and low for anything at all that could account for it, like writing on a wall or in a stained glass window or anything else that could possibly have caused the effect. There was absolutely nothing that we could see -- anywhere.

Later that night back at the hotel, I was contemplating this extraordinary turn of events and it occurred to me that the writing might be in reverse; that is to say that it might have been on the other side of the orb and showing through its transparent body. So I took out my makeup mirror and held it up to the camera screen to get the reverse view of the picture. Suddenly I saw with quite a shock that it very closely resembled the nickname that some of my family and oldest friends call me 'Toni'-- a diminutive of Antonia!

The orb at top right is the orb with writing in it -- taken at the jazz festival in Juan-les-Pinson12th July 2008.

Practically nobody has called me 'Toni' for more than thirty years. I hate it! It's a right only reserved for family and childhood friends and even then I have to grit my teeth, grin and bear it but I wondered if the Light Beings were intrigued by hearing this and were letting me know that they had heard me being called 'Toni' all day by the two cousins, and were testing my reaction to it in a teasing kind of way. If this is the case, then there should be no further doubt in anybody's mind that these are very intelligent little creatures indeed! Capable of thought, they obviously know what's going on around us and they are showing that they have a good sense of humour too!

Four days later on 12th July, just in case I had any doubts whatsoever in my mind about the orb with the writing in it (and probably to make sure that it got into the book), the 'Light Beings' obviously decided to provide further proof for me. I was invited to a concert given by jazz singer Al Jarreau and I was taking photos when . . . . . ah yes you guessed it! Another orb with writing in it!

The intriguing thing about these two orbs is that by shape and size they are almost identical. The writing is almost identical too but with tiny almost imperceptible differences. Is it the same orb? The space and time between the two photos was about 350 kilometres and four days. Did the orb follow me from Aigues-Mortes to Cannes and then to Juan-les-Pins where the concert was held?

<u>BOTH ORBS SET SIDE-BY-SIDE FOR COMPARISON</u>

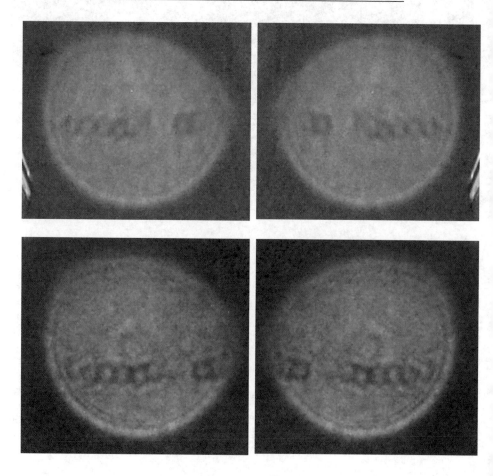

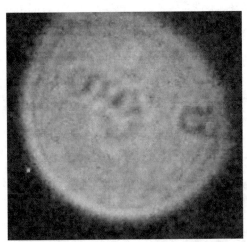

The Surprises Were Not Quite Over.

I had just about finished writing this 'Stop Press' when I happened to be going through the photos taken up on the Col de Vence on the night of the 28th June just after the Summer Solstice. I stopped dead in my tracks – for there was a photo taken that night which I had not noticed before and which also contained writing in it. Therefore the date of the 28th June is when the 1st writing appeared in my photos – not the 8th July. And I am ready to bet any money that it is the same orb – Old Flatface!

With this new and incredible phenomenon of the 'Light Beings' manifesting themselves with writing on their surface, I would like to say that I truly have no idea where the 'Light Beings' are going or where they are leading us but I am totally convinced that they do indeed have a definite plan and that they are working up to the next 'phase' of their development which, with their usual impeccable timing, will probably be scheduled for sometime soon after this book is on the shelves and a wide segment of the public is familiarised with them and fully aware of their existence in a non-threatening, non-scary way. As I said right at the very beginning of this book I am 100% convinced that they are not here to harm us.

FACING PAGE -- TOP PAIR: 8th July 2008. Orb photo taken in the Church of 'Our Lady of the Sands' in Aigues-Mortes. The photo on the top left is the original orientation of the photo. When reversed as in mirror writing (picture on top right), the orb seems to very closely spell my nick-name 'Toni' (a diminutive of Antonia), with a lower-case 't' preceded with a capital 'D'.

LOWER PAIR: 12th July 2008. Orb photo taken four days later at the Al Jarreau open-air concert in Juan-le-Pins, French Riviera. Photo on left is the original orientation of the photo. When reversed as in a mirror (picture on lower right), the writing very closely resembles the July 8th orb. The Capital 'D' is present but the writing although extremely similar has very slight differences. I have deliberately reproduced them here in sepia as I think that the writing shows up to its best advantage in this colour as it takes out all the pixels in various hues which tend to confuse the eye.

Before I close(please note that I don't dare say anything about 'final words' or 'ending this book'!) I would just like to draw your attention to the huge physical evolution in the orbs since I first began photographing them in 2000. From those first fuzzy ill-defined white spheres, they have variously taken on a beautiful luminosity, different colours, shown a diversity of definite patterns on their surfaces which have varied considerably over the years and some people have even said that they can see faces in them. Quite recently they have started to show that they can change shape too and now their latest trick is turning up with writing in them!

There is no doubt in my mind that we are seeing a script of some sort. But what script is it? And what could it possibly be trying to say? There's something vaguely familiar about it like a faint echo from a distant past. But what? If there's anybody out there who recognizes this style of writing or has any ideas about it, please let me know.

Will one small word possibly spelling out someone's name gradually become a more complex text containing an important message something like the message encoded in the 'Crabtree Farm E.T.' crop circle? I would not be at all surprised -- but only time will tell and I for one am very excited about the prospect of being there when that happens.

I hope you will be too - so keep your cameras on hand and never lose an opportunity to get out there and try to capture the 'Light Beings' in action because . . . . .

this my friends, is *definitely* not the end!

14th July 2008.

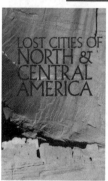

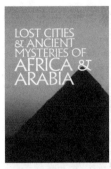

LOST CITIES & ANCIENT MYSTERIES OF AFRICA & ARABIA
by David Hatcher Childress
Childress continues his world-wide quest for lost cities and ancient mysteries. Join him as he discovers forbidden cities in the Empty Quarter of Arabia; "Atlantean" ruins in Egypt and the Kalahari desert; a mysterious, ancient empire in the Sahara; and more. This is the tale of an extraordinary life on the road: across war-torn countries, Childress searches for King Solomon's Mines, living dinosaurs, the Ark of the Covenant and the solutions to some of the fantastic mysteries of the past.
423 PAGES. 6x9 PAPERBACK. ILLUSTRATED. $14.95. CODE: AFA

LOST CITIES OF ATLANTIS, ANCIENT EUROPE & THE MEDITERRANEAN
by David Hatcher Childress
Childress takes the reader in search of sunken cities in the Mediterranean; across the Atlas Mountains in search of Atlantean ruins; to remote islands in search of megalithic ruins; to meet living legends and secret societies. From Ireland to Turkey, Morocco to Eastern Europe, and around the remote islands of the Mediterranean and Atlantic, Childress takes the reader on an astonishing quest for mankind's past. Ancient technology, cataclysms, megalithic construction, lost civilizations and devastating wars of the past are all explored in this book.
524 PAGES. 6x9 PAPERBACK. ILLUSTRATED. $16.95. CODE: MED

LOST CITIES OF CHINA, CENTRAL ASIA & INDIA
by David Hatcher Childress
Like a real life "Indiana Jones," maverick archaeologist David Childress takes the reader on an incredible adventure across some of the world's oldest and most remote countries in search of lost cities and ancient mysteries. Discover ancient cities in the Gobi Desert; hear fantastic tales of lost continents, vanished civilizations and secret societies bent on ruling the world; visit forgotten monasteries in forbidding snow-capped mountains with strange tunnels to mysterious subterranean cities! A unique combination of far-out exploration and practical travel advice, it will astound and delight the experienced traveler or the armchair voyager.
429 PAGES. 6x9 PAPERBACK. ILLUSTRATED. FOOTNOTES & BIBLIOGRAPHY. $14.95. CODE: CHI

LOST CITIES OF ANCIENT LEMURIA & THE PACIFIC
by David Hatcher Childress
Was there once a continent in the Pacific? Called Lemuria or Pacifica by geologists, Mu or Pan by the mystics, there is now ample mythological, geological and archaeological evidence to "prove" that an advanced and ancient civilization once lived in the central Pacific. Maverick archaeologist and explorer David Hatcher Childress combs the Indian Ocean, Australia and the Pacific in search of the surprising truth about mankind's past. Contains photos of the underwater city on Pohnpei; explanations on how the statues were levitated around Easter Island in a clockwise vortex movement; tales of disappearing islands; Egyptians in Australia; and more.
379 PAGES. 6x9 PAPERBACK. ILLUSTRATED. FOOTNOTES & BIBLIOGRAPHY. $14.95. CODE: LEM

A HITCHHIKER'S GUIDE TO ARMAGEDDON
by David Hatcher Childress
With wit and humor, popular Lost Cities author David Hatcher Childress takes us around the world and back in his trippy finalé to the Lost Cities series. He's off on an adventure in search of the apocalypse and end times. Childress hits the road from the fortress of Megiddo, the legendary citadel in northern Israel where Armageddon is prophesied to start. Hitchhiking around the world, Childress takes us from one adventure to another, to ancient cities in the deserts and the legends of worlds before our own. In the meantime, he becomes a cargo cult god on a remote island off New Guinea, gets dragged into the Kennedy Assassination by one of the "conspirators," investigates a strange power operating out of the Altai Mountains of Mongolia, and discovers how the Knights Templar and their off-shoots have driven the world toward an epic battle centered around Jerusalem and the Middle East.
320 PAGES. 6x9 PAPERBACK. ILLUSTRATED. BIBLIOGRAPHY. INDEX. $16.95. CODE: HGA

TECHNOLOGY OF THE GODS
The Incredible Sciences of the Ancients
by David Hatcher Childress
Childress looks at the technology that was allegedly used in Atlantis and the theory that the Great Pyramid of Egypt was originally a gigantic power station. He examines tales of ancient flight and the technology that it involved; how the ancients used electricity; megalithic building techniques; the use of crystal lenses and the fire from the gods; evidence of various high tech weapons in the past, including atomic weapons; ancient metallurgy and heavy machinery; the role of modern inventors such as Nikola Tesla in bringing ancient technology back into modern use; impossible artifacts; and more.
356 PAGES. 6x9 PAPERBACK. ILLUSTRATED. BIBLIOGRAPHY. $16.95. CODE: TGOD

VIMANA AIRCRAFT OF ANCIENT INDIA & ATLANTIS
by David Hatcher Childress, introduction by Ivan T. Sanderson
In this incredible volume on ancient India, authentic Indian texts such as the *Ramayana* and the *Mahabharata* are used to prove that ancient aircraft were in use more than four thousand years ago. Included in this book is the entire Fourth Century BC manuscript *Vimaanika Shastra* by the ancient author Maharishi Bharadwaaja. Also included are chapters on Atlantean technology, the incredible Rama Empire of India and the devastating wars that destroyed it.
334 PAGES. 6x9 PAPERBACK. ILLUSTRATED. $15.95. CODE: VAA

LOST CONTINENTS & THE HOLLOW EARTH
I Remember Lemuria and the Shaver Mystery
by David Hatcher Childress & Richard Shaver
Shaver's rare 1948 book *I Remember Lemuria* is reprinted in its entirety, and the book is packed with illustrations from Ray Palmer's *Amazing Stories* magazine of the 1940s. Palmer and Shaver told of tunnels running through the earth—tunnels inhabited by the Deros and Teros, humanoids from an ancient spacefaring race that had inhabited the earth, eventually going underground, hundreds of thousands of years ago. Childress discusses the famous hollow earth books and delves deep into whatever reality may be behind the stories of tunnels in the earth. Operation High Jump to Antarctica in 1947 and Admiral Byrd's bizarre statements, tunnel systems in South America and Tibet, the underground world of Agartha, the belief of UFOs coming from the South Pole, more.
344 PAGES. 6x9 PAPERBACK. ILLUSTRATED. $16.95. CODE: LCHE

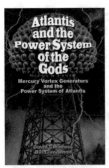

ATLANTIS & THE POWER SYSTEM OF THE GODS
by David Hatcher Childress and Bill Clendenon

Childress' fascinating analysis of Nikola Tesla's broadcast system in light of Edgar Cayce's "Terrible Crystal" and the obelisks of ancient Egypt and Ethiopia. Includes: Atlantis and its crystal power towers that broadcast energy; how these incredible power stations may still exist today; inventor Nikola Tesla's nearly identical system of power transmission; Mercury Proton Gyros and mercury vortex propulsion; more. Richly illustrated, and packed with evidence that Atlantis not only existed—it had a world-wide energy system more sophisticated than ours today.

246 PAGES. 6x9 PAPERBACK. ILLUSTRATED. $15.95. CODE: APSG

THE ANTI-GRAVITY HANDBOOK
edited by David Hatcher Childress

The new expanded compilation of material on Anti-Gravity, Free Energy, Flying Saucer Propulsion, UFOs, Suppressed Technology, NASA Cover-ups and more. Highly illustrated with patents, technical illustrations and photos. This revised and expanded edition has more material, including photos of Area 51, Nevada, the government's secret testing facility. This classic on weird science is back in a new format!

230 PAGES. 7x10 PAPERBACK. ILLUSTRATED. $16.95. CODE: AGH

ANTI–GRAVITY & THE WORLD GRID

Is the earth surrounded by an intricate electromagnetic grid network offering free energy? This compilation of material on ley lines and world power points contains chapters on the geography, mathematics, and light harmonics of the earth grid. Learn the purpose of ley lines and ancient megalithic structures located on the grid. Discover how the grid made the Philadelphia Experiment possible. Explore the Coral Castle and many other mysteries, including acoustic levitation, Tesla Shields and scalar wave weaponry. Browse through the section on anti-gravity patents, and research resources.

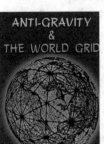

274 PAGES. 7x10 PAPERBACK. ILLUSTRATED. $14.95. CODE: AGW

ANTI–GRAVITY & THE UNIFIED FIELD
edited by David Hatcher Childress

Is Einstein's Unified Field Theory the answer to all of our energy problems? Explored in this compilation of material is how gravity, electricity and magnetism manifest from a unified field around us. Why artificial gravity is possible; secrets of UFO propulsion; free energy; Nikola Tesla and anti-gravity airships of the 20s and 30s; flying saucers as superconducting whirls of plasma; anti-mass generators; vortex propulsion; suppressed technology; government cover-ups; gravitational pulse drive; spacecraft & more.

240 PAGES. 7x10 PAPERBACK. ILLUSTRATED. $14.95. CODE: AGU

THE TIME TRAVEL HANDBOOK
A Manual of Practical Teleportation & Time Travel
edited by David Hatcher Childress

The Time Travel Handbook takes the reader beyond the government experiments and deep into the uncharted territory of early time travellers such as Nikola Tesla and Guglielmo Marconi and their alleged time travel experiments, as well as the Wilson Brothers of EMI and their connection to the Philadelphia Experiment—the U.S. Navy's forays into invisibility, time travel, and teleportation. Childress looks into the claims of time travelling individuals, and investigates the unusual claim that the pyramids on Mars were built in the future and sent back in time. A highly visual, large format book, with patents, photos and schematics. Be the first on your block to build your own time travel device!

316 PAGES. 7x10 PAPERBACK. ILLUSTRATED. $16.95. CODE: TTH

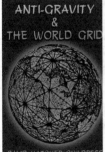

MAPS OF THE ANCIENT SEA KINGS
Evidence of Advanced Civilization in the Ice Age
by Charles H. Hapgood
Charles Hapgood has found the evidence in the Piri Reis Map that shows Antarctica, the Hadji Ahmed map, the Oronteus Finaeus and other amazing maps. Hapgood concluded that these maps were made from more ancient maps from the various ancient archives around the world, now lost. Not only were these unknown people more advanced in mapmaking than any people prior to the 18th century, it appears they mapped all the continents. The Americas were mapped thousands of years before Columbus. Antarctica was mapped when its coasts were free of ice!
316 PAGES. 7x10 PAPERBACK. ILLUSTRATED. BIBLIOGRAPHY & INDEX. $19.95. CODE: MASK

PATH OF THE POLE
Cataclysmic Pole Shift Geology
by Charles H. Hapgood
Maps of the Ancient Sea Kings author Hapgood's classic book *Path of the Pole* is back in print! Hapgood researched Antarctica, ancient maps and the geological record to conclude that the Earth's crust has slipped on the inner core many times in the past, changing the position of the pole. *Path of the Pole* discusses the various "pole shifts" in Earth's past, giving evidence for each one, and moves on to possible future pole shifts.
356 PAGES. 6x9 PAPERBACK. ILLUSTRATED. $16.95. CODE: POP

SECRETS OF THE HOLY LANCE
The Spear of Destiny in History & Legend
by Jerry E. Smith
Secrets of the Holy Lance traces the Spear from its possession by Constantine, Rome's first Christian Caesar, to Charlemagne's claim that with it he ruled the Holy Roman Empire by Divine Right, and on through two thousand years of kings and emperors, until it came within Hitler's grasp—and beyond! Did it rest for a while in Antarctic ice? Is it now hidden in Europe, awaiting the next person to claim its awesome power? Neither debunking nor worshiping, *Secrets of the Holy Lance* seeks to pierce the veil of myth and mystery around the Spear. Mere belief that it was infused with magic by virtue of its shedding the Savior's blood has made men kings. But what if it's more? What are "the powers it serves"?
312 PAGES. 6x9 PAPERBACK. ILLUSTRATED. BIBLIOGRAPHY. $16.95. CODE: SOHL

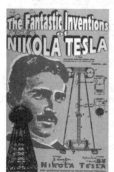

THE FANTASTIC INVENTIONS OF NIKOLA TESLA
by Nikola Tesla with additional material by David Hatcher Childress
This book is a readable compendium of patents, diagrams, photos and explanations of the many incredible inventions of the originator of the modern era of electrification. In Tesla's own words are such topics as wireless transmission of power, death rays, and radio-controlled airships. In addition, rare material on a secret city built at a remote jungle site in South America by one of Tesla's students, Guglielmo Marconi. Marconi's secret group claims to have built flying saucers in the 1940s and to have gone to Mars in the early 1950s! Incredible photos of these Tesla craft are included. •His plan to transmit free electricity into the atmosphere. •How electrical devices would work using only small antennas. •Why unlimited power could be utilized anywhere on earth. •How radio and radar technology can be used as death-ray weapons in Star Wars.
342 PAGES. 6x9 PAPERBACK. ILLUSTRATED. $16.95. CODE: FINT

REICH OF THE BLACK SUN
Nazi Secret Weapons & the Cold War Allied Legend
by Joseph P. Farrell
Why were the Allies worried about an atom bomb attack by the Germans in 1944? Why did the Soviets threaten to use poison gas against the Germans? Why did Hitler in 1945 insist that holding Prague could win the war for the Third Reich? Why did US General George Patton's Third Army race for the Skoda works at Pilsen in Czechoslovakia instead of Berlin? Why did the US Army not test the uranium atom bomb it dropped on Hiroshima? Why did the Luftwaffe fly a non-stop round trip mission to within twenty miles of New York City in 1944? *Reich of the Black Sun* takes the reader on a scientific-historical journey in order to answer these questions. Arguing that Nazi Germany actually won the race for the atom bomb in late 1944,
352 PAGES. 6x9 PAPERBACK. ILLUSTRATED. BIBLIOGRAPHY. $16.95. CODE: ROBS

THE GIZA DEATH STAR
The Paleophysics of the Great Pyramid & the Military Complex at Giza
by Joseph P. Farrell
Was the Giza complex part of a military installation over 10,000 years ago? Chapters include: An Archaeology of Mass Destruction, Thoth and Theories; The Machine Hypothesis; Pythagoras, Plato, Planck, and the Pyramid; The Weapon Hypothesis; Encoded Harmonics of the Planck Units in the Great Pyramid; High Freqquency Direct Current "Impulse" Technology; The Grand Gallery and its Crystals: Gravito-acoustic Resonators; The Other Two Large Pyramids; the "Causeways," and the "Temples"; A Phase Conjugate Howitzer; Evidence of the Use of Weapons of Mass Destruction in Ancient Times; more.
290 PAGES. 6x9 PAPERBACK. ILLUSTRATED. $16.95. CODE: GDS

THE GIZA DEATH STAR DEPLOYED
The Physics & Engineering of the Great Pyramid
by Joseph P. Farrell
Farrell expands on his thesis that the Great Pyramid was a maser, designed as a weapon and eventually deployed—with disastrous results to the solar system. Includes: Exploding Planets: A Brief History of the Exoteric and Esoteric Investigations of the Great Pyramid; No Machines, Please!; The Stargate Conspiracy; The Scalar Weapons; Message or Machine?; A Tesla Analysis of the Putative Physics and Engineering of the Giza Death Star; Cohering the Zero Point, Vacuum Energy, Flux: Feedback Loops and Tetrahedral Physics; and more.
290 PAGES. 6x9 PAPERBACK. ILLUSTRATED. $16.95. CODE: GDSD

THE GIZA DEATH STAR DESTROYED
The Ancient War For Future Science
by Joseph P. Farrell
Farrell moves on to events of the final days of the Giza Death Star and its awesome power. These final events, eventually leading up to the destruction of this giant machine, are dissected one by one, leading us to the eventual abandonment of the Giza Military Complex—an event that hurled civilization back into the Stone Age. Chapters include: The Mars-Earth Connection; The Lost "Root Races" and the Moral Reasons for the Flood; The Destruction of Krypton: The Electrodynamic Solar System, Exploding Planets and Ancient Wars; Turning the Stream of the Flood: the Origin of Secret Societies and Esoteric Traditions; The Quest to Recover Ancient Mega-Technology; Non-Equilibrium Paleophysics; Monatomic Paleophysics; Frequencies, Vortices and Mass Particles; "Acoustic" Intensity of Fields; The Pyramid of Crystals; tons more.
292 pages. 6x9 paperback. Illustrated. $16.95. Code: GDES

THE TESLA PAPERS
Nikola Tesla on Free Energy & Wireless Transmission of Power
by Nikola Tesla, edited by David Hatcher Childress

David Hatcher Childress takes us into the incredible world of Nikola Tesla and his amazing inventions. Tesla's fantastic vision of the future, including wireless power, anti-gravity, free energy and highly advanced solar power. Also included are some of the papers, patents and material collected on Tesla at the Colorado Springs Tesla Symposiums, including papers on: •The Secret History of Wireless Transmission •Tesla and the Magnifying Transmitter •Design and Construction of a Half-Wave Tesla Coil •Electrostatics: A Key to Free Energy •Progress in Zero-Point Energy Research •Electromagnetic Energy from Antennas to Atoms •Tesla's Particle Beam Technology •Fundamental Excitatory Modes of the Earth-Ionosphere Cavity

325 PAGES. 8x10 PAPERBACK. ILLUSTRATED. $16.95. CODE: TTP

UFOS AND ANTI-GRAVITY
Piece For A Jig-Saw
by Leonard G. Cramp

Leonard G. Cramp's 1966 classic book on flying saucer propulsion and suppressed technology is a highly technical look at the UFO phenomena by a trained scientist. Cramp first introduces the idea of 'anti-gravity' and introduces us to the various theories of gravitation. He then examines the technology necessary to build a flying saucer and examines in great detail the technical aspects of such a craft. Cramp's book is a wealth of material and diagrams on flying saucers, anti-gravity, suppressed technology, G-fields and UFOs. Chapters include Crossroads of Aerodynamics, Aerodynamic Saucers, Limitations of Rocketry, Gravitation and the Ether, Gravitational Spaceships, G-Field Lift Effects, The Bi-Field Theory, VTOL and Hovercraft, Analysis of UFO photos, more.

388 PAGES. 6x9 PAPERBACK. ILLUSTRATED. $16.95. CODE: UAG

THE COSMIC MATRIX
Piece for a Jig-Saw, Part Two
by Leonard G. Cramp

Cramp examines anti-gravity effects and theorizes that this super-science used by the craft—described in detail in the book—can lift mankind into a new level of technology, transportation and understanding of the universe. The book takes a close look at gravity control, time travel, and the interlocking web of energy between all planets in our solar system with Leonard's unique technical diagrams. A fantastic voyage into the present and future!

364 PAGES. 6x9 PAPERBACK. ILLUSTRATED. BIBLIOGRAPHY. $16.00. CODE: CMX

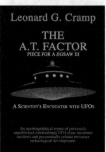

THE A.T. FACTOR
A Scientists Encounter with UFOs
by Leonard Cramp

British aerospace engineer Cramp began much of the scientific anti-gravity and UFO propulsion analysis back in 1955 with his landmark book *Space, Gravity & the Flying Saucer* (out-of-print and rare). In this final book, Cramp brings to a close his detailed and controversial study of UFOs and Anti-Gravity.

324 PAGES. 6x9 PAPERBACK. ILLUSTRATED. BIBLIOGRAPHY. INDEX. $16.95. CODE: ATF

THE FREE-ENERGY DEVICE HANDBOOK
A Compilation of Patents and Reports
by David Hatcher Childress

A large-format compilation of various patents, papers, descriptions and diagrams concerning free-energy devices and systems. *The Free-Energy Device Handbook* is a visual tool for experimenters and researchers into magnetic motors and other "over-unity" devices. With chapters on the Adams Motor, the Hans Coler Generator, cold fusion, superconductors, "N" machines, space-energy generators, Nikola Tesla, T. Townsend Brown, and the latest in free-energy devices. Packed with photos, technical diagrams, patents and fascinating information, this book belongs on every science shelf.

292 PAGES. 8x10 PAPERBACK. ILLUSTRATED. $16.95. CODE: FEH

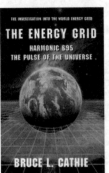

THE ENERGY GRID
Harmonic 695, The Pulse of the Universe
by Captain Bruce Cathie

This is the breakthrough book that explores the incredible potential of the Energy Grid and the Earth's Unified Field all around us. Cathie's first book, *Harmonic 33*, was published in 1968 when he was a commercial pilot in New Zealand. Since then, Captain Bruce Cathie has been the premier investigator into the amazing potential of the infinite energy that surrounds our planet every microsecond. Cathie investigates the Harmonics of Light and how the Energy Grid is created. In this amazing book are chapters on UFO Propulsion, Nikola Tesla, Unified Equations, the Mysterious Aerials, Pythagoras & the Grid, Nuclear Detonation and the Grid, Maps of the Ancients, an Australian Stonehenge examined, more.

255 PAGES. 6x9 TRADEPAPER. ILLUSTRATED. $15.95. CODE: TEG

THE BRIDGE TO INFINITY
Harmonic 371244
by Captain Bruce Cathie

Cathie has popularized the concept that the earth is crisscrossed by an electromagnetic grid system that can be used for anti-gravity, free energy, levitation and more. The book includes a new analysis of the harmonic nature of reality, acoustic levitation, pyramid power, harmonic receiver towers and UFO propulsion. It concludes that today's scientists have at their command a fantastic store of knowledge with which to advance the welfare of the human race.

204 PAGES. 6x9 TRADEPAPER. ILLUSTRATED. $14.95. CODE: BTF

THE HARMONIC CONQUEST OF SPACE
by Captain Bruce Cathie

Chapters include: Mathematics of the World Grid; the Harmonics of Hiroshima and Nagasaki; Harmonic Transmission and Receiving; the Link Between Human Brain Waves; the Cavity Resonance between the Earth; the Ionosphere and Gravity; Edgar Cayce—the Harmonics of the Subconscious; Stonehenge; the Harmonics of the Moon; the Pyramids of Mars; Nikola Tesla's Electric Car; the Robert Adams Pulsed Electric Motor Generator; Harmonic Clues to the Unified Field; and more. Also included are tables showing the harmonic relations between the earth's magnetic field, the speed of light, and anti-gravity/gravity acceleration at different points on the earth's surface. New chapters in this edition on the giant stone spheres of Costa Rica, Atomic Tests and Volcanic Activity, and a chapter on Ayers Rock analysed with Stone Mountain, Georgia.

248 PAGES. 6x9. PAPERBACK. ILLUSTRATED. BIBLIOGRAPHY. $16.95. CODE: HCS

GRAVITATIONAL MANIPULATION OF DOMED CRAFT
UFO Propulsion Dynamics
by Paul E. Potter

Potter's precise and lavish illustrations allow the reader to enter directly into the realm of the advanced technological engineer and to understand, quite straightforwardly, the aliens' methods of energy manipulation: their methods of electrical power generation; how they purposely designed their craft to employ the kinds of energy dynamics that are exclusive to space (discoverable in our astrophysics) in order that their craft may generate both attractive and repulsive gravitational forces; their control over the mass-density matrix surrounding their craft enabling them to alter their physical dimensions and even manufacture their own frame of reference in respect to time. Includes a 16-page color insert.

624 pages. 7x10 Paperback. Illustrated. References. $24.00. Code: GMDC

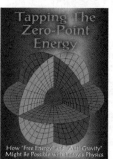

TAPPING THE ZERO POINT ENERGY
Free Energy & Anti-Gravity in Today's Physics
by Moray B. King

King explains how free energy and anti-gravity are possible. The theories of the zero point energy maintain there are tremendous fluctuations of electrical field energy imbedded within the fabric of space. This book tells how, in the 1930s, inventor T. Henry Moray could produce a fifty kilowatt "free energy" machine; how an electrified plasma vortex creates anti-gravity; how the Pons/Fleischmann "cold fusion" experiment could produce tremendous heat without fusion; and how certain experiments might produce a gravitational anomaly.

180 PAGES. 5x8 PAPERBACK. ILLUSTRATED. $12.95. CODE: TAP

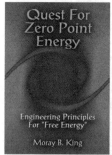

QUEST FOR ZERO-POINT ENERGY
Engineering Principles for "Free Energy"
by Moray B. King

King expands, with diagrams, on how free energy and anti-gravity are possible. The theories of zero point energy maintain there are tremendous fluctuations of electrical field energy embedded within the fabric of space. King explains the following topics: TFundamentals of a Zero-Point Energy Technology; Vacuum Energy Vortices; The Super Tube; Charge Clusters: The Basis of Zero-Point Energy Inventions; Vortex Filaments, Torsion Fields and the Zero-Point Energy; Transforming the Planet with a Zero-Point Energy Experiment; Dual Vortex Forms: The Key to a Large Zero-Point Energy Coherence. Packed with diagrams, patents and photos.

224 PAGES. 6x9 PAPERBACK. ILLUSTRATED. $14.95. CODE: QZPE

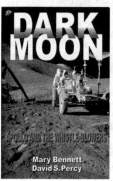

DARK MOON
Apollo and the Whistleblowers
by Mary Bennett and David Percy

Did you know a second craft was going to the Moon at the same time as Apollo 11? Do you know that potentially lethal radiation is prevalent throughout deep space? Do you know there are serious discrepancies in the account of the Apollo 13 'accident'? Did you know that 'live' color TV from the Moon was not actually live at all? Did you know that the Lunar Surface Camera had no viewfinder? Do you know that lighting was used in the Apollo photographs—yet no lighting equipment was taken to the Moon? All these questions, and more, are discussed in great detail by British researchers Bennett and Percy in *Dark Moon*, the definitive book (nearly 600 pages) on the possible faking of the Apollo Moon missions. Tons of NASA photos analyzed for possible deceptions.

568 PAGES. 6x9 PAPERBACK. ILLUSTRATED. BIBLIOGRAPHY. INDEX. $25.00. CODE: DMO

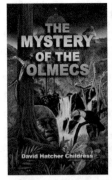

THE MYSTERY OF THE OLMECS
by David Hatcher Childress

The Olmecs were not acknowledged to have existed as a civilization until an international archeological meeting in Mexico City in 1942. Now, the Olmecs are slowly being recognized as the Mother Culture of Mesoamerica, having invented writing, the ball game and the "Mayan" Calendar. But who were the Olmecs? Where did they come from? What happened to them? How sophisticated was their culture? Why are many Olmec statues and figurines seemingly of foreign peoples such as Africans, Europeans and Chinese? Is there a link with Atlantis? In this heavily illustrated book, join Childress in search of the lost cities of the Olmecs! Chapters include: The Mystery of Quizuo; The Mystery of Transoceanic Trade; The Mystery of Cranial Deformation; more.

296 PAGES. 6x9 PAPERBACK. ILLUSTRATED. BIBLIOGRAPHY. COLOR SECTION. $20.00. CODE: **MOLM**

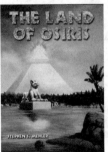

THE LAND OF OSIRIS
An Introduction to Khemitology
by Stephen S. Mehler

Was there an advanced prehistoric civilization in ancient Egypt who built the great pyramids and carved the Great Sphinx? Did the pyramids serve as energy devices and not as tombs for kings? Mehler has uncovered an indigenous oral tradition that still exists in Egypt, and has been fortunate to have studied with a living master of this tradition, Abd'El Hakim Awyan. Mehler has also been given permission to present these teachings to the Western world, teachings that unfold a whole new understanding of ancient Egypt . Chapters include: Egyptology and Its Paradigms; Asgat Nefer—The Harmony of Water; Khemit and the Myth of Atlantis; The Extraterrestrial Question; more.

272 PAGES. 6x9 PAPERBACK. ILLUSTRATED. COLOR SECTION. BIBLIOGRAPHY. $18.00 CODE: **LOOS**

ABOMINABLE SNOWMEN:
LEGEND COME TO LIFE
The Story of Sub-Humans on Six Continents from the Early Ice Age Until Today
by Ivan T. Sanderson

Do "Abominable Snowmen" exist? Prepare yourself for a shock. In the opinion of one of the world's leading naturalists, not one, but possibly four kinds, still walk the earth! Do they really live on the fringes of the towering Himalayas and the edge of myth-haunted Tibet? From how many areas in the world have factual reports of wild, strange, hairy men emanated? Reports of strange apemen have come in from every continent, except Antarctica.

525 PAGES. 6x9 PAPERBACK. ILLUSTRATED. BIBLIOGRAPHY. INDEX. $16.95. CODE: **ABML**

INVISIBLE RESIDENTS
The Reality of Underwater UFOS
by Ivan T. Sanderson

In this book, Sanderson, a renowned zoologist with a keen interest in the paranormal, puts forward the curious theory that "OINTS"—Other Intelligences—live under the Earth's oceans. This underwater, parallel, civilization may be twice as old as Homo sapiens, he proposes, and may have "developed what we call space flight." Sanderson postulates that the OINTS are behind many UFO sightings as well as the mysterious disappearances of aircraft and ships in the Bermuda Triangle. What better place to have an impenetrable base than deep within the oceans of the planet? Sanderson offers here an exhaustive study of USOs (Unidentified Submarine Objects) observed in nearly every part of the world.

298 PAGES. 6x9 PAPERBACK. ILLUSTRATED. BIBLIOGRAPHY. INDEX. $16.95. CODE: **INVS**

PIRATES & THE LOST TEMPLAR FLEET
The Secret Naval War Between the Templars & the Vatican
by David Hatcher Childress

Childress takes us into the fascinating world of maverick sea captains who were Knights Templar (and later Scottish Rite Free Masons) who battled the ships that sailed for the Pope. The lost Templar fleet was originally based at La Rochelle in southern France, but fled to the deep fiords of Scotland upon the dissolution of the Order by King Phillip. This banned fleet of ships was later commanded by the St. Clair family of Rosslyn Chapel (birthplace of Free Masonry). St. Clair and his Templars made a voyage to Canada in the year 1298 AD, nearly 100 years before Columbus! Later, this fleet of ships and new ones to come, flew the Skull and Crossbones, the symbol of the Knights Templar.

320 PAGES. 6x9 PAPERBACK. ILLUSTRATED. BIBLIOGRAPHY. $16.95. CODE: PLTF

TEMPLARS' LEGACY IN MONTREAL
The New Jerusalem
by Francine Bernier

The book reveals the links between Montreal and: John the Baptist as patron saint; Melchizedek, the first king-priest and a father figure to the Templars and the Essenes; Stella Maris, the Star of the Sea from Mount Carmel; the Phrygian goddess Cybele as the androgynous Mother of the Church; St. Blaise, the Armenian healer or "Therapeut"- the patron saint of the stonemasons and a major figure to the Benedictine Order and the Templars; the presence of two Black Virgins; an intriguing family coat of arms with twelve blue apples; and more.

352 PAGES. 6x9 PAPERBACK. ILLUSTRATED. BIBLIOGRAPHY. $21.95. CODE: TLIM

THE HISTORY OF THE KNIGHTS TEMPLARS
by Charles G. Addison, introduction by David Hatcher Childress

Chapters on the origin of the Templars, their popularity in Europe and their rivalry with the Knights of St. John, later to be known as the Knights of Malta. Detailed information on the activities of the Templars in the Holy Land, and the 1312 AD suppression of the Templars in France and other countries, which culminated in the execution of Jacques de Molay and the continuation of the Knights Templars in England and Scotland; the formation of the society of Knights Templars in London; and the rebuilding of the Temple in 1816. Plus a lengthy intro about the lost Templar fleet and its North American sea routes.

395 PAGES. 6x9 PAPERBACK. ILLUSTRATED. $16.95. CODE: HKT

OTTO RAHN AND THE QUEST FOR THE HOLY GRAIL
The Amazing Life of the Real "Indiana Jones"
by Nigel Graddon

Otto Rahn led a life of incredible adventure in southern France in the early 1930s. The Hessian language scholar is said to have found runic Grail tablets in the Pyrenean grottoes, and decoded hidden messages within the medieval Grail masterwork *Parsifal*. The fabulous artifacts identified by Rahn were believed by Himmler to include the Grail Cup, the Spear of Destiny, the Tablets of Moses, the Ark of the Covenant, the Sword and Harp of David, the Sacred Candelabra and the Golden Urn of Manna. Some believe that Rahn was a Nazi guru who wielded immense influence on his elders and "betters" within the Hitler regime, persuading them that the Grail was the Sacred Book of the Aryans, which, once obtained, would justify their extreme political theories and revivify the ancient Germanic myths. But things are never as they seem, and as new facts emerge about Otto Rahn a far more extraordinary story unfolds.

450 pages. 6x9 Paperback. Illustrated. Appendix. Index. $18.95. Code: ORQG

EYE OF THE PHOENIX
Mysterious Visions and
Secrets of the American Southwest
by Gary David

GaryDavid explores enigmas and anomalies in the vast American Southwest. Contents includes: The Great Pyramids of Arizona; Meteor Crater—Arizona's First Bonanza?; Chaco Canyon—Ancient City of the Dog Star; Phoenix—Masonic Metropolis in the Valley of the Sun; Along the 33rd Parallel—A Global Mystery Circle; The Flying Shields of the Hopi Katsinam; Is the Starchild a Hopi God?; The Ant People of Orion—Ancient Star Beings of the Hopi; Serpent Knights of the Round Temple; The Nagas—Origin of the Hopi Snake Clan?; The Tau (or T-shaped) Cross—Hopi/Maya/Egyptian Connections; The Hopi Stone Tablets of Techqua Ikachi; The Four Arms of Destiny—Swastikas in the Hopi World of the End Times; and more.

348 pages. 6x9 Paperback. Illustrated. Bibliography. $16.95. Code: EOPX

THE ORION PROPHECY
Egyptian and Mayan Prophecies
on the Cataclysm of 2012
by Patrick Geryl and Gino Ratinckx

In the year 2012 the Earth awaits a super catastrophe: its magnetic field will reverse in one go. Phenomenal earthquakes and tidal waves will completely destroy our civilization. These dire predictions stem from the Mayans and Egyptians—descendants of the legendary Atlantis. The Atlanteans were able to exactly predict the previous world-wide flood in 9792 BC. They built tens of thousands of boats and escaped to South America and Egypt. In the year 2012 Venus, Orion and several others stars will take the same 'code-positions' as in 9792 BC!

324 PAGES. 6x9 PAPERBACK. ILLUSTRATED. $16.95. CODE: ORP

PRODIGAL GENIUS
The Life of Nikola Tesla
by John J. O'Neill

This special edition of O'Neill's book has many rare photographs of Tesla and his most advanced inventions. Tesla's eccentric personality gives his life story a strange romantic quality. He made his first million before he was forty, yet gave up his royalties in a gesture of friendship, and died almost in poverty. Tesla could see an invention in 3-D, from every angle, within his mind, before it was built; how he refused to accept the Nobel Prize; his friendships with Mark Twain, George Westinghouse and competition with Thomas Edison. Tesla is revealed as a figure of genius whose influence on the world reaches into the far future. Deluxe, illustrated edition.

408 pages. 6x9 Paperback. Illustrated. Bibliography. $18.95. Code: PRG

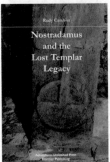

NOSTRADAMUS AND THE LOST TEMPLAR LEGACY
by Rudy Cambier

An analysis of the verses of Nostradamus' "prophecies" has shown that the language spoken in the verses belongs to the medieval times of the 14th Century, and the Belgian borders. The documents known as Nostradamus' prophecies were not written ca. 1550 by the French "visionary" Michel de Nostradame. Instead, they were composed between 1323 and 1328 by a Cistercian monk, Yves de Lessines, prior of the abbey of Cambron, on the border between France and Belgium. According to the author, these documents reveal the location of a Templar treasure.

204 PAGES. 6x9 PAPERBACK. ILLUSTRATED. BIBLIOGRAPHY. $17.95. CODE: NLTL

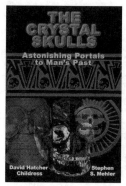

THE CRYSTAL SKULLS
Astonishing Portals to Man's Past
by David Hatcher Childress and Stephen S. Mehler

Childress introduces the technology and lore of crystals, and then plunges into the turbulent times of the Mexican Revolution form the backdrop for the rollicking adventures of Ambrose Bierce, the renowned journalist who went missing in the jungles in 1913, and F.A. Mitchell-Hedges, the notorious adventurer who emerged from the jungles with the most famous of the crystal skulls. Mehler shares his extensive knowledge of and experience with crystal skulls. Having been involved in the field since the 1980s, he has personally examined many of the most influential skulls, and has worked with the leaders in crystal skull research, including the inimitable Nick Nocerino, who developed a meticulous methodology for the purpose of examining the skulls.
294 pages. 6x9 Paperback. Illustrated. Bibliography. $18.95. Code: CRSK

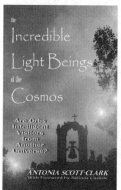

THE INCREDIBLE LIGHT BEINGS OF THE COSMOS
Are Orbs Intelligent Light Beings from the Cosmos?
by Antonia Scott-Clark

Scott-Clark has experienced orbs for many years, but started photographing them in earnest in the year 2000 when the "Light Beings" entered her life. She took these very seriously and set about privately researching orb occurrences. The incredible results of her findings are presented here, along with many of her spectacular photographs. With her friend, GoGos lead singer Belinda Carlisle, Antonia tells of her many adventures with orbs. Find the answers to questions such as: Can you see orbs with the naked eye?; Are orbs intelligent?; What are the Black Villages?; What is the connection between orbs and crop circles? Antonia gives detailed instruction on how to photograph orbs, and how to communicate with these Light Beings of the Cosmos.
334 pages. 6x9 Paperback. Illustrated. References. $19.95. Code: ILBC

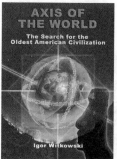

AXIS OF THE WORLD
The Search for the Oldest American Civilization
by Igor Witkowski

Polish author Witkowski's research reveals remnants of a high civilization that was able to exert its influence on almost the entire planet, and did so with full consciousness. Sites around South America show that this was not just one of the places influenced by this culture, but a place where they built their crowning achievements. Easter Island, in the southeastern Pacific, constitutes one of them. The Rongo-Rongo language that developed there points westward to the Indus Valley. Taken together, the facts presented by Witkowski provide a fresh, new proof that an antediluvian, great civilization flourished several millennia ago.
220 pages. 6x9 Paperback. Illustrated. References. $18.95. Code: AXOW

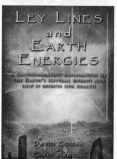

LEY LINE & EARTH ENERGIES
An Extraordinary Journey into the Earth's Natural Energy System
by David Cowan & Chris Arnold

The mysterious standing stones, burial grounds and stone circles that lace Europe, the British Isles and other areas have intrigued scientists, writers, artists and travellers through the centuries. How do ley lines work? How did our ancestors use Earth energy to map their sacred sites and burial grounds? How do ghosts and poltergeists interact with Earth energy? How can Earth spirals and black spots affect our health? This exploration shows how natural forces affect our behavior, how they can be used to enhance our health and well being.
368 PAGES. 6x9 PAPERBACK. ILLUSTRATED. $18.95. CODE: LLEE

ORDER FORM

**10% Discount
When You Order
3 or More Items!**

One Adventure Place
P.O. Box 74
Kempton, Illinois 60946
United States of America
Tel.: 815-253-6390 • Fax: 815-253-6300
Email: auphq@frontiernet.net
http://www.adventuresunlimitedpress.com

Please check: ✓

☐ This is my first order   ☐ I have ordered before

Name

Address

City

State/Province   Postal Code

Country

Phone day   Evening

Fax   Email

Item Code	Item Description	Qty	Total

Subtotal ▶	
Less Discount-10% for 3 or more items ▶	
Balance ▶	
Illinois Residents 6.25% Sales Tax ▶	
Previous Credit ▶	
Shipping ▶	
Total (check/MO in USD$ only) ▶	

Please check: ✓

☐ Postal-Surface

☐ Postal-Air Mail
  (Priority in USA)

☐ UPS
  (Mainland USA only)

☐ Visa/MasterCard/Discover/American Express

Card Number

Expiration Date

10% Discount When You Order 3 or More Items!